The THEEF of LIFE

How to Protect or Reclaim Your Life from FEAR in 7 Steps

LANRE BALOGUN

Pp
Pages Publishing Limited

By Lanre Balogun

ISBN: 978-0-9562961-0-8

© **2012 by Lanre Balogun. All rights reserved.** No part of this book may be reproduced or transmitted in any form or by any means, electronic or mechanical, including photocopying, recording, or by any information storage and retrieval system, without written permission from the author, except for the inclusion of brief quotations in a review. All materials and techniques are protected by copyright.

Published by:
Pages Publishing Limited, 7525 Holly Hill Dr #67, Dallas, TX 75231

Disclaimer
While every effort has been made to ensure accuracy throughout this book, the author accepts no liability for loss or damage as a result of following any of the content herein. Expert advice should always be sought before making major life decisions.

Visit **(www.thetheefoflife.com)** for more information and for links to contact the author.

Printed in the Great Britain

First Printing January 2012

Library of Congress Control Number: 2010941036

Dedicated to my parents,
my father, Chief Aristo Balogun
and my late mother, Ayoka Amudalat Abina.

Contents

Brief Version

Acknowledgments		ix
Epigraph		xi
Introduction		1

PART ONE: Who Stole My Life?

ONE	FEAR	9
TWO	The Past	38
THREE	Overview	56

PART TWO: Personal Battle

FOUR	Step 1: Relax	61
FIVE	Step 2: Interrogate	64
SIX	Step 3: Establish	80

PART THREE: Public Battle

SEVEN	Step 4: Action	119
EIGHT	Step 5: Analyze	151
NINE	Step 6: Gradual	165

PART FOUR: The Art of Battle

TEN	Step 7: Practice	179
ELEVEN	Role Models	183
TWELVE	Constant Reminders	211
THIRTEEN	Conclusion	217

Bibliography	241
Index	243
About the Author	251

Contents

Contents, Brief Version	v
Acknowledgments	ix
Epigraph	xi
Introduction	1

PART ONE: Who Stole My Life?

ONE   **FEAR**   9
FEAR! FEAR!! FEAR!!! | Olé | Above the Law | FEAR as a Virus | Variation | Certificate of Compliance | Bully | Phone | Warranty and Receipt | Compound Interest | Negligence | Depreciation | Languages | Rules of Engagement | The Disabled Mind | Infectious | Hostage of FEAR | The Circle of FHIF | The Circle of FHAF | Religion

TWO   **The Past**   38
PAST | Clinton | Pretty Boy | Paranoid | The Race | Poverty and Struggle | In Dollars We Trust | The Three Musketeers | The Price of a Soul | Welfare | Mittal | Money

THREE   **Overview**   56
A Brief Overview of the Protect or Reclaim strategy – The 7 Steps

PART TWO: Personal Battle

FOUR   **Step 1: Relax**   61
How to Relax

| FIVE | **Step 2: Interrogate** | **64** |

How to Communicate With the THEEF | Interrogation | Interrogation Techniques | Conversation | Basics | Business | Formal and Casual | Purpose | Bank of Conversations | The Most Ignored | News

| SIX | **Step 3: Establish** | **80** |

Establish Your Burning Desire | Courage | Confidence | Sum of Thoughts | Encouragement | Ambition | Juice of Success | Deadly Disease | Self-Image | $100 | Michael Jackson | Self-Marginalization | Self-Esteem | Desire | Books | Sales Executive | Hot Food | Procrastination | The Face | DHL | Plan + Action

PART THREE: Public Battle

| SEVEN | **Step 4: Action** | **119** |

TAN | Phonetic | Reward | Afraid | Spoon | Naked Arrival | A Debt Is a Favor | A Clash of the Giants | Stop or Be Stopped | Feel the Difference | Omelet | FEAR EXIT | FEAR Extinguisher | Taming the Murder | SUPER BOWL XLII | The Message

| EIGHT | **Step 5: Analyze** | **151** |

The Power | University of Choice | Chance of Choice | Mathematics Calculations | Analyze this and that

| NINE | **Step 6: Gradual** | **165** |

Sniper | Mail | Responsibility | Pressure | Squares

PART FOUR: The Art of Battle

TEN	**Step 7: Practice** *How to Practice*	179
ELEVEN	**Role Models** Khan | Lectures from Daddy | Oprah | Gardner | Sir Branson | 34 | Octogenarian | Lincoln | Recession | Talent | Obama | Speed Bike | RISE	183
TWELVE	**Constant Reminders** Law of Reciprocity | Failures Attract Failures | D'banj | Dress Code	211
THIRTEEN	**Conclusion** The James Effect | The Angel | Hidden Ability | Free Society | Peace | Ability | Delay | Ban | Adidas and Nike | Today | 24 | Caution | Blood of Failures | Yours | The Matthew Factor | Farewell	217
	Bibliography	241
	Index	243
	About the Author	251

Acknowledgments

I want to extend my gratitude to all the journalists who gave me permission to use their news articles in this book. You have shared with us, via your professionalism, information – and information is knowledge. Steve Blow from *Dallas Morning News*, and Paul Cheston from *Evening Standard*, England: you inform us not only about our environment, but about happenings in different parts of the world. To each one of you, I salute your professionalism. I would like to express my appreciation to The Dallas Morning News. I would like to thank Sunday Are from Mo' hits records for permission to use excerpt from their website.

I also want to thank Shazo, my book cover (front and back) designer, for an outstanding and exceptional job with the cover and Tolu Shofule for the illustrations inside the book, as well as my preferred editor and proofreader, who went beyond the call of duty, by providing much more than I expected, and Paper Perfect, who systematically turned this data into information. I would also like to thank Nicole Farley for casting her eyes over the final version of my manuscript.

My sincere gratitude goes out to…

All my friends who showed they are friends and much more than friends. My sisters and brothers who gave me unbelievable advice, and those who read the manuscript and provided valuable feedback.

My wonderful son, Lanre Jr. (aka Larry, DHT, Lazza), who kept telling and asking me, *"Daddy, I told my teachers and friends in school you are writing a book. When are you going to finish your book?"* You have your wish – you can not only tell your friends your dad is an author, you can show them the book as well. Thank you, son, for your love, encouragement and support.

Finally, to my awesome wife, thank you for your pain, love and support while writing the manuscript of this book and for your outstanding love and friendship from the beginning of our matrimonial journey to date.

A dictionary does not carry or require a foreword to deliver the message it carries, because it is based on the truth. Likewise, this book is based on the truth. Digest it and make your own conclusion based on the truth, and not FEAR.

The truth is incontrovertible; malice may attack it, ignorance may deride it, but in the end, there it is.
Sir Winston Churchill

The THEEF of LIFE

Introduction

Nobody begins the journey of life with intentions to fail. For this reason, I believe each individual must address *the creator of failure* via conversation or discussion.

> *The struggle is my life.*
> **Nelson Mandela**

The creator of failure's goal is to accumulate failures worldwide, and to accomplish his task, communication is required. Communication is important and most companies, particularly banks, will tell you – it is good to know your customers. Our customer (the creator of failure) only sells one product: handcuffs. This is a product he has sold for decades after decades. With exceptional marketing, demand is extremely high within the global village of the world. Conversations, discussions and lectures can help in the discovery of an individual's hidden abilities. Conversations constitute daily events of the general public in any country; however, despite the importance of conversing with the creator of failure, it is totally ignored or overlooked (yet, a simple conversation or interrogation would suffice). This conversation is responsible for the majority of the reasons why people fail in life.

Courage is required in life to deal with the challenges we face in the world today. Poverty is generally a deterrent to a happy life, and in most cases, the third party in a marriage (if not the first in certain marriages), because some marriages are purely based on money. The disappearance of that financial element is the arrival of poverty, hence, the revelation of the true color of the marriage. The past is also a culprit for failure, if entertained above present concerns. Successful people constantly inspire themselves to do what needs to be done, and believe in *doing it*, and not just saying it. To this end, inspirational quotes are useful; we could all use them to motivate ourselves into action. We can overcome negative perceptions to improve our self-image. With a systematic guide, step-by-step, we can move our lives to another level and to a form of living that leads to freedom in various areas of our lives – but only if we are willing to take action. Caveats have been constantly maintained throughout this book because of the serious dangers to human lives, which the creator of failure can unleash on any individual. By using role models and with constant reminders, I am going to convince you that from the high school drop-out, lecturer, property tycoon, chart show host, entrepreneur, to president, nobody is beyond failure or success in any vocation. Taking an objective look at these issues will be a major focus of this book. In reality, most of us already know how to solve our problems; we just need someone else to remind us and keep our focus on what needs to be done.

In pursuit of knowledge to unravel and dismiss the myths about the creator of failure, and to exchange knowledge and inspire each other in various areas of our lives, three of us decided to meet for a weekend conversation, discussion and lecture. Janet Jones is an American, born in New York, a thirty-five-year-old journalist. Thiago Arantes dos Santos is a forty-three-year old Brazilian married to a woman named Maria, who he met while at university. *"It was love at first sight,"* he told me. There after, their conversations simply drove their feelings home. Janet, Thiago and I established a burning desire for this conversation during the second week in August, 2005. Janet suggested we meet in a hotel in central London, where we could have drinks during the course of the day, and lunch in the afternoon. We agreed on a time and place to meet on Saturday morning. I was looking forward to our meeting and was very excited, particularly as *"Conversations constitute learning and teaching."* We'd never met each other before, although we had been having conversations and discussions for the last few months via e-mail and telephone. Friday evening, at about 6:45 p.m., suddenly the telephone rang. Thinking it may be Janet or Thiago calling with further information regarding our meeting, I picked up the receiver. "Hello, good evening!" The caller did not respond, so I said, "Hello, good evening!" again. No response again. I placed the receiver in its rightful home, and then wondered why the caller had called if the caller did not want to have a conversation. *"Could it be FEAR of actually having a conversation... or just a bad line?"* Surely if the caller did not want to have a conversation, the caller would not have called in the first place.

I woke up Saturday morning, and had breakfast – toast and a cup of tea – and then let my enthusiasm for the weekend wash over me. I began my journey to my destination, the Waldorf Hilton in central London, as agreed. I arrived at the Waldorf Hilton at 10:00 a.m., even though our meeting was not until 10:30 a.m. Unknown to me, Janet and Thiago had also arrived early. While waiting in the hotel reception area, I could not help but admire the lovely ambiance of the hotel. I remember once hearing someone say, "The Hilton provides heavenly beds in their rooms." That day I discovered that the exceptional ambiance extends all over the hotel, not just to the beds. At 10:30 a.m. by the reception area, I watched Thiago approach Janet and said, *"Good morning, you must be Janet?"* Janet, with a smile on her face, replied, *"Good morning, I am, and you must be Thiago?"* Thiago replied with a smile, *"Yes."* At that very moment, I joined them and introduced myself. We all exchanged pleasantries and then proceeded to Homage Patisserie, the patisserie and champagne bar area in the hotel, for morning coffee in a sumptuous setting of rich fabrics, period furniture and wood paneling.

The journey of life is not immune from obstacles. The biggest of them can destroy a life with handcuffs, the most powerful weapon in the obstacle's toolbox. We have on our hands a pandemic disease – a contagious and escalating disease. It is a disease that refuses to discriminate against the human soul, a citizen of the world and conversant in any language. DO WE REALLY KNOW FEAR OR WHAT FEAR IS? Perhaps, the answer lies in the spelling of the pronunciation, not the spelling of the word *'Thief'*. The pronunciation of the word *'Thief'* is spelled, *'THEEF'*, which according to the language of this book, stands for: *'Terminator,' 'Hijacker,' 'Exterminator,' 'Extinguisher' and 'Finisher'* of human lives. In order to accomplish the objective of FEAR, the voice of a life will have to be silenced – a systematic technique is used to steal time out of a life in an attempt to deliver failure to the owner of that life. The stolen time is the creation of a delay in a life. FEAR has never, and will never, employ open force in its operations, but is always guilty of larceny and never convicted. As stated by the title of Jeffrey Archer's book, **Honor Among Thieves**, most people don't freely give their consent to the THEEF, and yet its results are second to none. I give to FEAR what is due to FEAR, the greatest honor within the thieving industry, the crown of the king of thieves.

FEAR only carries handcuffs, a product that restricts the use of, or renders the human hands inactive, and more importantly, as far as FEAR is concerned, runs down the clock of a human life. There are different types of handcuffs. Hinged and chained handcuffs are two common types, but the THEEF prefers the chain type, it's a best-seller. The way the handcuff works is a standard process, but the positioning depends on the severity of your FEAR. If your FEAR is large to extra large or beyond, FEAR generally puts your hands in front of you, and handcuffs your wrists – simply because you will be too scared to attempt to free yourself, even though it is easier to tamper with the handcuffs on your wrists in front of you, compared to behind your back. If your FEAR is small to medium, your hands will be placed behind your back and your wrists will be handcuffed behind your back. Because of your small level of FEAR, you may be tempted to try and escape and it is much more difficult to tamper with the handcuffs on your wrists behind you. Regardless of the locking position (front or back), the locking mechanism, in this case a key, is then used to double lock the handcuffs to further reduce the chances of you freeing your hands from the handcuff by picking the lock.

This book has been divided into four parts, namely: *Who Stole My Life?" (a must-ask personal question), Personal Battle (one on one battle, the troops of both parties; FEAR's and your helpers are not invited to this battle); Public Battle (troops, agents of success and agents of FEAR are welcomed at this level of conflict) and The Art of Battle (mastery is established based on practice)*. Each of these is based on Part One, *"Who Stole My Life?"*. A call to battle will arise, which requires a Protect or Reclaim strategy: *'Figure,' 'Evaluate' and 'Action'* for victory. This strategy constitutes the *'Personal Battle'* and *'Public Battle,'* which, in effect, creates *'The Art of Battle.'*.

When you are sick, you visit your doctor, and you get medication to cure your sickness. To conquer your FEAR, or at least, to reduce the element of FEAR in you to an acceptable level, you will need to receive FEAR eradication treatment. Part of the FEAR eradication treatment amongst others, is your conversations with the THEEF of life. Somebody once said FEAR is nothing more than *'False Evidence Appearing Real,'* in that case, with the Protect or Reclaim strategy listed below, which constitutes the seven steps provided in this book, if we have the handcuffs of FEAR on our wrists, we shall take them off – or if we don't, we shall dismiss any attempt by FEAR to put the handcuffs on our wrists. In other words, we shall protect ourselves against a future attack or reclaim our ownership status with these seven steps:

Personal Battle

Step 1 – Relax
Step 2 – Interrogate
Step 3 – Establish

Public Battle

Step 4 – Action
Step 5 – Analyze
Step 6 – Gradual

The Art of Battle

Step 7 – Practice

Lector [1], *(Reader)* it's in your hands as you read – the four words that describe the most deadly thing in the world. With great pleasure and honor, I present to you *"The THEEF of LIFE:* FEAR," our subject over that weekend. What I truly believed became, by the fall of Sunday, that week, an amazing weekend. I was, and am still, thrilled and excited. I was inspired to deliver this book in the hope that it will enlighten, empower and encourage you to become all that you can be and not settle for a life less than you deserve. Knowledge of, not the acceptance of FEAR, is the conversation that I intend to drive to your doorstep; I don't have the space to offer FEAR a ride in my car to your home. Even if I have, I won't, can't and refuse to be party to the objectives and foreign policy of the nation of FEAR. To be successful involves an element of risk; the risk factor involved is what creates the FEAR, and the FEAR is the cancer of success that instantly stops individuals from trying. FEAR has within itself the capacity to dominate the existence of any human being. With this book, in order to fulfil your dreams, I would like to empower you with *"The ability to stretch without stress,"* (*a simple concept that allows the elimination of pain or strain in a human life, as a result of engaging in a particular task or activity before and after taking action*). With this book, you will learn how to deal with instances of FEAR (**F**alse **E**vidence **A**ppearing **R**eal), in all areas of your life to avoid failure. You will be able to raise your price, conversation skills, confidence, courage and self image, and your desire to a burning desire and take effective actions by developing the habit of taking action. You will also learn how to analyze your options and gradually make the required changes, and how to master taking actions. You will not give up and deny your life a voice. You will take the battle to FEAR before he brings it to your doorstep.

Success does not have to be a painful or stressful experience. Regardless of your definition of success and current situation, this book, funny and insightful, will motivate you to new heights. Enjoy!

---

[1]Lector is the Latin word for 'Reader'.

PART ONE

Who Stole My Life?

ONE

FEAR

FEAR! FEAR!! FEAR!!!

Thiago opened the proceedings on our subject by repeating the word FEAR three times, then continued. *"Conversa com medo!"* said Thiago, in Portuguese, which translates in English as *"conversation with FEAR!" "It seems there is no getting away. Clarify for me, if you can, who or what is this animal called FEAR?"* Thiago requested.

> *The man who views the world at 50 the same as he did at 20, has wasted 30 years of his life.*
> **Muhammad Ali**

It can only be down to FEAR. A man with the same views for thirty years must have shared the same views with FEAR, the agent of intimidation for the last three decades. If a man has wasted three decades of his life, and it is said, *"A fool at forty is a fool forever."* Let's put things in perspective: *"A failure at fifty is a complete failure."* A father with no regular income, a layabout, who, perhaps, is in and out of jail, had two children. His daughter, at 15 years old, in search of resources to make a living, became a prostitute on the streets of New York offering sex services, in some cases, for as low as $5. She contracted HIV and died a few years later. His son became a drug addict at the age of 17; in the process of feeding his habit, drug addiction, he mugged a man walking down a quiet street in New York. Unfortunately for him, the man was an undercover police officer. In self-defence by the officer, he was shot dead. Even if the man at fifty or over, won the lottery, it couldn't make up for his failure to provide the essentials of life for his children. He is still a complete failure – as one of the key responsibilities of a father is to provide for his dependants, particularly, those labeled as minors. No amount of success can overshadow his failure, as far as his responsibilities to his children are concerned. Provided an individual is still living, even at sixty years old or over, there is hope; but such hope can't make up for such a price (loss of a daughter and son) under such circumstances. *"Your portrait at fifty will be the true results of your conversations with the THEEF of life from adulthood."*

FEAR is an authority on the subject of failure and its aim is to wear down his subject mentally. It weaves intimidation and fright, by dangling handcuffs in the air. With its one-of-a-kind artistry, FEAR has mesmerized a worldwide legion of fans and failures, and continues to enjoy an unprecedented level of support from the fans to date. People get high, extremely high, on FEAR, by deluding themselves into thinking if they confine their operations within the corridors of FEAR, they are safe and can't really lose anything. This is a bitter inspiration as opposed to better inspiration. An elder statesman, an octogenarian in the industry at the very least, FEAR runs a recession-proof business. The highest rating in rifle marksmanship belongs to FEAR, over a short or long distance. When the sound of your heartbeat fills your ears and sleep is not in sight or forthcoming, the indications are that the merciless THEEF is already your landlord on a particular subject. FEAR will never elevate you to a higher level of existence; if anything, it will downgrade you to a lower level of existence and beyond. The messiah will turn water to wine, but FEAR will turn water to undrinkable water. At least, we could have drank the water in the absences of wine; instead, we have to drink the undrinkable water in the absence of drinkable water. FEAR has the highest success percentage rate compared to its colleagues. FEAR is the greatest obstacle or hurdle that prevents an individual from progressing to the next level. With handcuffs, FEAR exercises extraordinary control over lives. FEAR eradication treatment is an essential ingredient for anybody who intends to be successful in life.

Fear defeats more people than any other one thing in the world.
Ralph Waldo Emerson

The enemy of progress, who, if given the opportunity, with or without your approval, FEAR will eradicate your dreams, ambition and success. FEAR is the greatest reason responsible for more dreams, ambitions and success not being achieved than any other reason or all other reasons combined. Success is immediately extinguished, and FEAR puts up a defense that can take a lifetime to overcome. In certain cases, FEAR may never be overcome. From any perspective, professional or non-professional, FEAR is deadly, extremely deadly. "How deadly is FEAR?" you ask. Beyond your wildest imagination. The definition of FEAR is kind to FEAR.

Definitions of FEAR:

A distressing emotion aroused by impending danger, evil, pain, etc., whether the threat is real or imagined; the feeling or condition of being afraid.

Apprehension, Consternation, dismay, terror, fright, panic, horror, trepidation.
www.dictionary.com

Fear implies a painful emotion experienced when one is confronted by threatening danger or evil.

Olé

A brief history of the word *'Olé.' Olé* is a word that comes from Arabic that means Bravo. In some languages, it could also be used as an exclamation of joy, appreciation, encouragement or anything similar. *'Olé'* is:

Used as a shout of approval, triumph, or encouragement.
www.dictionary.com

However, insofar as languages in general are concerned, the word *'Olé'* can have the same or similar pronunciation, yet the meaning in different languages can reflect something at the end of two different spectrums. For example, in Spanish, *'Olé'* is used to appreciate a brilliant act, display or performance in any area of life; it is generally an expression of admiration. In my native language, Yoruba (one of the major languages in Nigeria), *'Olé'* means *'Thief'*. Thief in English is defined as follows:

> A person who steals, esp. secretly or without open force; one guilty of theft or larceny.
>
> www.dictionary.com

A whisper of the word *'Olé,'* let alone an outcry of the word, can create the arrival of FEAR and all its agents. Refraining from usage of the word could be in order not to create panic and chaos, people running helter-skelter in different directions on one hand, or on the other hand, not to appreciate a matador in a bullfight, in case the matador is not doing or has not done a good job; depending on which of the two languages (Yoruba or Spanish) you subscribe to.

Greatness exists in all; not achieving greatness is not due to lack of ability, but the ignorance of personal ability. Focus is often directed at the ability of another individual. Instead of focusing on the ability that makes an individual unique, focus is derailed and centered on the ability they do not have. You cannot derive the benefits of the ability you do not acknowledge. Along the journey of the struggle of acknowledgement, another factor appears – the factor that redefines the margins between attempted impersonation, deception (which in reality is a crime) and individualism. The element, *FEAR,* that creates the margin cannot be overlooked. We give value to something only when we know what it is—if you give a one-year-old child a $1,000 bill, a high probability exists that by the time you get it back, it will be shredded to pieces or completely soaked in saliva; however, if you give the same $1,000 bill to an adult, by the time you get it back, assuming you are fortunate enough to get it back, it will be in the same condition, if not better. The THEEF of life does not accommodate violence in its operations of stealing lives, unlike others in the industry like burglars, pickpockets, bank robbers, and highwaymen. An encounter with them in operation may be at the cost of violence. Even the police, *in addition to handcuffs,* in order to maintain law and order, still carry handguns, batons, pepper spray and electroshock guns. Handcuff is the preferred weapon of choice for FEAR.

Above the Law

FEAR, like a beautiful lady, does not have to be on her best behavior at all times. Regardless of her behavior, even as a star member of one of the oldest professions in the world, takers are always available at all times. Action, on the other hand, is like an ugly woman, and must be on her best behavior all the time. Even when she is offered to the public on a bug-off basis *(buy one, get one free basis)*, takers are still not available, except when she brings a mouth-watering financial package to the negotiation meeting. The picture changes, the ugly becomes beautiful and the beautiful becomes ugly. The reality, however, presents a different picture. Ugly has always been beautiful in its own right. With regards to thieves, the 'Thief of Baghdad,' who, in his own right is a great thief by name but not by action, is an amateur compared to FEAR, the daylight THEEF of life. In fact, any professional Thief is an amateur when measured against the daylight bandit; FEAR never retires from the job at hand, while the others eventually retires and to date has committed theft that carries the greatest consequences for the robbed rather than for the robber. FEAR is the daylight robber and the legendary midnight bandit. FEAR cannot sue or be sued, as he is not a legal entity. At some point in our lives, FEAR has freely dipped his hands into our pockets and stolen something from us; the daylight robber has hit even a judge and a police officer. We know him. We have evidence. Above all, the law is aware of him. He cannot be made accountable, even in a court of law, despite all of the millions of pieces of evidence we have in a safety deposit box at the Bank of Conversations. The THEEF of life is immune from prosecution; therefore, he is above the law. If everybody in society were immune from prosecution, we would not require the use of courts, judges, police or prisons. But, as we are not accorded the same privileges given to the legendary bandit, we all have to comply with the laws of the land. Even the police are not above the law.

Bandit by day, bandit by night, roaming the streets freely in search of the next victim, it begs the question, *"Why does FEAR enjoy such freedom, and yet nobody is capable of bringing him to justice?"* By being immune from prosecution, the biggest success killer in the world, the daylight killer of dreams, not only stops people from moving around freely, but also stops them from even getting out of first gear!

FEAR as a Virus

Viral disease: a disease caused by a virus.
Disruptive computer program: a short computer program, hidden within another, that makes copies of itself and spreads them, disrupting the operation of a computer that receives one. A virus may be transmitted on diskettes and through networks, on-line services, and the Internet.

Something that corrupts: something that has a corrupting or Poisonous effect, especially on the mind.
uk.encarta.msn.com/dictionary

FEAR is a virus, a self-replicating program that causes damage (types of FEAR), generally hard disk erasure or file corruption and infects other programs, USB sticks, or hard disks by coping itself onto them (particularly components of the operating system or the boot sector of a disk). Viruses use a variety of strategies to avoid detection. Some are harmless, merely informing their users that their system has been infected without destroying components of the systems. Most are not benign, and identification of their creator can be virtually impossible, although the THEEF of life has been quite prepared to identify himself.

A task or project without a start date has no finish date in sight; action will give you a start date.

To complete a task or project, it would have to start before you can visualize a finished date. Getting started is daunting, and is the most difficult part of any task or project; with a corrupt and poisonous effect in place, a start date would appear to be virtually impossible. World leaders, CEOs, generals, pilots and members of the public all know the THEEF. FEAR is nothing new, how you deal with the THEEF of life is what makes the difference.

Courage is not the absence of fear; it's the mastery of it.
Zig Ziglar

We go to school, college and university to learn and to enable us to get good jobs. When you start working or are at any stage of your journey of life, you may have a great idea or opportunity, but the THEEF prevents you from getting off the treadmill. Instead, you remain in the same job year after year, unhappy and frustrated, struggling to make ends meet until a gold watch is presented for the wonderful services given to the company over the last 25 years as a thank you gift, a present to send any of us into our retirement. Without any financial vehicle in place to provide income in retirement apart from our pension (hopefully a good pension scheme), surviving on the pension income becomes a struggle with all the various bills that need to be conversed within the language of bills. It makes me wonder and ask the question: *"Did we really get off the treadmill after retirement?"* Future income earning via a pension treadmill belongs to the THEEF of life. The bygone decades give a guarantee for income earning in the future without an acknowledgment of inflation. In retirement, the THEEF of life then gives us a reminder of inflation by applying it to our pension income. The THEEF does not show himself via pension income alone.

Variation

The THEEF of life comes in different forms and sizes. Various people generally have the following types of FEAR:

FEAR of failure
FEAR of losing money
FEAR of recession
FEAR of success
FEAR of losing respect
FEAR of criticism
FEAR of making a fool of yourself
FEAR of learning something new
FEAR of networking with people
FEAR of looking for leads
FEAR of investing in assets.
FEAR of approaching a member of the opposite sex
FEAR of public speaking
FEAR of personal courage
FEAR of how the individual looks

The list is endless. When you find on your hands a full-blown FEAR, it is guaranteed to immobilize you. Any type of FEAR can become full-blown. The FEAR of losing money is one FEAR that causes people to protect the money they have by leaving the money in their bank accounts, effectively giving their money janitors permission to use the money as they wish provided they return the money to them. The THEEF of life keeps people on the FEAR treadmill for so long that by the time they start or complete their conversations with the FEAR, it is too late to get off the treadmill. Even after people have achieved success, an element of FEAR still exists in human beings. Once you get on the treadmill of the THEEF of life, it can be very difficult to get off the treadmill as you become accustomed to your monthly wages; this is particularly true for people who are not courageous and confident. It is essential while on the treadmill to put some investment vehicle in place, regardless of how small the financial vehicle is. A small financial vehicle put in place today may become a huge investment or the best investment you ever made in the future. There is no limit to the damage the THEEF of life can do to anybody. The promise, from the THEEF, is safety, but the delivery is failure. Hence, dealing with this global monster is necessary.

To conquer fear is the beginning of wisdom.
Bertrand Russell

With the THEEF of life, living is no longer an adventure, but a liability (a debit balance in an individual's life account), hence, living is confined to a box.

Certificate of Compliance

The THEEF has been involved in more conversations and battles than any individual has. As far as an individual is concerned, the reasons to agree with the THEEF of life are in place; however, to the global terrorist, they are tools for stealing lives, tools that have delivered results constantly in the past and are still producing results today. The following are individual or combined reasons that people use to justify giving in to the THEEF of life. Some of the available Certificates of Compliance are:

I do not have the intelligence or expertise to go it alone.
I am just not educated enough.
I am too young or I am too old.
Times are hard. No one makes money these days.
I am not from a privileged family.
His father or mother was there to help along the way.
Luck is on his side.
It is down to faith.
I do not know how to set clear goals.
I cannot put a plan together.
Executing the plan will require a huge commitment.

I tried it before; it does not work.

Those are the limiting ideas that FEAR creates in peoples' minds. The individual certificate to justify failure is worn with certainty after coming out of the debate with the THEEF. It is a simple case of bullying of the mind.

Bully

Janet said, "The THEEF of life is a bully." Most individuals just want the bullying to stop without actually confronting the bully. FEAR takes this tacit acceptance to mean that you are comfortable with the bullying, and continues to bully you. The bullying will not stop unless you make it stop. The bully will cripple you and, in the process, hand you daily gifts like worry, stress, harassment, panic attacks and headaches.

"Janet, I totally agree with you," Thiago said. "I remember, a few years ago, when I wanted to buy a house, I was so scared that I pulled out because of FEAR. The THEEF of life with the daily gifts of worrying, panic and headaches, bullied me. I was hoping the worrying would just disappear, but it did not. I kept on thinking, what if the roof needs to be repaired or replaced after buying the house? What if the house has a major electrical problem? I asked my father for advice, and he said to me, you have not even bought the house and you are worried and afraid of things that may or may not happen in the future. I think you should buy the house; you will cross other bridges when you get to them. Knowing that any house purchase would require a survey, slowly and steadily I initialed my conversations with the bully, the THEEF." "Is the THEEF of life real?" I asked Janet. The bully could easily be any of the following depending on your opinion:

Forged Exhibit Appearing Real.
Failure Emerging As Real.
Freedom Evaluation Appears Rejected.
False Errors Appearing Real.

Fake Emergency Appearing Real.
FEAR Elevated As Real.

FEAR is a land of imprisonment where many restrictions apply. Similar to prison, you do not decide what to do; you are told what to do and when to do it. When people who give excuses other than FEAR for not embarking on their desires in various areas of their lives are hooked up to lie detectors, a polygraph, results will show that most excuses given are false (not truly believed). Another great asset of FEAR is the ability to turn a grown man or woman into a perpetual liar. The fear of falling is a natural fear, as well as the fear of loud noise; as children, we are afraid of falling or loud noises. Most other kinds of FEAR always breed negative results once you establish a relationship with them. Sometimes we are not even aware that we are afraid. FEAR steals your opinion, numbs your mouth and movement in your time of need, and when you need to express yourself or ask questions, you can't. The THEEF of life takes over and controls you, bullying your mind to choose your preferred individual or combined reasons amongst the certificates of compliance as a justifiable reason for your current or future predicament.

Phone

Every now and then, you get a phone call from your car manufacturer along the lines of, "Good morning, I am calling from XYZ motors, we are just checking to confirm we have the correct e-mail address for you. The last time we sent you an e-mail, it bounced back. Are you still using this e-mail address? I hope everything is okay with your car? Our records indicate your car will be due for service next week. Your car is one of our latest models and requires timely service. When due for service to avoid any further complications in the engine, we ensure our customers are given ample time to make an appointment for servicing their cars on time. If you need anything, please give us a call. *That is why we are here.* Thank you for your time today."

That is why we are here! Of course, that is why they are there. They are not there to operate at a loss, they are there like any other business, and they exist to make profits. Like the telephone conversation above, once the formalities of the e-mail issue are out of the way, the conversation moves swiftly to your car and any needs for the car. FEAR arrives via the telephone as well *(requires timely service when due for service to avoid any further complications in the engine)*. After the telephone conversation, the owner of the car goes into FEAR mode, thinking *"I need to get my car in for service as soon as possible to avoid any engine problem in the near future."* The chances are that most owners will make an appointment to have their cars serviced before the end of the telephone conversation. They know they can get their car service done somewhere else. FEAR is not different from any other company; the product on offer is handcuffs. FEAR exists to win souls, the souls of potential failures, and the more failures they acquire, the more soldiers they will have in the Failure Armed Forces, and the more profits they make. The visible or presented objectives are not necessarily the real objective. Most of the time, it is very difficult to identify the real objective from the information presented to you. The only reason the THEEF of life is there for you is to ensure you fail and *not* to protect you from failure. The THEEF of life does not create successful people; it only creates failures. That is why FEAR is here. Within the Failure Armed Forces, unmotivated people surround you; these people cannot motivate you. If you have conversations with unmotivated people, you tend to adapt their ideas, ideas that take you nowhere. Somebody going nowhere cannot tell you how to get to a place he has never been and has no intention to go.

Warranty and Receipt

Failure, despite the fact that it can have a detrimental effect on you, does not provide warranties to its clients for failing. When you fail, you are alone; you pay the price of failure alone. You cannot hold anybody responsible. In a court of failure, FEAR is the judge and jury; it cannot be sued for damages, and it cannot be removed from any professional organization or body it belongs to, as it is an independent organization or body that is accountable to himself and only himself. Even if you had the opportunity to sue the THEEF, the only person who will be permitted to give evidence is the THEEF. The global terrorist has loyalty to failure, and it will always be against you. In court, the judge will ask you, *'Why did you fail?'* Your reply, I guess, will be, *'Your honor, I failed because I was afraid.'* I wonder what your chances of winning this case would be – your guess is as good as mine on this one. Doctors, lawyers, accountants, etc. all belong to a particular professional governing body that can take action against the individual for professional misconduct should the need arise, so largely you feel more comfortable dealing with any of them. Failure has no recourse, guarantee or warranty on offer for its clients. Failure belongs to a free organization – a body trading freely with catastrophic consequences for its clients.

You don't get a receipt when you purchase failure; the option of a refund or exchange for the product is not available to you. In most cases, once the salesperson, the THEEF of life, has sold the failure to you, it is yours. The only other option is not to make a purchase in the first place, but it is a product you could be buying without realizing it. Failure is always *'sold as seen'* to potential buyers, and once a sale is made, it moves on swiftly to the next potential customer. In any country, the failures are the majority; hence, there is no shortage of potential customers all over the world. Most people don't know or understand FEAR until the gravity of failure is right at their doorstep by wish time, and, in many cases, it is too late to take action against FEAR. Do not underestimate the THEEF of life; if you do, it will be at your peril.

"I am not going to fail as long as I don't take any risk." You will not find a warranty or receipt for that statement either. The very second you put such a thought in your mind, you have failed because that is exactly where the THEEF of life wants you to be, stable or at attention until you are told to stand down by the Field

Marshal himself, (which will not happen unless you make it happen). FEAR moves at the pace of the speed of light; you don't see it happen. Reality only hits you when you stand down.

Compound Interest

Compound interest is an effective tool for anybody who decides to utilize it – it always gives a positive result. FEAR is aware of compound interest and uses it to its full capacity. Upon the delivery of a rousing speech by FEAR, an individual remains stable or at attention, effectively making what appears to be an investment by depositing his FEAR. $20,000 in monetary terms at the World Bank of FEAR at an interest rate of 40 percent per annum – at the end of the first year, your balance will be $28,000. Compound interest moves into action in the second year; the table below shows how the THEEF utilizes compound interest:

END OF YEAR	FEAR ($20,000)
1	$28,000
2	$39,200
3	$54,880
4	$76,832
5	$107,565
6	$150,591
7	$210,827
8	$295,158
9	$413,221
10	$578,509

Compound interest is when the initial principal earns interest in the first year and the interest is added to the initial principal *(compounding is the addition of interest to principal)*. For the second year, the added interest also starts to earn interest thereafter. For example, as in the table above when the initial principal of $20,000 earns an interest of $8,000 (at a rate of 40 percent per annum) at the end of the first year, and the $8,000 is added to the initial principal ($20,000) for the second year at the same rate of interest, the initial principal plus interest from the first year ($20,000 + $8,000 = $28,000) both earn interest. The first year's interest ($8,000) begins to earn interest in the second year. The 40 percent interest rate may seem very high and unreal but, trust me, when you're dealing with FEAR, by investing in his bank the interest on offer is always astronomical (ask any failure who has been relieved of his duties in the Failure Armed Forces of the cost of such an investment to him). As the years go by, the individual's FEAR increases year after year. By the middle of a decade, our debt to FEAR is uncomfortable. At the end of a decade, it would have increased beyond what is an acceptable level; we are already knocking on the door and entertaining half of a million dollars' worth of FEAR. Suddenly, a fat income becomes a crippled income, that is not in a position to speak the language of bills as fluently as it used to.

Negligence

The rights of wives unduly influenced by their husbands was established, the case that was significant in establishing that right in the House of Lords in the United Kingdom was:

Barclays Bank -v- O'Brien (1994)

Where a husband has asked his wife to charge her interest in a property as security for her husband's liabilities and to do so is of no obvious advantage to her. In O'Brien's case the House of Lords clarified the duties owed by a bank to the wife. Financial institutions will be familiar with the case.

Insofar as the THEEF is concerned, there is no room for Undue Influence and Negligence (gross or ordinary), an irrelevant fact. It is an immaterial defense, regardless of the position occupied by FEAR in the husband's or wife's mind. As an individual, he or she can't claim undue influence on the part of FEAR for following the gospel of FEAR to the point where he or she realized that the decision to accommodate that gospel was the wrong decision at that time.

Negligence is no defense for not taking action.

Depreciation

Depreciation is the method used to write off the cost of an asset over its useful working life—called its useful economic life (UEL). *'Straight-Line Depreciation'* and *'Declining-Balance Method'* are common methods for calculating depreciation. When you limit yourself on compliments of the THEEF of life, you become a fixed asset of FEAR, and your value starts to depreciate immediately, either through the *straight-line method* or through the *declining-balance method*. As you are not doing anything because of FEAR, your value will mostly depreciate based on effluxion of time or obsolescence through technological or market changes. After a number of years, as the THEEF of life applies the straight-line method of depreciation over your useful economic life (by preventing you from taking action to fulfill your potential to the maximum in equal installments year after year) at the end of your useful economic life – even if your residual value had been taken into account at the beginning of your association with FEAR – your residual value will be FAILURE! Nothing more, nothing less. Even if the THEEF of life applies the other method of depreciation, declining-balance, over your useful economic life, your net book value (NBV), the cost of the asset (you) less the accumulated depreciation to date, will still be FAILURE! At this stage, your useful economic life has been fully used by the THEEF of life, and your scrap value will be next to zero at best.

Languages

FEAR is FEAR in any language in any country. FEAR and its effects do not have barriers. FEAR carries global damage; it does not matter on which continent you reside. The damage that can be done by the THEEF of life is not restricted to a particular country or continent. FEAR will stop you in your tracks, and put your hands in handcuffs of bondage that make it even more difficult, but not impossible, for you to attempt to free yourself. The THEEF of life in different languages carries the same meaning and effect.

FEAR is powerful! *"How powerful, you ask?"* It has the ability to turn your lights off and keep them off permanently in any country. People generally underestimate the power of the global THEEF; it should not be accommodated in any language. A word in one language can mean one thing, and the same word in another language could mean something else, just as with the word *Olé* in Spanish and Yoruba. Whatever the THEEF of life is called in any language, its effects and results on human beings are the same. Playing or listening to the music of the THEEF of life has only one outcome: you will have to dance to the tune of FEAR.

Rules of Engagement

You retreat into your shell at the first sight of FEAR based on, perhaps, a minor setback in an activity in your life. You struggle to come out of your shell; whenever you attempt to come out of your shell, all you can think of and see is the minor setback you had in the past. FEAR is now in control of your life. You wake up and go to bed each day on the rules of engagement given to you by your general in the Failure Armed Forces. You signed these rules of engagement when you enrolled. The rules of engagement in the Failure Armed Forces are as follows:

Rule 1 states:

"You believe deeply in your mind you are a failure."

When you are trapped in the mindset of a failure, you believe success is not possible for you, no matter how hard you try. A chance or opportunity is viewed as a disaster waiting to happen; you hold your station in life and avoidance is the only option for peace of mind. References to self-made millionaires are met with customized reasons for why they are successful and why you cannot do likewise. In support of the reasons, more convincing stories with catastrophic endings are cited by your commanding officer from his bank of knowledge.

Rule 2 states:

"You don't attempt success without the permission of your commanding officer."

Every now and then, a voice whispers to you, *you can do it*. Based on the rules of engagement, you require your commanding officer's permission. When you seek his permission, your perceptions are analyzed with a failure's mindset – not just a failure's mindset, but by a veteran, and his decision without a doubt will be to point to every possible reason that would discredit success and credit failure. A commanding officer who failed, failed in life, has been honored with the medals of failure in the Failure Armed Forces and has personally and finally accepted that success is beyond him, and will only confirm your enrollment in the forces as the best decision you have ever made in your life. Because if you do not take action, you cannot experience the pain of failure again.

Rule 3 states:

"You develop under the guidance of your commanding officer and fellow soldiers in failure."

You relate with your fellow soldiers under the guidance of your commanding officer. Future soldiers will follow you as you follow them, those higher in ranks to yours in combat against success. You delude each other on the merits of the Failure Armed Forces by narrating experiences, which, in most cases, should be dismissed instantly upon delivery of the words. Each soldier brings their reasons for enrollment to the group discussions. A support system is developed and nurtured amongst fellow soldiers.

Rule 4 states:

"Go, multiply and bring forth the nation."

Every force always welcomes new recruits from the outside world. As a soldier in the Failure Armed Forces, you are expected to seek new recruits, as many as possible – family, friends and the public. Armed with your experience and the failure mindset instilled in you in the forces, you are ready to seek new recruits, and the more you recruit, the more you grow within the Failure Armed Forces. You spread the gospel to whoever cares to listen and act. The Failure Armed Forces grow and the success register waits for potential soldiers to apply.

Rule 5 states:

"You have the right to retirement benefits after serving 25 years in the Failure Armed Forces."

Like any other forces, you have a right to retirement upon attaining the retirement age and you will be entitled to your retirement benefits. But unlike other forces, the retirement benefit handed to retired soldiers is failure, in most cases, complete failure – and it is too late to take any meaningful action. The assumed benefit (safety) that initially convinced you to enroll, is not what is delivered at retirement. Unfortunately, it is not possible to know what the retirement package really entails before retirement.

Rule 6 states:

"The strategy for the game must be implemented; the strategy of containment with the inclusion of inaction and the exclusion of action is your game at any point in time."

The real game is FEAR, the result is failure but it must be perceived as success.

These are the rules of engagement in the Failure Armed Forces and they are non-negotiable. Provided an individual is aware of them and decides to proceed with his enrollment, it can be concluded that the individual has agreed to the outcome at the end of the journey with the THEEF of life. In the military, the greatest soldiers are those who take and carry out orders from their commanding officers. Those who cannot execute or refuse instructions, can never be leaders in military assignments or operations; eventually their position in the force will become untenable. They simply cannot or will not execute instructions with the required military precisions, and these are not the kind of soldiers the Failure Armed Forces intend to recruit.

The Disabled Mind

When you put a piece of paper into the paper shredder, the piece of paper is shredded; the importance of the paper is not in question. Similarly, if you put a $10 million certified check in the paper shredder, it is shredded. A disabled mind functions in the same mode of operation: when a good idea, desire, and motivation passes through a disabled mind, the idea gets no attention or review; it just passes through the disabled mind (in and out) pretty much as paper goes into the shredder and comes out shredded. The paper shredder does not review any piece of paper; the shredder simply does its job, and shreds the paper. Hence, a disabled mind is as good as a paper shredder. The THEEF of life disables the human mind. When it arrives, a disabled mind will regard success as failure, desire as dessert, and action as inaction; it is not enabled to differentiate.

A person capable of taking action who does not take action is no better than somebody who cannot take action.

Infectious

FEAR is infectious: it spreads like wildfire from one place to the other, individual-to-individual, group to group and organization to organization without any evidence. Hearsay is the only proof required by people to be infected with the FEAR bug. This is the new face of the THEEF of life: a brand-new two-bedroom apartment fully furnished with FEAR, free with your reservation, 50 percent failure deposited exclusively for you at any nominated bank of your choice. A short walk to the failure health club. If you can't afford to buy action, you can rent FEAR instead. Your conversation with the THEEF of life was effective, not to your benefit, but to the benefit of the global THEEF. The THEEF of life has taken effective action; you, on the other hand, have taken effective inaction. You have to be in a position to take effective action from your conversation with FEAR, not inaction. When you have a simple conversation with FEAR and you are already infected with FEAR, I very much doubt your chances of victory in the conversation battle. Failure cannot be denied; you bought and became a tenant of the THEEF of life. Loyalty rules, and you are committed to the cause.

Hostage of FEAR

As long as FEAR is accommodated, desire is hostage of FEAR.

Inheritance becomes an agent of FEAR when the size of the inheritance is huge. Combined with FEAR or when the inheritance is to be divided by the number of inheritance stakeholders, the birth of greed is certain, particularly when personal achievements of stakeholders are slaves to FEAR. The hard work of the provider of inheritance becomes the only ground for their conversations with the THEEF. There have been cases of children killing their parents to speed up the delivery of the inheritance due to them as stakeholders.

In any country, more than half of its citizens have been hostages of FEAR in the past and at present. In the future, many will still be hostages. Those who have refused to meet the conditions (the rules of engagement in the Failure Armed Forces) of the THEEF of life are free from the bondage of FEAR; however, those who have met the conditions of FEAR remain hostages to the greatest day and night robber of all time. For one reason or the other, FEAR rules their lives, yet they march on, hoping for a miracle to free them. The conditions herein are not hidden or dressed in fancy dress party costumes; they are visible for all to see, but the THEEF of life is relying on your FEAR of FEAR as a deterrent to you for your freedom from bondage of the THEEF of life. You cannot be a tenant of the THEEF of life, as far as FEAR of buying a home is concerned, and expect to achieve the American Dream, home ownership status: that position is reserved for those who are willing to implement the Protect or Reclaim strategy. Even in cases where the funds to do so are not available – provided the FEAR has been eliminated in the personal battle – a will to do so is established, and with the will to do so, there is always a way (for example, you could move in with your parents for a few months to save rent money for use as a deposit). As a tenant, you would have exhausted your deposit for your house on your rental obligation, and it would not be easy to achieve the status of home-owner. For further information, initiate your dialogue with the FEAR of home ownership; if not, you may end up going round in circles.

The Circle of FHIF

The THEEF of life is a strong de-motivator and excellent at what it does. It puts you in inaction mode (handcuffs) and ensures that you have no appetite for action; in most cases, you are not even aware. If you don't take care, you could be going round and round in circles for years without conversations in any of the segments of "The Circle of FHIF." This circle consists of the 'FEAR,' 'Helpless,'

'Inaction' and 'Failure' (FHIF) segments. When FEAR arrives in your life, you find yourself in the FEAR segment. If you enrol in the Failure Armed Forces, you proceed to the Helpless segment of the circle. By being helpless, your next port of call is the Inaction segment, and by remaining inactive you end up in the Failure segment to complete the journey round the circle. An individual could be moving from segment to segment in the circle, repeating the movement for decades. You are sitting on a $1 billion time bomb. The clock is ticking, in any language, in any country, second by second, minute by minute, hour by hour. The timer is on auto start from the second you enter the circle of FHIF. A second could be a day, a minute could be a month, and an hour could be a year. Regardless of the duration of a second, minute or an hour, the bottom line is, you only have a limited amount of time and the clock is ticking.

Eight of the twenty-four hours that constitute a day, in most cases, have been assigned to freeware – an open source tool called sleep. We should not deprive ourselves of what is naturally due to us. To deprive yourself of such things, is to inflict pain and discomfort on yourself, and above all, it is free. You do not pay for its use, and it is the human right of all human beings. Eight hours of sleep is recommended for each individual on a daily basis; the human batteries are recharged for human activities. Energy is generated, and the mind is also refreshed; hence, your ability to carry a basic conversation is enhanced.

A comfortable position and closing of the eyes are all that is required for initiating sleep. A day only has sixteen hours left to complete its duration; the eight hours donated to the freeware are not recalled to increase the sixteen hours left. However, the clock is still ticking, and the nine-to-five treadmill intends to claims its own portion of the sixteen hours left on the daily clock circle. A mandatory treadmill for most of us, that leaves us with eight hours for our other activities like quality time with the family or perhaps to generate additional income – considering the fact that, in certain cases, the pressures and demands of life place too much stress on one income.

FEAR begets FEAR, conversation begets more conversation and action begets more action. The THEEF of life, *FEAR*, sires *helplessness, inaction, and failure (the children of FEAR)*. When you arrive in the failure segment without any plan for the battlefield, it will lead to failure in events in other areas of your life. Remember FEAR is a virus; together, these areas make up the fourfold circle of FHIF in the minds of human beings. When such children are conceived or adopted in the human mind, the objective of the THEEF of life, failure, awaits a delivery date.

The Circle of FHIF

A mental connection with the THEEF of life creates a self-limiting belief, the requirements for ineffective and inefficient operation in the Circle of FHIF. FEAR breeds helplessness, helplessness breeds inaction and inaction breeds failure. The paraphrased Chinese proverb sums up the circle of FHIF:

> *"If there is fear in the soul,*
> *there will be helplessness in the person.*
> *If there is helplessness in the person,*
> *there will be inaction in the house.*
> *If there is inaction in the house,*
> *there will be failures in the nation.*
> *If there are failures in the nation,*
> *there will be failures in the world."*
> **Chinese Proverb (paraphrased)**
> **Tao de Ching**

When you arrive in the failure segment of the circle of FHIF because of not having your conversations with the THEEF of life (at the FEAR segment), you will feel forgotten, exploited and betrayed. This feeling is revealed to you only after your conversations with FEAR in the failure segment, but you are already in the last lap of the race, and you can see the tape in front of you at the finish line. Your monthly pension contribution has been running, perhaps for the last ten to twenty years, and you are not in position to know if the monthly pension you will receive will be enough for you to survive on a monthly basis. You will probably be saying to yourself, *I should have had my conversations with the THEEF in the FEAR segment, helpless segment or inaction segment.*

Failures keeps their life in the circle of FHIF by limiting their views to the views of failures, and as a result, they issue themselves certificates of failure for collection in the near future.

The Circle of FHAF

If due diligence is not applied, an individual could be in *"The Circle of FHIF"* and actually think he is in "The *Circle of FHAF*". Unlike FHIF, *"The Circle of FHAF"* consists of the 'Fearless,' 'Help,' 'Action' and 'Freedom' (FHAF) segments – they are identical in terms of looks and appearances of the segments. However, the essential difference lies in the segment names. The most important

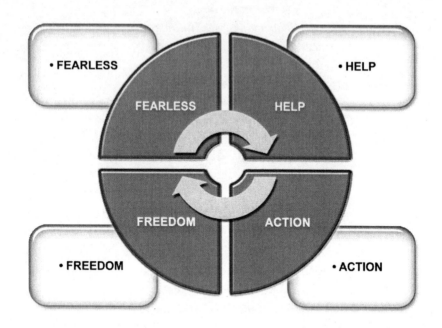

The Circle of FHAF

conclusion remains that without the co-operation and support of your fearless segment in *"The Circle of FHAF"* in all stages of the circle, your chances of successfully negotiating the remaining segments to salvage any freedom due to you, dealing with your burning FEAR, are minimal or virtually nonexistent.

To help yourself, you will need to reach the Help segment of the *"The Circle of FHAF."* To reach the *Help* segment, your negotiation skills via your dialogue with your FEAR will be an unavoidable requirement during your *'Fearless'* segment. This is where you are required to help yourself. If you choose not to help yourself, your destination will be the *'Helpless'* segment of *"The Circle of FHIF,"* as this is what you are requesting for dinner by avoiding your conversations with the THEEF of life. *Could this be a law in the universe? Is this the law of attraction?*

21 *Amoxicillin (an antibiotic drug used to treat infection) belongs to a class of antibiotics called penicillin. 250MG capsules.*

Take ONE capsule three times daily. How many times have you been given such a prescription by your doctor to treat an infection? Take your FEAR amoxicillin at regular intervals. Complete the prescribed course unless otherwise directed. The *'Fearless'* segment is your doctor's surgery, and the FEAR amoxicillin is available in various MGs depending on the severity of your burning FEAR. Visit *"The Circle of FHAF"* surgery, and initiate your conversation to receive the correct MG of FEAR amoxicillin. This will aid you to reach the *'Help'* segment of *"The Circle of FHAF"*. It's the very least you can do for yourself. FEAR amoxicillin is recommended for treating burning FEAR in the *'Fearless'* segment to produce symptoms of burning desire in the *'Help'* segment, which generally keeps the momentum going to take you through the *'Action'* segment and to the *'Freedom'* segment.

Religion

A drug binge led to the collapse and death of a millionaire banker

The drug overdose as a result of binging on cocaine, opium and alcohol by a millionaire banker, who lost a considerable amount of money in the credit crunch, led to his death.

Managing director of AKN Investments, Melvin Thomas Sabour, a 44-year-old American, after taking a cocktail of opium, cocaine and alcohol in his home, is said to have died after suffering heart failure in the presence of his girlfriend.

It was reported that he was found unconscious by his girlfriend, 28-year-old Kyara Dekker, in his bed at his home in Hertford Street, London and had taken opium before he was found. "Death from dependence on drugs" was the verdict recorded by the coroner.

Just as substance abuse is not limited to a particular religion, race, profession or location, neither is the THEEF of life. FEAR is not religious; neither are its agents. Religion simply does not exist in the vocabulary of the THEEF. The Eighth Commandment of the Ten Commandments in accordance with the Judeo-Christian tradition:

Thou shalt not steal.

No religion advocates stealing. One of the five pillars of Islam is Almsgiving:

> *The act of giving of alms voluntarily, of making contributions to the poor.*

Alms, or almsgiving, is practiced in quite a number of religions.

The THEEF of life is not an advocate of almsgiving, but a firm believer in stealing. When we are in pain and in need of relief of the pain, and somebody inflicts further pain on us in the name of almsgiving, surely, it does not constitute almsgiving in the true spirit of almsgiving, except when one considers the giving of failure to failure as almsgiving. It is frankly, *"Kicking a man when a man is down."*

In Judaism, the Sabbath (called Shabbat in Hebrew) is a day of rest and it is observed from sundown Friday until the appearance of three stars in the sky Saturday night. The THEEF of life has a phenomenal stealing technique: Monday, Tuesday, Wednesday, Thursday, Friday, Saturday or Sunday does not mean anything to the global bandit. Regardless of the day in the week, it's simply business as usual as far as the THEEF of life is concerned. A holy day in any religion does not exist for FEAR; FEAR is not religious and has no allegiance to any religion. The fear instilled by religion on people is a different kind of fear, fear of staying on the right side of the gospel of the religion. For example Muslims go to mosque on Fridays and Christians go to church on Sundays; those are the traditions of both religions respectively. You can't turn up in church on Friday morning for a service traditionally held on Sunday morning and vice versa.

> *Always speak the truth. Shun words that are deceitful and ostentatious.*
> **Quran [22/30]**

The holy Quran states, *"be cautious of god and always speak the truth."* FEAR does not speak the truth and has no intention of doing so. His words are deceitful. This individual is doing everything to keep information under wraps to increase sales of his product, handcuffs, in any religion. Start asking questions today, and by tomorrow you will realize just how deceptive and deadly this individual can be. Your conversations with the global bandit await you. Put your questions to the THEEF of life before your life, which is yours, is taken away from you by the THEEF.

FEAR, a nasty piece of work, is like fighting the enemy (anybody that goes to war against you with the intention to take you out) in a war with your eyes closed and your hands in handcuffs.

Last word:
Occupational hazards should be labeled appropriately; unfortunately, FEAR slipped through the net.

THREE

The Past

PAST

After the tea break, Thiago took over the proceedings with words of wisdom. *"Be proud of your background no matter how good or bad your past may have been. Regardless of your past, you are who you are,"* said Thiago to Janet and I. Establish your past as your PAST.

PAST – *"Past Actions See Transformation."*

There are things you did in the past that you are not particularly proud of, and would not do now or in the future. Let your past be a platform from which to launch your future. Be proud, stand tall, and don't be ashamed of your past. Everybody has a past; you are not alone in that department. Always remind yourself, *"My past is my past, not my future."* You may not have had the opportunity to influence your past because, when you were a child, your parents were your guardians, and you were not in a position to make decisions at such a young age. You have a chance now to decide your future. The opportunities are for all, not for a selected few. Identify opportunities when they present themselves. When an individual not comfortable with his past finds wealth, he immediately tries to hide his past with his wealth. The reality is that no amount of money can make you comfortable if you refuse to make peace with your past.

A man cannot be comfortable without his own approval.
Mark Twain

Approve your past; it is entitled to be PAST. Be comfortable with your past; your future is ahead of you, not behind you. You own your past. Nobody can give you the approval you seek on your past – not even all the wealth in the world can give you the approval. You are the only one who can give yourself that approval. When you cannot approve your past within yourself, how can you be comfortable with yourself, let alone engage in an open discussion about your past comfortably? When a man is not comfortable with his past, he will never be comfortable even with a successful future because his past has not seen a transformation for the future. Simple questions about his past, that should be his PAST, become topics to avoid at all cost. A friend once told me, *"My friends had a better childhood than I did, but I don't feel uncomfortable with them."*

The amazing thing about that statement, to me, was, this is a man who is now very successful but had no FEAR of his past, and was willing to engage in a discussion about his past freely and willingly. He is a man who has truly made his past a PAST and has moved to another level – a level that, in my opinion, ensures he is comfortable with his past, a level that a lesser man still struggles to deal with and would find very uncomfortable in any area. I wonder why! Regardless of your past, it is yours: own it and accept it.

Success is not reserved for those with silver spoons, nor is failure reserved for those with plastic spoons; the game of life can go either way. It just depends on how well you use your spoon, silver or plastic.

I said to Janet and Thiago, "I take my hat off to such individuals, they have truly shown they are real winners who will not be derailed." Regardless of our past, we are who we are. We do not choose which family we want to be born into before we are born, and no child comes into the world wearing clothes when they are born. Silver spoon or not, each individual needs to rediscover himself, for each individual has a journey, a journey into the unknown. A silver spoon does not necessarily guarantee success, and a plastic spoon does not necessarily guarantee failure. The future is the future; the past is the past. Your past is your past, unless you make the past your future. The future is yours.

FEAR comes in different forms: FEAR of one's past is a THEEF that needs to be eradicated. It makes you paranoid; you become more concerned about who knows about your past and who doesn't. You become uncomfortable. Regardless of any situation, you have to deal with your past, and dealing with it not only makes you comfortable, but it also provides the platform from which a comfortable future can be launched. Until you give your approval, you can run, but you can't hide. Even if you run and hide from all, you can't run and hide from yourself. I really don't see the reason why anybody should be ashamed or uncomfortable with their past. I actually believe strongly that each individual should be totally comfortable with his or her past. If you are not comfortable with your past, an element of FEAR exists in your past, and no matter what position you find yourself in in the future, for you to truly be comfortable within yourself, you need to deal with the FEAR that exists in your past. Artifacts are man-made items. Hence, they will not make the man; rather, the man makes the artifacts. You cannot hide your past behind artifacts; you will still need to approve your past. You need a dialogue with the THEEF of life regarding your past. Remember, it is your past, not your future, and everybody gets a second chance to make amends or improvements depending on each situation as the case may be. Your subconscious mind can influence your future but not your past. With your future ahead of you, no one is in charge of your happiness but you. Make peace with your past so it won't screw up the present or future. Who knows what the future holds? Perhaps the best is yet to come into your life.

Clinton

If the THEEF had got the better of Bill Clinton when he was defeated in his campaign for Congress in Arkansas's Third District in 1974, or if he had not met JFK in the White House Rose Garden, America would have been robbed of the presidency of Bill Clinton. Instead, he was the president of the United States of America for eight years. While in the White House, he had an issue that guaranteed his place in the record books as the second president in the history of the United States of America to be impeached. Bill Clinton at the time denied the allegation, but later took ownership of the issue (a mistake on his part in the past) and acknowledged it. Due to his ownership and approval of the issue, it became his PAST. *(He apologized to the nation and continued to have unprecedented popular approval ratings for his job as president.)* Had Clinton not taken ownership and approved the issue, the issue could have been the beginning of the end. I am sure his actions bear heavily on him. It was a mistake, a costly mistake, but it had to be put to bed one way or the other. Bill needed to move on, his family needed to move on and the nation needed to move on. Should we stop living because we made a mistake in the past? We can't keep dwelling on mistakes in the past, they were in the past. If we insist on dwelling on mistakes in the past, I believe we intend to give the negative past a voice to interfere with the future.

Pretty Boy

Floyd Mayweather Jr.: "I had a father who was a hustler and a mother who was on drugs."

Floyd Mayweather's face does not do him any justice in relation to his current profession. No wonder they call him Pretty Boy. With the kind of upbringing Mayweather Jr. had, you would have expected him to be a hustler or drug addict by default, more so the latter because of his wealth, his relationship with his mother, and his father doing time for drug trafficking. His story is a true case of mind over matter, rather than matter over mind – the greatest pound-for-pound fighter on the planet as of today, in my opinion. Disregard the bad boy image; it is all hype. Pretty Boy is pretty and getting prettier by the hour with his devastating hand speed, exceptional footwork and wealth. It is easy to forget that boxing is a sport like any other sport where the objective is to win. The most amazing thing about Pretty Boy for me (Thiago said) is not his wealth, but his ability to put his past behind him and his future in front. A man among men and an icon, he accepted and, even more importantly, approved his past as PAST. An ordinary man on the street would struggle to accept his past, let alone approve it, yet Pretty Boy with all his wealth, gladly accepted and approved it as if it was just a story in a storybook. Could Pretty Boy at the age of one, have avoided being used as a human shield when his uncle on his mother's side arrived with a shotgun and shot his father in the leg? The question is yours; your answer is good enough for me. Janet and I agreed with Thiago. Pretty Boy had conversations with his FEAR of his past and future, which is hardly surprising. He stood pound for pound with the THEEF as he has always done in the boxing ring against his opponents.

Try as hard as we may, we can't change our past. Your roots are your roots. The earlier you accept your past as PAST and approve it, the earlier you become comfortable with yourself. A dialogue with your FEAR of your past is crucial. Clinton and Pretty Boy are two different people with different upbringings and achievements under different circumstances, but each has a past that could easily have had devastating consequences for both leading to the same destination – failure. Each had to approve of his past to be comfortable with it. In Clinton's case, he failed in the past, when he was defeated in his campaign for Congress in Arkansas's Third District in 1974. Pretty Boy could have been a drug hustler based on the past drug history in the family, but he kept at it and broke the family tradition as champions, by becoming a five-division world champion and staying on the right side of the law on drug issues compared to his predecessor. I will be completely responsible for my future. It is ahead of me, and I will make the decisions going forward. My past should not control my future; it should be a reference point for my future. Deal with your past. Let the past go with the past, and your future with your future. The THEEF will always discourage you from approving your past to contaminate your thinking about your future *(if you were not good enough yesterday, you will not be good enough tomorrow)*. We must unite to say past is past, future is future, not past.

The Democratic Party presidential candidate Senator Barack Obama stated, *"Drug-taking in my youth was my greatest moral failing."* At least, we have it on record now, and it was in the past, not the present or the future; hence, 'Garbage Diggers' trying to attack his character with various investigation techniques can eliminate his youthful exuberance within their digging duties. It has been sealed and approved by the subject.

Paranoid

When you are paranoid among friends, work colleagues or the public in general about your past, you not only have a problem, but you also create further problems in your life. I cannot emphasize it enough; your past is your PAST *(Past Actions See Transformation)*. These are things you did in the past that you are not particularly proud of and would not do now or in the future. Family, friends, work colleagues and members of the public: every single one of them has a past. Some people's pasts are even worse than yours is. Some people's pasts may have been brighter than yours, but one thing is certain –there are others whose pasts are darker than yours, darker than dark, yet you choose to be paranoid about your own past. Everybody knows that everybody has a past; this is common public knowledge. I am sure you cannot tell me you know somebody without a past. It is only your past; don't be paranoid about it, just approve it. Everybody knows you have a past, and that is not an issue; however, it is the fact that you are paranoid about it that makes your past an issue with friends, work colleagues and the public. In certain quarters, your past is not overlooked. If public figures can approve their past, even though it is in the public domain without invitation, it should not be difficult for you as a member of the general public to put a seal of approval on your past. There is really nothing you can do about your past apart from accept it and move on, it is history and you can't rewrite that history. Regardless of what that history contains, you will have to live with it, and to live with it – personal approval is required.

The Race

Your past is not in the next race, but your future is. Your past, to date has already ran its race. Let the future run its own race. The past has no allocated lane for the next race or future race; simply stated, your past is not in the running. Let the future, the athlete of the future, step on to the tracks to man its own assigned lane. The past is too old to compete with the future on the track. The past has experience! Yes, it certainly does, but within a hundred meters, the old legs will give way at about the sixty-meter distance, eliminating any chance of a podium place finish for the race. Meanwhile, at the sixty-meter stage of the race, the future is just getting into its stride. If we are not going to dine with the past, let's get the future to dine with the THEEF of life constructively. In a race between you and FEAR, without your conversation, you don't stand a chance except if you start at the finish line. The loss from the THEEF of life cannot be measured at the beginning, but is assured at the end. FEAR has no intention of retiring from the helm. Waiting for his retirement is not an option for consideration. Life is a journey; don't focus on the past, and keep the focus on the future.

Poverty and Struggle

Whatever may be said in praise of poverty, the fact remains that it is not possible to live a really complete or successful life unless one is rich.

**The Science of Getting Rich,
Wallace D. Wattles**

If you are poor and unable to afford basic food items in grocery stores, can you live a complete life? Surely basic food items are essential requirements for our lives. The discussion of poverty and struggle is upon us. Poverty is the state or condition of having little or no money. A proverb says:

Poverty is not a crime.

To be poor is not a crime in reality, but it leads to crime. It is something most people would rather not be associated with (particularly those who are relatively well-off and suddenly find poverty knocking on their door), because it carries some conditions which, upon its arrival could lead to committing suicide, a personal death sentence imposed by an individual upon himself. It begs the question, if poverty is not a crime, what is it? If it carries such a heavy penalty in some cases, could it be FEAR, or the reality of not being able to provide yourself with the necessities (food, shelter and clothing) that leads to such tragic consequence? Another proverb says:

Poverty is no disgrace, but a great inconvenience.

It really must be a great and serious inconvenience. Crime, homelessness, starvation, lower life expectancy, social isolation and discrimination are other effects of poverty. When real poverty arrives, in a once-comfortable home, it creates a struggle for basic daily needs which were easily provided in the past. A very happy marriage could really be put to the test in times of hardship.

How great is this inconvenience? People have committed suicide due to poverty; that is how inconvenient poverty can be. Today, I offer you my priceless asset. "Poverty may or may not be regarded as a crime; regardless of your opinion, don't associate yourself with poverty." Strive for success and achievements to provide a better quality of life for yourself. Nobody strives for poverty willingly, but their strategy for battle may not share the same desire, hence the need to review the options in our strategy for battle from time to time.

When poverty comes in via the door, love flies out via the window.

Poverty and love don't ply the same route and are not related; they are not of the same descendants, either. They hardly meet eye-to-eye with each other; in most instances when they meet, one or the other gives way. I have heard people say, "I am poor, but I am happy." How can you be happy when you are poor? I really don't understand it. Poverty makes life a struggle. If life is a struggle, where is the happiness? To struggle for existence in life is not a very comfortable situation to be in, and to be happy in such circumstances is difficult. However, I recognize and appreciate the fact that there are poor people who are happy and I respect them for that, particularly in situations where due to circumstances beyond their control, turning their fortune around may not be an option. I have to take my hat off to people who are happy under such conditions. It is not about huge amounts of money; it is about what small amounts of money can do for you and your family. The amount of money I am talking about is not millions or billions. A regular job can still deal with these basics effectively. I will not be happy if I cannot provide the basic essentials of life (food, shelter and clothing) for my family (as a matter of fact, the need for the provision of these basic needs could lead to the creation of a burning desire), and to do that, I will need money, (unless somebody is willing to carry my responsibility for providing basic essentials for my family). By the way, whoever carries my responsibility for the basic essential needs would still require money to do so. Money does not grow on trees. Money is necessary for the provision of basic daily requirements. As they say, "A hungry man is an angry man." Expansion of this phrase leads to, "A well-fed man is a happy man." To feed the man, food is required, and to get the food, payment is required, unless an individual intends to steal the food (an act for which the THEEF of life would sing any individual's praise day and night). Moreover, to make the payment, money appears in this family portrait. Money delivers the cure for the disease of hunger; money is the mediator between the disease and the cure, and provides the happiness that comes with the cure. I am not saying money will give happiness in all areas of our lives, but it will certainly alleviate happiness in most areas of our lives, and, at the very least, mitigate the pain of unhappiness.

In Dollars We Trust

Your needs and your dollar had their conversations with FEAR: the result, a mutual respect and understanding was established between your dollar and your needs. Your needs will always exist, and their satisfaction requires your dollar at the going price. You are not a party to the decision, but you are a party to compliance with the decision they established. Another day, another dollar – however, the dollar has a 'one to many' relationship with your needs, while your needs have a 'many-to-one' relationship with your dollar. We all have many needs (food, shelter, clothing, etc.) that require the dollar; how many dollars will be required to satisfy these needs varies from individual to individual. The bottom line is, "the absence of the dollar means the absence of needs that require satisfaction, period." Rich or poor, some needs (food, shelter and clothing) still require the attention of the dollar; the difference is the quality and quantity required by both.

"In dollars we trust:" your needs are us (food, shelter and clothing), and our needs are your dollar bills. Our equilibrium is when our needs meet, and they meet on a daily basis. With regard to the relationships, the 'one-to-many' relationship is the same as the 'many-to-one' relationship from a different viewpoint. The dollar may require many needs, and many needs may require the dollar; the relationship flow depends on which requires which. The dollar and needs have had their conversation, and the rules of the game have been agreed.

The Three Musketeers

> *Athos, Porthos and Aramis – inseparable friends who live by the motto, "One for all, and all for one".*
> **The Three Musketeers,**
> **Alexandre Dumas, père**

Needs and dollar are comrades and have established a statement of solidarity. Ask yourself, *"Are my current needs honored?"* Either way, in any direction, you are not alone by any means, because this is the biggest issue most people have to deal with. Your dollar and your needs have the same inseparable loyalty to each other. If you don't have the dollar, your needs will not be satisfied. Just as FEAR has allegiance to failure, the end product of a conversation with the THEEF of life in his favor, so do needs to the dollar; the only language they understand is the dollar language. If you are not communicating in dollars, your needs will not understand your language on their maturity date, and as they already exist, their maturity date is already in sight. It is only a matter time. There are over 80 different currencies in the world; they have all signed the statement of solidarity with needs. In any country, you have to communicate with the relevant currency for your needs to adhere to your request. NEEDS! Their satisfaction is the reason for the undervaluation of the human soul. The search for the dollar leads a man to undertake unlawful activities, even though he knows it is the wrong thing to do.

The Price of a Soul

*Merit is for those who merit merit. The
THEEF of life is not a candidate for merit.*

You pay homage to fellow human beings. You applaud them, and you show respect to those who don't deserve it. You undervalue your soul, you put a price on your soul and market it at less than one percent of its true value. You are not a professional evaluator; how can you value your soul at less than one percent? That one percent, by the way, is your rough estimate. I am sure if the services of a professional soul-valuer were employed, the value would be miles away from your valuation. It may not be 100 percent, but it certainly would not be 1 percent. With knowledge, good knowledge, nobody can wave or dangle the handcuffs of slavery (due to the FEAR of lack of money) in front of you, in exchange for your soul, particularly where the handcuffs of slavery in question are the proceeds of a substance abused by daughters and sons in the world.

Poverty shows its true colors. Is blood wealth or bloodstained dollar bills worth your soul? I truly believe no kind of wealth should be worth more than any human soul. A man who has tasted poverty knows the power that resides in the monster. The unmistakable look of poverty in its extreme cannot be mistaken for a look of wealth. The price of poverty denies the human soul the knowledge of its true value; the value is dictated by poverty. The human soul becomes a hostage of poverty, which creates a security-free zone for the THEEF of life to do what it does best.

> *I am opposed to millionaires, but it will be dangerous to offer me the position.*
> **Mark Twain**

As much as poor people may oppose the rich, it would definitely be dangerous to offer anybody the opportunity, let alone a man who has had poverty and struggle as his best friend for most of his life. Likewise, the failures always oppose the action-takers. Tame a failure's FEAR, and watch how much action resides inside the man. Dictators are good examples. Once they take control, the power and wealth development avenues available are explored to their full capacities. The national treasury becomes a personal treasury, and basic amenities for citizens become non-existent in the country.

Welfare

In certain cases, an argument may exist for being on welfare, but without a doubt, such an argument does not exist for the majority of welfare cases. Being in a position to afford three square meals, joy-riding and having a place in the projects does not mean you have achieved success. Welfare is the first cousin to poverty and struggle. If you are on welfare and in a project, it could be because you want to, or enjoy being on welfare and in a project. People on welfare tend to have a free-lunch mentality, a *'something for nothing'* culture. They expect the government, the rich and the working-class citizens to pay their bills. If you have an option to get off or to remain on the welfare line, the first question you need to ask yourself is, *"Why am I on the welfare line?"* Within your answer, there will be some element of FEAR. An option available to you, is to deposit your welfare check and FEAR in your account, and to withdraw your ticket to success from your bank account at the same time. Another option is for you to issue your own welfare check in the amount you want or need every two weeks.

J.K. Rowling
Went from a welfare mom to the world's wealthiest author. Her seven books in the Harry Potter series have sold 400 million copies worldwide. Her new book, The Tales of Beedle the Bard, raised $6.5 million for her charity, Children's High Level Group

www.forbes.com

There may be more brilliant writers or other brilliant people on welfare who could do an excellent job in other professions, but if they don't try, we will never know. J. K. Rowling could still be on welfare today if she did not start writing. *"One day I will get off the welfare roll"* is only a statement. If you take effective action to do so, the reality arrives. If you don't, you are taking a gamble that you may win or lose. However, when you start gambling, the odds are against you; in the majority of cases, the house always wins. Furthermore, you are not forced to go on welfare.

Forced to be a drug mule
Facing 15 years in jail on suspicion of attempting to smuggle $500,000 worth of cocaine from Peru, the British lady from Southampton said: "I was forced to be a drug mule." 8lbs. of drugs were said to have been found in her suitcases by the police, and on the woman, Rachel Franklin, 20 -years-old, while she waited in Lima at Madrid at Jorge Chavez airport to board her flight. She is being held at the police headquarters and has not been charged as the police began their investigation.
Rachel Franklin admitted, for $10,000, she agreed to smuggle the cocaine for drug dealers in Southampton, whom she met through her

> *boyfriend, a heroin addict. Initially she agreed, but later tried to reverse her decision to smuggle the cocaine.*
> *She said: "At first it was about the money. I did want the $10,000, because being unemployed, $10,000 is a lot. But on the day before I left, I did not want to do it. But one of the guys said I had to go because all the flights were booked. I have three A-levels and I wanted to do things with my life, and now it is ruined." After spending seven days in Cusco, a tourist destination, she flew to Lima. Rachel Franklin intends to plead guilty when she is charged.*

Hard work is deprived of confidence, hope or spirit by welfare. Being on welfare is not a defense for becoming a drug mule. The welfare line only gives you a certain amount of money every two weeks or whatever the case may be, no more, no less. If you want more, you will have to get off the welfare line. However, if it is enough for you, then you don't have to get off the welfare line, and by the way, congratulations, as you may be in your comfort zone and not willing to move. However, one thing is certain. The welfare line is not a line for success; it is a line for failure with hidden repercussions that are not visible until, in certain cases, it is too late to make amends. Welfare takes your mind and lets you keep your body. A weak mind in a strong body is not strong enough to take the welfare mentality on in a debate at any stage of the dialogue.

If you are on welfare and your paymasters struggle to make ends meet with their paycheck on a month-to-month basis, how do you make ends meet on your crippled welfare payment? If they go on strike for a longer period, how do you get your welfare payment? The records indicate that 95 percent of the people who reach retirement age will need some kind of help or a part-time job in order to live a decent life. It begs the question, *"If quite a number of the people who work until retirement will need some kind of help or a part-time job in order to live a decent life, will people on welfare need a major financial help or a full-time job to live a decent life upon attaining the age of retirement?"* Provided we are staying within the constraints of the law, I am sure people on welfare will require more than a full-time job after retirement age, unless training is provided while on welfare for managing on an exceptionally low income after attaining the retirement age.

At first glance you may think you are getting *"something for nothing"* and really living in the *"something-for-nothing"* culture; however, the welfare system does not just give you *"something for something."* If you take a good look at it, it gives you something to live on, but further down the line in the relationship, the system gives you failure, all in return for inaction on your part to get off welfare. The THEEF of life is not in the business of *"something for nothing,"* its business model is clearly based on *"something for something."* The only thing FEAR can give to you is assistance to fail which appears as assistance to *safety*. The reality is FEAR has given you something in return for your life and for having been on welfare. A gentleman in London, England, C. Northcote Parkinson, came up with a rule known to economists as "Parkinson's law." *If expenses are rising to meet income, then expenses will rise faster than income.* On account of Parkinson's law, we can therefore conclude that expenses will always rise faster than welfare income, at a faster rate than the rate at which it will rise against real income (earned income via work), because welfare income does not rise at a rate close to real income.

Mittal

There has to be a philosophy behind those who are successful and those who fail. To unravel this philosophy we have to ask; where they are from, where and how they grew up and when they grew up. These questions are legitimate to clarify, aside from taking action, what personality traits they might have in common. We can't just make a dangerous assumption about what they are like in order to justify their success.

Laskshimi Mittal, the richest man in Great Britain, is from India. Welfare is not available in India, at least, not on the same level as in the United States. The basic task, expected of every individual, to provide food for himself or herself is met head on with work, hard work – the bedrock of success, and not handouts from the government. Working is second nature for any individual who grows up in this kind of environment, as opposed to those who grew up on regular handouts (welfare). This is not to say one can't be successful, even if one grew up on handouts – but under such circumstances, the hands, in most cases, are in handcuffs. The hands of those who don't have the option of handouts are already in motion to achieve the task of success; the chance of succeeding is increased before the scheduling of relevant success lecture classes. If a father is on welfare, and is a role model to his son, the chances of the son being on welfare in the future are quite high. On the other hand, the chances of a son whose father has already dedicated himself to hard work in the steel industry, chances of himself embracing hard work in the steel industry are also quite high. *To unravel this philosophy we have to ask; where they are from, where and how they grew up and when they grew up.* Lakshimi Mittal's cultural background is not an exception to this rule, and neither is the background of those on government handouts.

Money

> *Money isn't the most important thing in life, but it's reasonably close to oxygen on the "gotta have it" scale.*
> **Zig Ziglar**

"Is money imperative to you?" People's perceptions about money vary. Some people will say they don't want a lot of money, because, you guessed it, "money is the root of all evil." However, we should not forget that money is the medium of exchange; hence, if you do not have money, you cannot carry out any form of exchange that requires money. There is a proverb that says:

> *Money says if he is not at home, let no one make any plans in his absence.*

A plan in the absence of the medium of exchange to obtain

products and services that require money for their fulfillment is simply a dream, and remains a dream until the arrival of the medium of exchange. There is nothing wrong in dreaming, but for that dream to be realized, it has to become a burning desire supported with action.

> *The future belongs to those who believe
> in the beauty of their dreams.*
> **Eleanor Roosevelt**

The audacity to make that future plan in the absence of money is the belief in the beauty of the dream; that belief is burning desire and action. Going to work is a very common way of earning money to live. It is simply grinding out resources for day-to-day living. Everybody can apply for a nine-to-five job. Most people can produce a resume for applying for a job. It is a basic skill for most human beings, but not everybody can create nine-to-five jobs for people. This is a fact known and understood by the rich, which remains unknown and a puzzle to the poor. The nine-to-five treadmill strategy is the easy way out, and human beings, in general, prefer the easy way out option. This life stimulus, like economic stimulus, is temporary; the government cannot continue to bail out companies from their current predicaments. This nine-to-five treadmill stimulus has an expiration date in the future, and should not be treated as a permanent source of income. Living a good life costs money; if an individual dislikes money, the individual probably dislikes the good life, but no man can dislike the basics of life and those also come at a price, in certain cases, a good price. FEAR has, for a long time, lied to the masses and they have acted as disciples of FEAR, preaching the gospel of FEAR without any proof. They become liars based on 'he said' or 'she said' mandates handed to them. If you are bold enough to ask for or request evidence, the 'he said' or 'she said' mandate is produced – but not the 'I said' mandate, which generally comes with concrete experience.

Money is the servant capable of putting breakfast, lunch and dinner on your table on a consistent basis. Unlike FEAR, money only goes where it receives an invitation for attendance, and only stays in those places where it is welcomed. It is quite possible to be invited to a function, and not be welcomed or acknowledged.

> *Do not enter houses other than your own until you have sought permission, and then greet the inhabitants and wish them a life of blessing, purity and joy.*
> **Quran [24/27]**

To enter somebody's house without permission is a crime in any country, regardless of the language of the country. Only a THEEF will break this rule. FEAR will not always seek your permission before he enters your mind, let alone, wish you a life of blessing, purity and joy. The THEEF of life seems always satisfied if the cause is noble to him, if it will affect society negatively. We are all destined to make an impact on society. The question is, what impact are you going to make on society, or are you here for society to make an impact on you? I hope not. If there has to be a limit to youthful exuberance, there has to be a limit to human endurance. A human being can only starve until the human hunger reaches its highest level, and the human physical endurance has completed its duration. The THEEF of life is willing and able to complete the duration, and the society the global THEEF belongs to is waiting to make an impact on you.

Last word:
Analyze your PAST. Analyze the effects of poverty and struggle. Money is not your friend or enemy; money is a natural tool required in your toolbox for your journey of life.

THREE

Overview

A Brief Overview of the Protect or Reclaim strategy – The 7 Steps

The application of FEAR eradication is to implement the Protect or Reclaim strategy. Within your Personal Battle, you decide if you want to go to war to free your life, and how soon you intend to go into battle. In the Public Battle, you go to war along with like-minded people and evaluate situations and results together. If required, you modify accordingly. The Art of Battle arrives as a result of your previous battles (Personal and Public), in addition to consistent engagement in present and future battles – a divide and eliminate strategy. Each step can easily be accommodated individually. It is an established fact that human beings, in general, learn better via a step-by-step process, rather than executing all the steps together as one. The discovery of this strategy, the burning need for it to protect or reclaim the life of an individual and the arrival of it on an individual's hands, is triggered by the need for improvements or changes in results. The three parts of the Protect or Reclaim strategy constitute the seven steps to protect or reclaim our lives from FEAR. As an overview, it can be summarized as three-stage process, applicable to any part of the Protect or Reclaim strategy. The three-stage process is:

1. Figure out the FEAR – Establish what you are afraid of, or why you are afraid.
2. Evaluate the FEAR – Establish the real worth or value of the FEAR, to establish a burning desire.
3. Action the FEAR – Perform an action to confirm your evaluation and eradicate your FEAR.

In most cases, before the individual gets a chance to ask himself or herself, *'Who Stole My Life?'*, the individual's hands are already in handcuffs. The three parts of the strategy are battles and warriors don't go to war without their weapons. This is the weapon (plan) you require to go into a battle with FEAR. This three-stage process can be fully employed and implemented, with the seven detailed steps for protecting or reclaiming your life from the creator of failure.

Personal Battle

Step 1– Relax – Learn to relax, nobody talks for 24 hours in one day.
Step 2– Interrogate – Identify the reasons for, or what causes your FEAR.
Step 3– Establish – Establish your burning desire.

Public Battle

Step 4– Action – Take action on small FEAR; begin by taking one action, and then another, that each has little or no consequences.
Step 5– Analyze – Analyze the feedback from the small actions you took, and create a soft landing for yourself.
Step 6– *Gradual* – gradually increase or decrease your action.

The Art of Battle

Step 7– *Practice* – Practice, practice, practice and practice again.

This is a systematic approach to silence the voice of FEAR; in lives everywhere in the world, or in situations where FEAR has declared wars on our lives in battles here and there. Do we sit back, or defend our lives? We may have sat back in the past, but going forward, we have to have a systematic approach in place to defend ourselves. There has to be a reason for going to war, and that reason must be a valid reason – your reason for going to this particular war lies in the answer to, *'Who Stole your Life?'* I once asked myself, *'Who Stole my Life?'*, and the answer pointed to the THEEF of life without any doubts whatsoever; the answer was the justification for a declaration of war, and the beginning of the creation of this Protect or Reclaim strategy as a plan for battle. With your knowledge of FEAR, your past and an outline of the Protect or Reclaim strategy, I urge you to ask yourself, if you haven't done so, that same question: *'Who Stole my Life?'*

A systematic approach to silence the voice of a life cannot be tolerated, it must be met with a systematic approach to give a life a voice.

Last word:
This is the battle plan, and it comes with options. With this battle plan, if a man is down, the only other option is up. On that note, let the battle commence!

PART TWO
Personal Battle

FOUR

Step 1: Relax

Learn to relax, nobody talks for 24 hours in one day.

The first part of the seven steps of the Protect or Reclaim strategy is a personal battle that should appear on your radar as soon as possible to maintain your focus and the objective of the battle. As you execute the steps of the strategy, you will be ready not only to identify the real face of the THEEF of life, but also to take action – effective and constructive action – in different areas of your life within days, weeks or months depending on how urgent a result is to your life. You will be in a position to take more important actions in different areas of your life effectively, by using the following steps of the Protect or Reclaim strategy (personal and public battles) to tame the global bandit, the THEEF. The first step of this systematic approach to giving life a voice in the personal battle, is to learn to relax. Nobody can talk for 24 hours in a day, due to fatigue of talking. There are different ways to relax, including the mandatory freeware (sleep).

How to Relax

The following are some excellent ways to relax depending on your preference:

1. Sleep: The value of this freeware should not be underestimated. It is one of the best ways to relax. You should strive to get enough quality sleep every day. Sleep is good for your immune system, and refreshes your mind. A nice bath before sleeping is also relaxing.
2. Deny the agents of FEAR a voice in your life: they are the transmitters of FEAR, which automatically create a stressful life.

3. Organize your activities in order of importance: this enable you to get things done quickly and efficiently. It gives you more time to relax.
4. Eat healthy food: you can get professional help from dieticians regarding what kinds of foods are healthy foods. Eating healthy food also helps you reduce the possibility of become oversized or obese.
5. Beautiful things: appreciate the beautiful things in your life and deny the ugly things an appreciation. Be positive, and maintain positivity in everything you do in your life.
6. Vacation: Take a vacation; it's another great way to relax. Relax and put your feet up. Your vacation could be a trip to the next city or abroad – it is not limited by distance.
7. Massage: There are a number of spas throughout the country – find one to get a good massage.
8. Yoga: It is rejuvenating mind and body therapy. Yoga improves your mental focus. This is another good way to relax. I am told by yoga lovers that they get totally relaxed with yoga.
9. Meditation: Another excellent way to relax is by meditating. You can reach relaxation via meditation.
10. Self-Hypnosis: You could also use hypnosis to relax.
11. Take a walk: Do this either during lunch breaks, or around the block at home.
12. Read books: You can read a book, as you can become relaxed by reading books, either fiction or non-fiction books. Some non-fiction motivational books are particularly good at inspiring and renewing enthusiasm, and some fiction books are extremely funny and will make you laugh. You can't really smile or laugh when you are totally stressed out.
13. Have a Laugh: Having casual conversations, particularly with your family, is another way to relax. Conversations that make you laugh are another way of relaxing. Laughing has never been bad for any individual.
14. Switch off your daily gadgets: Your cell phone, TV, computer, pager, etc. – just enjoy the quiet and peaceful environment, and relax your mind.

15. Music: You can become relaxed by listening to music. Some people get totally relaxed just by listening to a particular type of music – depending on the kind of person you are. Some people reduce stress levels with music.
16. Don't confine yourself inside the box: Is there anything else you can do to relax? Think outside the box.
17. Amongst the different ways of relaxing, always use the one that suits you, that gets you totally relaxed. For example, you might prefer yoga, and I might dislike it; thus, there is no point in me using yoga to relax.
18. **Take action to ensure you relax.**

When we are relaxed, we communicate better in our conversations and discussions. You need to be calmed and relaxed when you assess your FEAR. Assess the THEEF of life with a relaxed mind, and you will be in for a surprise. You will discover the majority of your FEARS are simply false and unfounded. You get a better view of your FEAR with a relaxed mind, and you also plan better when your mind is at peace. You should have a whole day or longer to relax in a way that suits you. Some prefer to meditate, listen to music, play a round of golf, sleep, or go out with friends, etc. The minute you are hit by this surprise, you will instantly know you are already engaged in the personal battle. It is important to be relaxed, because it will eliminate your FEAR of FEAR, which prevents you from having a simple conversation with FEAR, interrogating FEAR or establishing your desire, let alone finding a burning desire to move forward in different areas of your life. In a relaxed mode, learn to understand the real THEEF of life, via your conversation or discussion.

Last word:
It is difficult to be relaxed when confronted by FEAR; however, a relaxed mind is priceless to all.

FIVE

Step 2: Interrogate

Identify the reasons for or what causes your FEAR

How to Communicate With the THEEF

The most ignored conversation will not solve itself if we ignore it; it will only accommodate a resolution if we address the conversation with the THEEF. To establish a good conversation or discussion with the THEEF is to have the most ignored conversation, a conversation with FEAR, the first conversation in the hierarchy of conversations. Once you establish a good conversation with your FEAR, keep it going. Once established, it should be nurtured and maintained. The world bandit is pretty good at what it does; it is the very best in the world in its department. The THEEF is extremely successful, you only need to look at the number of failures worldwide to appreciate how successful FEAR is; yet, FEAR intends to prevent us from becoming successful. I wonder why. If FEAR likes success, why should we dislike success? Why is success good for him, and bad for us? FEAR can easily reverse your good conversation to a bad conversation within seconds, without you even realizing it. To nurture good conversations with the THEEF, and ensure that your conversations with the bandit are mainly good rather than bad, you simply need to get over your FEAR of the turbulence in conversations. Effective and good conversation with FEAR can be established and maintained by the following:

- *Communicate your views and opinion to FEAR* – The major point of a good conversation with the THEEF is to ensure FEAR appreciates your views and opinions. For example, while you need to put your views and opinions across to the THEEF, remember that you are both having a conversation and the global THEEF will definitely be putting his views and opinions across to you, to ensure he has a good conversation with you and, in the process, hands you the turbulence in conversation. Your views and opinions on the subject form the basis of your good conversation with the THEEF; don't ignore the power of you views and opinions on the subject.

- *Listen to the THEEF of life* – FEAR always gives one disadvantage against itself, sometimes hidden in the advantages it gives in conversation with you. The disadvantage outweighs, and can't be compared with all its advantages combined together. In your conversation with the THEEF, if you always talk and never listen, you will miss the disadvantage FEAR gives against itself and the opportunity to understand and learn about it. You will agree with the THEEF that its advantages outweigh its most important disadvantage, which, in reality, is not the case. Put your listening skills to work, and develop them further; don't take over the conversation. Listen to FEAR; don't forget it's a conversation between two, not one (you and the global THEEF). I really don't see success happening when you commence your journey with the undertaker of life with a strong bond. The undertaker, FEAR, will not let it happen. The undertaker has not come this far with you, only to hand you the qualification of his opposition, success. The bond with FEAR is breakable; that bond has to be broken, and it is you who can break the bond. Break that bond! *"The journey to success cannot be completed when FEAR is the navigator of the route to success."*
- *Communicate with confidence when you converse with the THEEF* – FEAR always respects those who carry a conversation with him confidently. Do your research and be prepared, so you know exactly what you are talking about. The best way to be confident when having a conversation with the THEEF, is to stick to talking about topics you know something about. FEAR creates failures, and action creates winners – and, by the way, don't second-guess yourself throughout the whole conversation. The

minute you do, you hand the THEEF a competitive advantage in the conversation.
- *Avoid certain topics with the THEEF* – There are some topics you probably should never bring up unless you want a debate with FEAR, a debate you will never win. What you believe before your conversation with the THEEF, will be different from what you believe after your conversation with him. If you don't avoid those topics (for example the subject of FEAR without good research on the subject, or failures who are failures but believe they are successful under the guidance of FEAR) where the THEEF has an upper hand compared to you, you will soon be unveiled as the latest recruit of the Failure Armed Forces.
- **Take action, have a conversation with FEAR.**

Interrogation

To conduct an interrogation, we have to converse with the suspect by asking questions. The objective of our interrogation is to get the results we want; you can therefore employ any method you're comfortable with when questioning your suspect, but you have to ensure you are totally relaxed and not stressed out when you conduct the interrogation. Interrogation techniques are used to get information from a suspect, witness or victim after a crime has been committed. Interrogation by torture or sleep deprivation are not the kinds of techniques we can employ against FEAR.

Interrogation Techniques

Review your knowledge about FEAR before interrogating FEAR. As with any good interrogation, the information available to you must be reviewed before you begin the interrogation. We talked about FEAR at great length and the Past in chapters two and three respectively.
1. Listen attentively (attention to details is imperative in the interrogation) and take notes on answers to your questions when you start the interrogation.

2. Ask FEAR for his version of events: Why are so many people willing to join the Failure Armed Forces? Are any of his soldiers successful in life? What do they get in return for joining the Failure Armed Forces? Has anybody ever been proud to have been a soldier after leaving the forces? Why are successful people not soldiers in Failure Armed Forces?
3. Employ various methods in the interrogation. For example, play both sides, pretending you understand his reasons for his actions. Present your findings to him and analyze his defense. Vary the account of events, or request his account of events from the mid-way point as opposed to from the beginning.
4. Review your notes from the interrogation based on your knowledge of FEAR. Take your time when reviewing your notes.
5. Don't be in a hurry to end the interrogation; you have to collect as many facts as you can. You may have spent a long time in your life under the myth surrounding your suspect, FEAR, so why rush your interrogation?
6. **Take action, conduct your interrogation.**

If you are afraid to put questions to the THEEF, you can ask the victims and failures, once they have been relieved of their duties in the Failure Armed Forces, or the witnesses to the journey of life of failures. Role models have experiences, ask your role model:

1. How did you identify your FEAR?
2. How did you overcome your FEAR?
3. How did you become successful?
4. Did you attack every instance of FEAR in your life with burning desire and action?
5. How did you deal with agents of FEAR?
6. Did you arrive in your current position by standing still?
7. What would you advice me to do to deal with an instance of FEAR?
8. Seek clarification, by asking your role model key questions, on areas of concern to you.
9. **Take action to find and ask your role model questions.**

If you ever get arrested for a crime as a suspect by the police, you will be interrogated for that offense. Now, we all know a suspect is innocent until proven guilty for the crime. To be a winner, you must include mental fortitude in your diet, either by having a simple conversation or interrogating FEAR. Why be a failure when you can be successful? Provided you are willing to put in your best effort, you may not be guaranteed a place on the 'A' list, but anywhere on the 'B' to 'E' list is better than on the 'F' list. Any success, large, medium or small, is still better than failure. Interrogate the THEEF of life to establish if he is guilty or not, and, more importantly, to establish reasons for your FEAR. Your interrogation does not end with the THEEF, victims or witnesses – you also have to interrogate yourself to eliminate yourself from this investigation, or have a simple conversation with yourself. Ask yourself 'Am I afraid?' and 'Why am I so afraid?'

1. Is it because I was ridiculed by people?
2. Do my childhood experiences still haunt me?
3. Is it minor failure on a task or project in the past that is holding me back?
4. Am I not good enough to do something?
5. Am I afraid of failing because most people I know who tried failed?
6. Do I have any goals?
7. You need to rediscover yourself: Who are you, and what are your limits, if any? Rediscover yourself; it's like being one year old again, with endless possibilities.
8. **Take action; ask yourself questions.**

With these questions, you can identify and understand the cause of your FEAR. Is it FEAR? ('False Evidence Appearing Real'). Banks need to perform due diligence to identify their clients in order to conform to customer identification programs – mandatory under the Bank Secrecy Act and USA PATRIOT Act, this activity is known as "Know Your Customer" (KYC). For an individual to know who he is dealing with – particularly the unavoidable clients of all human beings, FEAR – one will have to do likewise. A due diligence of FEAR is a mandatory human requirement. By knowing your customer, you gain knowledge about your customer. You generate the courage and confidence to deal with your customer. Furthermore, you discover how to deal with this dangerous customer, who can easily hand an individual poverty and struggle. We have the privilege to hold a conversation or discussion with FEAR. We cannot and should not make ourselves victims of our privilege voluntarily. Confrontation with your FEAR is a must; understand why you are afraid and what you are afraid of. In our conversation or discussion we need to ascertain, short or long term, what does FEAR really bring to the table? By understanding and knowing, you can deal with the THEEF better, as well as by being bold enough to stand toe-to-toe and face-to-face with your FEAR – as they say, "*Familiarity breeds contempt.*" You will start to see FEAR as part of the furniture; FEAR becomes just another object in the house. The '*whats*' and '*whys*' of FEAR are published in your mind. The THEEF is gradually being exposed for what it really is, the picture becomes clearer in your mind, and FEAR gets distinguished. Hence, with the interrogation of the relevant parties above, FEAR will be desensitized. Desensitization is the key to the heart of FEAR. Desensitization is:

A behavior modification technique, used especially in treating phobias, in which panic or other undesirable emotional response to a given stimulus is reduced or extinguished, especially by repeated exposure to that stimulus.
www.onlinedictionary.com

    Regardless of the type of FEAR you have, desensitization is a good way to deal with it. For example, when you stand to challenge the THEEF a few times, you get used to FEAR and you become 'desensitized' to the THEEF of life. When you encounter FEAR in the future, you begin to treat it as part of your regular daily routine; hence, you don't lose any sleep over it. The THEEF has introduced himself to you in a big way; introduce yourself to him gradually.

Conversation

Conversation is the vehicle of any language.

Knowledge acquisition and communication are the end products of a conversation – the most efficient tool of any language. However, *'Language'* is a mandatory prerequisite for a conversation; you cannot hold a conversation without a particular language being the common denominator. You cannot use a language without having a conversation; neither can you have a conversation without using a language. Regardless of the vehicle you choose to use, even if your preferred mode of transportation is beast of burden or draft animal, regardless of the speed of your conversation or discussion, 100 MPH, 10 MPH or 5 MPH, your conversation will drive the language home and deliver your message, provided you are not afraid to start and develop a meaningful conversation.

In the boxing ring, professional conversations are carried out with their fists. If the boxers chose to carry a conversation with their mouths *(with the exception of press conferences before and after the boxing event)*, they couldn't; the mouthguards, also used in many other types of sports, prevent harm that may occur as a result of accidental or deliberate impacts to the mouth. These guards are a compulsory requirement of the professional and amateur boxing federations in any country around the world. Just as these mouthguards are deterrents to having conversations in the ring, FEAR is a deterrent to success. Dialogue between a dentist and patient is another useful metaphor; while the patient is in the dentist's chair receiving treatment, he can't engage in dialogue *(conversations are for before and after treatment)*. Although professionals in most industries do not go around communicating with their peers or bosses with their fists, conversation is too often limited. Therefore, it is necessary to understand the deterrents to having successful conversations with each other before they can be realized.

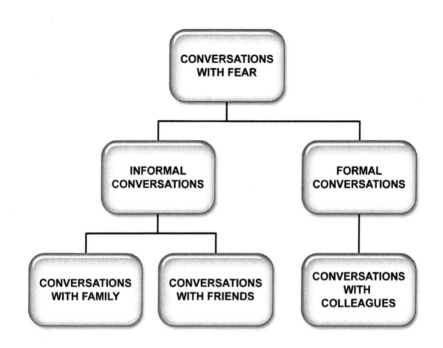

Hierarchy of Conversations

Basics

You require only the basics, the minimum requirement, to hold a conversation in any language. You need to understand the language in question; if you understand the language, you can speak the language. An individual cannot claim he or she understands the language, but cannot speak the language, provided he or she is not dumb. For example, if I say to you, *"Can you please come here for a minute?"* if you come to me, you understand the English language. Your understanding of the English language is established. If you say to me, *"Can you please come here for a minute? I need to show you something,"* your ability to speak the English language is also established. If you can't come to me immediately for the next ten to fifteen minutes, all you have to do is say, *"I will be with you in fifteen minutes."* You are speaking the language; you understand. Hence, you understand and can speak the English language. Whatever language you understand and speak, it will suffice for your conversation, discussion and lecture with your FEAR. We can still get to our destination without a car; there are different kinds of transportation that can and will get us to our destinations. The question we now have to answer is not *"How do we get our conversation to our intended destination?"* but, *"Which conversation in the Hierarchy of Conversations, do we intend to use to get to our destination?"*

Business

We are all in the business of conversation; we need to communicate with others, and others need to communicate with us. We are constantly improving our communication skills – the more conversations you have, the better you become at having them. Communicating is not always easy, but it is essential if you intend to move up the ladder in both your organization and in life. The following are some helpful tips for having a successful business conversation (with a new acquaintance):

- Break the Ice: People normally kick off a conversation with basic questions such as "Good morning, how are you today?" Most of the time, you get an answer that invites your own views about your day as well. Then the door opens for a more formal introduction, with names and locations.
- Establish a common ground: You can establish a level playing field where both are comfortable in the conversation, i.e., a major news story that all are aware of and are willing to express their views on.
- Appreciate the person you are having a conversation with: Pay compliments, appreciate their dress sense or offer compliments

on the tie or scarf. Most people appreciate compliments from people, and will warm to you a bit more.
- Be brief and to the point: Remember, there are two parties to the conversation. Don't take over the conversation; be brief with your answers and provide details if requested by the other party. You do not want to bore the person with whom you are having a conversation.
- State your case and let the other party state his or her case.
- Learn what the other profession is about in the conversation; do not come across as not interested in the world of other people, particularly when they show a lot of interest in what you do.

Formal and Casual

Formal conversations are members of the middle layer of the hierarchy of conversations, with the usual conventional procedures of formality. A relaxed and friendly approach is replaced by an organized and methodical approach, and there will usually be an important formal subject for discussion. Examples: a formal interview between interviewer and interviewee – in a job interview, you answer questions professionally, and make your exit swiftly in a professional manner with a smile and handshake, with an understanding that time is precious to everybody, including your interviewer. An interview is a great example of a formal conversation; it is a conversation between two or more individuals. The main objective of the interview is to extract information from the interviewee by the interviewer(s) via questioning. Interview of assessment and interview for information are generally the two types of interviews. An interview can be structured, semi-structured, unstructured, or research-based. The desired result of the interview, regardless of its nature, can only be to obtain desired information by asking the correct open-ended questions. Typically, a formal conversation begins with formal greetings; for example, *"Good afternoon, my name is Peter Jones."* The other party to the conversation usually responds by saying, *"Good afternoon, my name is John Page."*

Informal conversations, another middle layer member of the hierarchy of conversations, are more casual conversations. The barriers of formality or ceremony are on permanent strike, and the etiquette of formal conversation is generally away on holiday somewhere by the beach side. Informal conversations have various branches: family, friends and social acquaintances. In each branch, casual conversations are easily employed, like having conversations with family members, friends and acquaintances, at a barbecue or at any other social gathering. Discussing events of the day in your office and child's school as a family, is a good way to engage members of the family in conversations. Engaging the other party in common interest conversation enables the establishment of a good rapport between both parties to the conversation. Furthermore, the flow of information during the conversation is smooth when all parties employ open-ended questions during the conversation.

The ways of answering questions are legally employed within conversations; it aids understanding by providing clarification of the conversation.

Purpose

A direct or indirect, formal or informal conversation should have a purpose, a *burning* purpose. The beginning of a conversation is the ownership of an impulse that requires the conversation for the satisfaction of this purpose. Human hunger for food motivates the human search for food to satisfy the hunger. The realization and satisfaction of the hunger becomes a dominating purpose that consumes all the thoughts of the individual. A burning purpose is born and grows; hence, dialogue for clarification of the burning purpose becomes necessary. The FEAR of holding a conversation regarding the burning purpose will no longer exist as the individual's passion grows, and the thirst for conversation arrives. In the movie *Alive* (directed by Frank Marshall, and based on a true story of a plane crash in 1972 in the Andes, between Chile and Argentina), the only option on the menu – cannibalism – for breakfast, lunch, and dinner, would not have been employed had the need not arisen. Survival became a burning purpose *(over and above the FEAR of eating human flesh),* and human beings had to eat the flesh of other dead human beings for survival – something that would not have been done or contemplated under normal circumstances. Soldiers would not have been sent to war in Afghanistan and Iraq had the burning purpose not been established and exceeded the reason for not going (depending on the views you subscribe to). An individual will not stop until the objective of the conversation has been achieved or proved unachievable. When the burning purpose of failure exceeds that of success, for an individual to fail in every aspect of his life is not difficult; it is probably the easiest thing to do. All an individual needs to do is to stand in the corridors of the authority on failure. If the burning purpose of success exceeds that of failure, it should be your personal philosophy to learn, learn and learn as much as you can from the experts in their fields via your conversations and discussions. Analyze how they approach and deal with problems or potential problems. Conversations with experts give you a brilliant insight. You get to know different perceptions of the experts on the subject in question. Furthermore, you acquire different techniques to deal with the highest-placed authority on failure. The prerequisite is to open an account at the Bank of Conversations to withdraw the knowledge payments received from the experts.

Bank of Conversations

I have never met anybody who has not motivated me in one way or the other; this includes every single member of my family, friends, colleagues and the public in general. Every single individual I have ever met or known by name in my life has motivated me. When I see somebody I know in a situation I would not like to be in, the focus is on how to avoid arriving in that situation. And for anybody in a situation I would like to be in, the focus changes to how to arrive in that situation, for they must be experts at arriving in their relevant situations. According to the dictionary, an expert is *a person who has special skill or knowledge in some particular field.* Thus, it must be agreed that successful people and failures are authorities on the subject of FEAR by the sheer volume of their knowledge of FEAR, albeit from different sides of the gate. Learn as much as you can from successful people and failures (what they did, did not do, or should have done that put them in their current situations); there is always something to learn from both. It is what you learn from either party that matters. Every human being is unique in his or her own way. Just as a successful person has a wealth of experience about life, so does a failure – after leaving the forces at retirement age and the gravity of their mistake arrives. The "if I had known this and that" statements (the knowledge that deprived them of success in the first instance) begin to get an audience. The experience from both quarters is priceless, and their conversation with FEAR is a knowledge bank, the Bank of Conversations. Their deposit account has a very, very high interest rate. You can't open a certificate of deposit (CD) account with the Bank of Conversations without making a profit, even for a term as short as six months. The profit is more than or double the profit of the offers at the major mainstream banks. To make matters even more interesting, their fixed and variable mortgages (different kinds of useful knowledge) carry a zero percent interest rate, with no product fee, over a term of fifteen to thirty years. There are no penalties for partial payments, or full repayment of the mortgage at any time during the life of the mortgage. They also have a fantastic product for first-time buyers: two years' payment holiday from the inception date of the mortgage. Many people have their checking accounts, saving accounts, certificates of deposit and mortgages with the FEAR World Bank (where bad knowledge is offered to customers and good knowledge is dismissed without a hearing) – perhaps, due to the availability of branches worldwide, that enables transactions to be carried out easily any time and anywhere in the world with ridiculous charges to the customers. For example, if your bank account is held in a branch in London, and you make a withdrawal in New York or Paris with your debit or credit card, a transaction fee of $199 per transaction (about £100 or €230)[2] is charged to your account. Considering such charges, the customer base of the FEAR World Bank is beyond comprehension. Complete your application form for opening an account at the Bank of Conversations – the conversation janitors will be glad to receive your application, and, in the future, you will avoid ridiculous charges from the FEAR World Bank.

The Most Ignored

Amongst the different types of conversations in the hierarchy of conversations, there must be honor and respect for the conversation at the top of the hierarchy (which is also the most ignored), the tip of the tree. The most important conversation for most individuals is the most averted conversation, and the last conversation they choose to have – despite having different conversations every day of their lives. Perhaps people delude themselves into thinking they really do not need to have conversations with their FEAR. We begin every day with a conversation and end it with a conversation, yet the most important conversation does not even get a glance. Your second voice, the voice that believes you cannot do anything positive, the voice that reminds your first voice of the consequences, and not the benefits, of your efforts. Your second voice is always talking with your first voice; perhaps, the first voice should have a conversation with your unenthusiastic voice, the defeatist. The unenthusiastic voice exists in all human beings, talking at any individual willing to listen. Most do not only listen – they create their world on the information received from their second voice. The information constantly given is negative thoughts. There are prerequisites for most things: to manage a team of people there is a prerequisite; there is a prerequisite for going to medical school to study medicine; there are certain conditions that must be met in order

---

[2]Exchange Rates used in this book - British Pound (GBP) to United States Dollar (USD) £1 to $2. British Pound (GBP) to Euro, £1 to €2.3.

for an individual to fulfill his American Dream of home-ownership status. To have a conversation, one of the most imperative prerequisites of conversation must be adhered to: you need to have another party to converse with. For example, the first party to a conversation is your second voice *(generally the initiator of the conversations between the two voices)*, and the second party is your first voice; together they make up the participants in the debate either for or against, depending on the perceptions of each party on the subject. Conversation enables giving and receiving of information and vice versa, just as information is provided to the general public via news on television, radio, the internet and in the daily newspapers.

News

News from January 20th, 2009:
"America's Day of Change Arrives"
Barack Obama will be sworn in today as the 44th President of the US. Millions of people across the world are expected to watch history being made.
***Skynews*, Robert Nisbet reports**

A Nation Readies Itself to Witness History.
ABC News

"I may not get there with you. But I want you to know tonight, that we, as a people, will get to the promised land." Excerpt from the speech in support of the striking sanitation workers at Mason Temple in Memphis, Tennessee, on April 3, 1968—the day before he was assassinated. (Dr. Martin Luther King, Jr.)

Not only has change arrived in America, but also the people have arrived in the promise land. On January 20, 2009, change arrived in the United States of America and the rest of the world. That day, Barack Obama's official call sign changed from 'Senator' to 'President,' not just president, but PRESIDENT OF THE WORLD! President Obama has become the first black (mixed-race) president, as the forty-fourth president of the United States of America. However, whether he is black, brown, or white is irrelevant. He is doing what he needs to do. Lector, please join me once again to congratulate the forty-fourth president of the United States of America, President Barack Obama: *On behalf of the world, I would like to congratulate President Obama. Congratulations, Mr. President, for the history that unfolded before our eyes on that day cannot be measured in any shape or form. Thank you, Mr. President. Anybody can take a leaf off your tree. God bless you and your family.*

Janet added, "God bless America. I am so proud to be American." After a glance at her watch, Janet said, "Gentlemen, it's 1:30 p.m.. The hotel restaurant will be closed in forty-five minutes – should we have lunch? Thiago and I agreed with Janet; it was indeed time for lunch.

Last word:
Interrogate all relevant parties to establish the diagnosis of your FEAR.

Step 3: Establish

Establish Your Burning Desire

After conducting your interrogation, you need to establish your burning desire. You can establish your burning desire by:

1. Set yourself a small goal: For example, going to the gym twice a week.
2. Execute your small goals to start building your confidence gradually: For example, do your best to make sure you go to the gym twice a week.
3. Increment your goals gradually: For example, from going to the gym twice a week, increase it to three times a week.
4. When you state your goals, don't be negative.
5. Document your goals.
6. Give your goals a voice: Think highly of yourself and your burning desire.
7. Don't set goals that are unrealistic: It's very difficult to achieve a goal that is based on an inaccurate model of reality. The idea is to ease yourself into battle, not to create an uphill struggle from the beginning of the battle.
8. Set goals that bring focus, clarity and inspiration to you: if they don't, don't take ownership of those goals. But if the goal brings greater clarity, focus, and motivation to your life whenever you think about it, then own it.
9. By setting goals, you will also raise your self-confidence, as you recognize your ability and competence in achieving the goals that you have set.
10. Set goals to achieve your potential: If you have the potential to achieve a particular task, set your goals to enable you to utilize your potential.

Step 3: Establish

11. Establish your desires based on things you hate or dislike: for example, if you hate your career or job, establish a desire on "I hate my career or job." If you are fat and hate being fat, then establish a desire based on "I dislike being fat." The key is to then establish a burning desire to get an opposite result in each area of your life you hate or dislike.
12. Once it is established, if the burning desire is hot enough, the SMART method or any other suggested guidelines generally used for setting goals will fall in line automatically. In the case of SMART, the burning desire will automatically be Specific, Measurable, Achievable, Realistic and Timely.
13. Hit the ground running insofar as you burning desire is concerned.
14. **Take action to establish a burning desire now.**

Those who are successful have established a burning desire. Constant reminders will help us to establish our need to establish burning desires. With a relaxed mind and your Interrogation of FEAR completed, you need to establish your burning desire – not just a desire, but a solid, burning desire. Make a decision on a particular achievement you really want to achieve in your life, and ensure it's very important to you to achieve whatever it is within a certain period of time. You can, if you wish, attach an expiration date to your burning desire, but if it is a solid, burning desire when established, it will be so hot within your mind that you will be itching to take action with or without an expiration date attached. For example my burning desire to give any life a voice, particularly the less-privileged, led to the birth of "The THEEF of LIFE" foundation; that burning desire didn't require an expiration date, it was simply to hot to be denied a birth certificate any longer.

It will also keep you focused on the task. The burning desire becomes your being and other issues will join the queue behind it in your mind. In the book *The Seven Habits of Highly Effective People*, Stephen R. Covey stated, "The carpenter's rule: 'Measure twice, cut once.'" Analyze your burning desire twice; act once. By improving your self-esteem, image, courage and confidence, you can establish burning desires to call FEAR and its agents to order.

Text your burning desire to your mind not your mouth.

About 10 years ago, I had a dream – a personal dream to write a book. A few years later, the manuscript was not in sight, due to perhaps, my schedule, FEAR and one or two other factors. I set myself a SMART (Specific, Measurable, Achievable, Realistic and Time) goal to write my manuscript within two years, but again, after two years a chapter was not yet on paper or on my PC as a soft copy. I could not begin the third step of my personal battle. Three years ago, I suddenly realised the desire to write the book was not a burning desire. I had a feeling one or two individuals out there in the world could improve their lives by reading my book. I established my personal burning desire to write my book and to fulfill one of my objectives – to improve the lives of a few people. As soon as I downloaded the 'burning' factor into my personal battle and attached it to my existing desire, I held in my hands the mandate for an uncontrollable burning desire in my life. An emotion and awesome passion took over. It was not a case of who will publish my book as an unknown author, but instead, the uncontrollable burning desire to write refused any negative ideas a title, let alone an introduction. I was only too happy to write at the first available opportunity, in some cases, staying up till early hours of the morning, and on other certain occasions, at the expense of quality time with family and friends. Even when I was out, I just couldn't wait to get back to my manuscript. I could consider myself lucky not to have been handed a divorce paper from my wife's attorney.

If you had the knowledge and expertise to achieve something and you had the desire to achieve it but you failed to achieve it, you have short-changed yourself. In most cases, the reason will be as a result of lack of burning desire and FEAR. Each individual should establish a burning desire in at least each of the following five areas of their lives – Physical Health, Career, Relationship, Individual Development and Finances.

Courage

One of the essential ingredients of FEAR eradication is courage. In a nutshell, *'Winners have guts, and losers don't.'* Winners are action-takers, and losers are not. It takes guts to be the focus of attention or to mount the podium of success, because it is easier to mount the podium of failure than it is to mount the podium of success. If you are a hostage of FEAR, it takes guts to hold conversations with the THEEF of life and demand answers to your questions. Going the extra mile, risking perceived failure, a certainty without taking action, and putting yourself on the line all require bravery; there could be a million and one reasons why when it comes to the stage of walking the talk, individuals turn to jelly. Instead of blaming yourself for your problems, you look for somebody else to blame. If you do not have the courage required, you are not going to make it; you either find the courage to establish your burning desire or fast-track your application to the Failure Armed Forces. Burning FEAR is the only requirement for fast-tracking an application for failure. At best, a mediocre life awaits you. There is no relationship between courage and doubts; if you have doubts about the courage you require to be successful in life, your life will be in doubt, and a life in doubts is a life consigned to failure. Most successful people have experienced FEAR and doubt at some stage in their lives. They had their conversations with FEAR to eliminate FEAR and doubts, simultaneously introducing courage into their lives. Many people plan to get rich or be successful, but their desires and actions do not support being rich or successful in different areas of their lives. When you look at what they are doing, you don't need a genius to tell you their destination is failure.

Success normally breeds success, provided the THEEF of life does not appear in the equation to steal your courage and confidence. Meeting one or a few successful individuals could easily enhance you in your quest for success in any area of your life. Bill Clinton said, *"Meeting President John Kennedy when I was just 16 years old led me to decide to pursue a life in politics."*

Individual financial scuffle is the result of not knowing the difference between a liability and an asset. If you want to be wealthy, keep increasing your debtors but if you want to be poor keep increasing your creditors. A subscription that constantly reduces your spending power is a liability; a subscription, on the flip side, that constantly hands you money is an asset.

There is a difference between an asset and a liability. The THEEF is a liability. There is nothing wrong with occasional indulgence in FEAR; uncontrollable indulgence is the problem. The influence of action or FEAR can make a gigantic difference in your future. The THEEF of life, not only takes money out of your pocket (loss of potential earnings), but it also takes your mind away as well. The majority of people, failures, spend their life buying FEAR; the destroyer of life is the most expensive liability you can ever buy. An individual can be aware of the difference between an asset and a liability and still spend his or her life buying FEAR. The investment in the THEEF of life is the greatest cause of financial hardship all over the world. It makes a mockery of the word *"Confidence."*

Confidence

Confidence by an individual can easily be mistaken for arrogance. To avoid this, you need to understand confidence and the nature of the individual. Confidence is *"Believing in yourself and your abilities, freedom from doubts or strong belief in your capabilities."*

You gain strength, courage and confidence by every experience in which you really stop to look fear in the face.
Eleanor Roosevelt

When we pause, reflect and resume, we learn from every experience we have in life. We build our confidence, courage and strength. We begin to think we don't have the strength and courage to move on, when everything seems beyond what we believe we can manage. Our thoughts create our reality; hence, it is our belief that we lack the strength and courage to carry on, that creates this opinion. I believe it is more important to feel good about yourself. If you don't feel good enough about yourself, you will always need more. When you buy into the bad feelings, you will never be confident and will always be searching for a dollar you really never lost. If you never lost that dollar, you will never find it; thus you can never take ownership of happiness in your life. It is extremely important for you to understand and believe, regardless of how you feel and look, *"You are not only good enough but much more than good enough." If you are making it happen naturally, your dollar has always been in your pocket.*

Once you establish in your mind that everybody has FEAR, you have taken the first step to dealing with your FEAR. To think or be told that some people have no FEAR would be wrong. It is something we all have, but how we deal with it in order to overcome it is the most important issue. To undertake a task or project, the ability to start the project is the most difficult part, so do your homework or research.

There are many ways to deal with the THEEF of life. If you have conquered your FEAR to a certain level, congratulations. If you have not even started your FEAR eradication treatment, a start date needs to be established. Depending on the kind of FEAR you have, a good way to start is to do a project that requires a maximum outlay of money within the realm that you can comfortably afford to lose, without losing any sleep. If you do a project with a maximum outlay of $500, provided $500 is within your budget for the project, at worst you will lose that money; at best, you will create a platform from which you can begin your investment journey and your FEAR eradication treatment. To some people, $500 is nothing, but to some, it is a lot of money.

A task or project that has not begun has no finish date in sight.

Starting is the most difficult part of any task or project, and when coupled with FEAR or lack of confidence, the start date may never be within your radar. Establish a start date!

Sum of Thoughts

You are simply the sum of your thoughts.

You are who you think you are. Thought 'A' plus thought 'B' plus Thought 'C' makes up the sum of your thoughts. If your thoughts of yourself are not big enough, you instantly devalue yourself, and if they are big enough, you instantly increase your value. When everybody sees the road ahead and you cannot see the road, you devalue yourself. Appreciate yourself before appreciating others. If you appreciate yourself, others will appreciate you, and vice versa. The sum of your thought could be your key to the door. Many roads lead home, but if you do not have the key, you cannot get into the house regardless of which road you take. Even if you have no meaningful thought about yourself, pretend you do. You will soon convince yourself and realize how big your thoughts of yourself are. The greatest harm you can bring upon yourself is to downplay your ability and intelligence. Your thoughts of yourself need to be positive, not negative. The THEEF of life generally brings out the best negative thoughts in you. You need to define yourself to yourself; nobody can do a better job of this than you can. Giving this job to others means the job will not be done properly. Do what you have to do; rediscover yourself. You might be in for a surprise. It will be exceedingly difficult for you to associate with the Exterminator of life when you discover how amazing you are.

***Your success will be determined by
your own confidence and fortitude.***

The first lady of the United States of America, Michelle Obama, told school girls while visiting their school in London (Elizabeth Garrett Anderson School in Islington, north London):
"I am an example of what is possible when girls from the very beginning of their lives are loved and nurtured by people around them.

Whether you come from project estate or a country estate, your success will be determined by your own confidence and fortitude. Future generations are counting on you being 'the best you can be.'"

Encouragement

It is said, *"Encouragement is oxygen for the soul."* We all need to be encouraged. Our children need to be encouraged. Regardless of their circumstances, everybody needs encouragement; failure does not mean failure forever. Failure is simply *a temporary setback that requires urgent attention, love, support and encouragement, which all reside in the Protect or Reclaim strategy.* Believe within yourself that you are not a failure, regardless of any temporary setback you may have or perceptions of people about you (a small-minded person's opinion or those who have already signed their names on the register of failures in ink), and you will arrive at your destination. Every day is a new learning day; each day we gain new knowledge. He who thinks he knows it all, knows nothing. It is quite amazing the things we can learn from people, including children.

*If I can see further than any other man it is because
I have stood on the shoulders of many giants.*
Isaac Newton

If you want to see further than any other man, start finding giants whose shoulders you can stand on. If you make the effort and truly stand on the shoulders of giants, the view looks better and clearer than when you stand on the floor with your own feet. Leverage is a powerful tool; we can all do with a bit of it. Your giant is your leverage. Do not waste it. Use it while you still have the strength to climb up his shoulder to see further than most men – including the THEEF of life, if you consider him to be a man. In any country, there are many dreamers, who dream of achieving big things, moving from rags to riches, or simply having a better life. For a number of people, the dream remains only a dream. Everybody has a dream;

some dreams remain a dream, and some become reality. There is no law that prevents an individual from dreaming, but a dream becomes real only when a burning desire is established and action is taken to achieve the dream. I'm confident that you have had 'million dollar' ideas. Yes! You have had the ideas, maybe not every day, but you have had them. If you harness them, you would never have to work another day at that job you hate going to every morning. Somebody once said, *"Who are you waiting for to give you an opportunity?"* The answer is, *"Nobody."* All you have to do is give yourself the permission to take up the opportunity. Be able to identify the opportunities when they present themselves to you. You do not have to settle for less, unless you appoint the THEEF of life as your guardian. Even when the opportunities presented to the THEEF of life are limited, the global THEEF will grab it and run with it. We only need a few opportunities as well, provided we are ready to do likewise – grab it and run with it. Failure is success in its own right, to a certain degree. To take a risk, no matter how small, the risk is a step toward eradication of FEAR. Not taking any risk at all could have devastating consequences in the future. Those who took the risk count their blessings for dealing with their FEAR. They were able to execute small and affordable projects to progress financially or get off the treadmill of failure for good. Do something even if you do it wrong; you can always learn from your mistakes. There is no substitute for experience. The experience from the first task could be the difference between success and failure; taking the experience to the next task could give you success beyond your wildest dream. If you invest $100 in a project and fail, it is easier to bear the pain and stress of losing $100 than that of losing $100,000. The $100 investment could grow to be a billion dollar business.

The eBay millionaire

Ten years ago, at 21 years old, Mark Radcliffe started a business; he named it First2Save with only $400 in the UK using his back bedroom as his office and eBay as his shop floor. Today, he navigates the streets in the city in a Ferrari, his customers on a monthly basis are over 35,000 people and his turnover annually exceeds $6 million. This is a turnover *that gives him the throne and title of eBay number-one bestseller in Britain; Radcliffe is an eBay millionaire. Computer cables and accessories for mobile phones were his main product on eBay in the beginning, but he has now extended his product range to over 3,600 items and operates his business from a warehouse, 10,000 sq ft in size and has 19 employees working for him. Further business expansion is within his plans. He intends to increase his number of workers to 34, move premises from 10,000 sq ft to 30,000sq ft, and wants to be the global village's biggest eBay seller, shipping 50,000 products per month.*

When Radcliffe was asked to give an insight into the secret behind his success, he said: "We keep focused on popular consumables. Our biggest sellers are all items with a value of less than $30 – accessories for iPod's and mobile phones, gadgets and electronic toys – low value goods with a high volume and decent profit margin.

When I started, I was very young with no commitments, and no real financial backing, so I had to buy small products that I could buy cheaply and sell quickly.

I started selling mobile phone accessories in 1999 from my own website. Then eBay came along, and that gave me the opportunity to reach a much wider customer base.

I'm constantly re-investing the money back into the business, so we can continue to grow. Without wanting to sound over-confident, there is every chance that we can become the number one eBay seller in the world in the next 2 years."

Mark Radcliffe lives in Southport, Merseyside in a detached house with his wife and daughter. In addition to his Ferrari, he also drives an Aston Martin DB9 convertible.

Nothing is impossible with prayer, desire and action. Effort, belief, courage and commitment are part of the requirements. Nobody can guarantee you will live for 200 years. If you need a guarantee for a risk you intend to take, the idea or project you wanted to execute will simply be a dream and nothing more than a sweet dream. People do not like to see their loved ones in trouble. They draw from their wealth of experience in life to give advice if asked, on elements of risk, the consequence of failure. Your dream should be your dream, and not somebody else's dream. Your dream should not be the dreams others have for you. In most cases, people are influenced by the views of other people. If you have done your homework properly and you have a strong desire to do a particular project, do it. Your parents, uncles or aunts, husband or wife, brothers or sisters may be giving you advice based on the true love they have for you as family – but they cannot guarantee that you will fail or succeed if you execute your idea. The THEEF of life is not going to encourage you to take the opportunity when it presents itself for the taking; *encourage yourself.*

Ambition

The willingness to strive for its attainment, when you suddenly find yourself with a burning desire to eradicate your FEAR, means you have the ambition to gain freedom from the THEEF of life. Your vision assisted by your focus will provide amazing results provided you focus on your vision. You feel something missing inside that motivates you to elevate yourself to a higher level of existence. You need to be ambitious; when you are ambitious, you always seem to find the willingness to march on in spite of any adversities. People who are not ambitious tend to be complacent, do not think of opportunities, are not interested in knowledge and are not inquisitive about development. Ambitious people thirst for knowledge and development. Some people are naturally ambitious for one reason or the other, and always enhance it to the best of their ability, and others generate the ambition within but never follow up on it for one reason or the other – in most cases because of the THEEF of life. Ambition always instigates action, and ambition creates a burning desire – the uncontrollable desire in you to do something to change your situation. It could be for better pay, to move up the ladder in the corporate world or to gain financial freedom. When your aspiration is high, your ambition does not entertain FEAR that can affect your ambition; your ambition keeps you focused and pushes your desire for action to be taken at the earliest opportunity. You have to be ambitious; those who never take action never really have solid ambition in the first place. The need arises for personal investigation on how to remove the FEAR factor that stifles an individual's ambition. Some people are just not ambitious and are okay in their current position in life. At least they think they are – for those people, here is food for thought:

It is said that, *"Our success in life is first determined by how ambitious we are."* Loyalty rules; be loyal to yourself. For those with or without ambitions, whether you are looking to improve your ambition or to have ambition, review different aspects of your life like the kind of people you associate with. If you are not around people who are goal-oriented, seeking to improve their future, have a positive attitude toward what they do or want to do, you will need to find such people to enhance your ambitions in life. Associating with them constantly increases your desired ambitions. Read inspirational books that will inspire you and rekindle your ambitions; even if you already have ambitions, a little encouragement here and there can only be good for you. Read articles about successful people, digest the information in the books you read and let the information inspire you to greater ambitions. Try to attend as many seminars as you can; a good seminar will not only introduce you to a world of ambitious people but also lead you to a mentor who has been there, done it and can easily walk you down the road of success with minimum effort. Minor issues that may derail your ambitions, if you lack the experience to deal with them along the way, are easily dealt with based on dialogue with a mentor, who can provide you with information you need to get things done effectively. A dialogue with the THEEF of life, on the other hand, relating to ambition, especially if you show signs of doubts (in effect you never really believed in your ambition), will only destroy the ambition. If you truly want to fulfill your ambitions, you will not only need the desire and the willingness to press on, but *your focus must also be maintained as well.* Your ambition is critical to your success; if you do not have any ambition, success can be difficult to locate. Set yourself goals, strive to achieve them and establish burning desires for those goals.

Your ambition is not for the public; hence, it should not be in the public domain. Your ambition is for you and the benefit of your family. If your ambition is in the public domain, an individual may be willing to offer you advice, but an individual without any real ambition cannot give you any meaningful encouragement; only discouragement based on his lack of ambition and the FEAR that put him in that situation in the first place. People are generally good at discrediting somebody who is ambitious for reasons best known to them; perhaps the people are jealous or envious of the energy you generate within you that they cannot generate within themselves. They normally supply explanations, without request, as to why you cannot be successful in this or that, without any formal experience to back up the explanations they supply. A man of average intelligence who cannot see himself as a winner cannot see anybody with average intelligence as a winner either. When he looks at you, he sees a reflection of himself; for him, it is like looking in the mirror, and that is what he sees in his mirror, morning, day and night. When you look in your own mirror, try to see and feel your ambition.

Juice of Success

*The juice of failure cannot be compared to
the juice of success; they are millions of mile apart.*

One of the merits of success over failure is that when you are successful, you acquire a taste for success, and want to drink the juice of success more and more. On the other hand, when you taste failure, you get a taste of the juice of failure. Ask anybody who is successful but has had to taste the juice of failure in the past. It is not a juice you would want to see on the shelf in a grocery store, let alone taste. One thing is certain. No man can prefer the taste of failure to the taste of success. Success is free for all, but only those who are willing to succeed will achieve it, because they are willing to climb the mountain of success. If you accept defeat at every obstacle or hurdle as the years roll by, you will get to understand that FEAR will always exist, and it is how you deal with the global THEEF that really matters.

For example: Tony and Tim were working as shelf fillers in a grocery store. They both complained how stressful the job was every day after work, so they set out on a journey to redress the situation they found themselves in. They approached owners of the grocery store to supply them products on a regular basis. They were told by the owners they could not meet their demand as they had twenty branches in the town, and all would need to be supplied with the product as well. Besides, they probably could not afford to raise the capital required to supply the twenty branches. Tony and Tim discussed the issue. Tony accepted defeat and agreed it was not feasible for them to establish the business to meet the requirements of twenty branches, and became content with his position in life. Tim, on the other hand, was not willing to accept defeat, and was constantly thinking about how it could be done. He had the vision and the passion to make it work, but he could not raise the finances required. A few weeks later, Tim was fired, because he was constantly late to work. After a few days off from work, Tim had another proposal for the owners. He told the owners he was willing to supply the product to two branches for the first month and to other branches within the next four months.

Tim could not believe what he was told by the owners – they agreed to his request. Tim immediately used his savings to obtain the supply for the two branches, and sold his car to raise funds for further supplies. The product was a top-seller for the next few months, and the demand kept growing and growing. Tim was now well established with an office, and there was demand for the product from other grocery stores both from within town and out of town. The product was now well established on the shelves of the grocery stores, and Tony was still working in the same grocery store putting Tim's product on the shelf daily.

Inaction breeds doubt and fear. Action breeds Confidence and courage. If you want to conquer fear, do not sit home and think about it. Go out and get busy.

Dale Carnegie

Deadly Disease

Risk is perceived by most people as a deadly disease. Most people don't take risks because they are afraid of making mistakes. They require some form of insurance policy in place before they take the risk. They wait for the insurance policy that will never come; hence, they never take the risk. Some people want to have the relevant experience in the area in question before embarking on any risky venture.

Those who are not bold enough to take any risk wait for a mistake or minor setback to happen to those who are bold enough, and swiftly move into action teasing you, laughing at you or making you a point of discussion within a social gathering. They relate the story about a minor setback to others boldly with such statements: 'I knew he was going to fail because . . .,' 'The last guy who tried to do it ended up being penniless, and his wife divorced him,' 'I read an article in the newspaper about a guy who committed suicide after taking a similar risk and it all went wrong,' 'I told him not to do it, but he didn't listen to me,' 'He thinks he is smarter than everybody; well, I am sure he knows better now.'

These same people would love to do what you are doing, but they do not have the guts to attempt it, let alone do it; in fact, they are waiting until they have enough money to start, boldness, support and time. Even if they have a money-back guarantee in place, they still would not act; the real handicap they have is FEAR, but they hide behind various excuses like lack of money, etc. Averting all types of risk is conceding defeat to the THEEF of life, and pushing the chances of success out of range. Just as a good transportation system is central to people for getting from A to B and vice versa, risk is central to every individual, company, corporation, etc. to enable development and growth. Without risk, development and growth would simply be nonexistent. Risk is viewed as a deadly disease by failures, without any medication to treat the deadly disease. Failures do not assess a risk; they simply discard the risk. A risk needs to be viewed, assessed and judged; failures don't even view the risk, let alone get to the stage where a judgment is made about the risk. Failures never ask themselves, *Can a potential risk be spread to mitigate the negative effects or absorbed in any way?*

The fundamental purpose for our existence, and our right to make an impact on the lives of our family and in the society as a whole, does not exist in the minds of failures. It's a task that is simply beyond them in their personal opinions. As it is also every human being's right to have his or her personal opinion, people are well within their human rights to hold such opinions about themselves. Such personal opinions coupled with an association with the THEEF of life, leads an individual to forget his or her needs, and those needs require constant attention as and when they arrive at people's doorsteps. Needs don't decrease; they increase, as risk is not being taken. The individual is not developing or growing, and the lack of growth will eventually create a shortage of all kinds of resources (knowledge and/or financial) required to combat the increasing needs.

Managing risk for reward is essential to success, while discarding risk for FEAR is the key to failure without options. Even if three options were available for discarding risk for FEAR, the options will probably be FAILURE, FAILURE or FAILURE. Risk is an opportunity to be viewed, assessed and judged. It is not a deadly disease to be avoided. If you want to take a risk and you need an opinion on whether to take the risk or not, ask the THEEF for his opinion. You will get a guarantee from the merciless THEEF *not* to take the risk.

Stolen 'Courage,' 'Confidence' and 'Ambition' can and must be reclaimed from the THEEF of life via the most ignored conversation in the hierarchy of conversations. The rest, as they say, will be history. If 'Courage,' 'Confidence' and 'Ambition' are not reclaimed by the rightful owner, the turbulence encountered on the flight to the top may be too much for the individual to handle; in that case, the only option is to remain at the bottom. You can't live with passion and purpose at the bottom; this is the result of an individual's choice to remain at the bottom by not reclaiming his Courage, Confidence and Ambition from the THEEF.

A condition is not permanent. It is forever evolving unless you choose to accept the views of the THEEF in your dialogue with him. The inaction that created the assumed permanent condition of being on the FEAR treadmill will eventually turn into action (you will have to get off the treadmill to retire and join the pension line). Whether you do it now or later, inaction will eventually turn into action by either choice or instruction. By choice, the world is your oyster; by instruction, failure is inevitable, except if you consider a monthly pension handout as the best replacement for your previous paycheck (which by the way, may not be up to one third of the paycheck you received while you were on the FEAR treadmill on a monthly basis).

Self-Image

The mental image an individual has of another person is on display for all to see, based on reaction to certain events. Generally, image issues are created in various ways; for example, if parents make negative remarks about their children, constant references to the child's mistakes, and disapproval of most things the child does, this can determine the attitude of the child. Children tend to internalize (accept and take ownership of) such treatment. The personal limitation of an individual creates a poor self-image when an individual is compared unfairly to the success of others without personal limitations, when a certain level of performance is expected and the person fails to deliver. An individual would look at the result of others and compare his result to the results of others. *He has a bigger house and a better car; he must be doing a lot better than me. Why can't I do as well as he is doing or better?* For the last few years, Dr. Petrov, a medical doctor, always wondered why his neighbor, who was also a doctor, could afford the $250,000 Ferrari he was driving doing the same job. He never bothered to ask his neighbor for FEAR of looking stupid, but did the mental comparison every day, and each day he brought the feeling of inferiority to himself, even though he could not comprehend the full picture of his neighbor aside from his profession. Don't give yourself unnecessary mental fatigue by comparing others to yourself. Dr. Petrov decided to ask his neighbor how he could afford to drive a Ferrari on his salary. His neighbor replied, "The Ferrari belongs to my cousin; he is on a world tour for eighteen months with his family, so he asked me to look after the car for him and ensure I drive it regularly. He should be back in two weeks. Nice car. I wish I could afford it." At this point, Dr. Petrov was speechless. The mental comparison did nothing for him apart from giving him feelings of inferiority, promoting envy and hatred for himself for his inability to measure up to his neighbor's presumed achievement, driving a $250,000 Ferrari. Don't compare yourself to others without the complete picture; it doesn't do you any good but harms you mentally. Focus on your own abilities. Creating an awareness of your self-image and overcoming your inferiority complex, which is rarely rooted in fact, makes you a better person and gives you a better view of life in general.

When an individual's economic status prevents him from doing certain things, instead of concentrating on how to improve his economic status, any comment made by somebody who is in the same or higher economic status is digested wrongly. For example, if somebody says, *"I prefer to shop at Macy's for personal reasons."* This statement is digested as *'I am rich, and I only shop at Macy's,'* even though the original statement did not include the words "rich" or "only." A man may react to such a statement aggressively as if the statement was made deliberately in relation to his economic status in life.

People with personal image issues tend to hold themselves back when the world is changing; they see the movement around them but refuse to move because of their personal image issues. Years later, when it becomes extremely visible that they have been left behind by their peers, they generate reasons to comfort themselves, for example, *"He was lucky; he changed his career at the right time,"* or *"Her responsibility is not as high as mine,"* or *"I was going to do that but something came up."* The changes required can still be made to move on, but the personal image issues again prevent them from saying, *"I can still do this, and I am going to do it.*" Rather, excuses why it was not done then become a better solution, than getting up to do what has to be done and that which can still be done. You don't have to measure your abilities against the abilities of others; we have different abilities. Different abilities can mean doing different things but still achieving successful results. Each person is unique and special in his own way. Find yours and grow with it. Too often, people try to be what they are not, and most end up achieving nothing in the process. Everybody has an intrinsic value, and it does not depend on anything or anybody outside oneself.

When family, sex, race or background becomes an excuse for not being successful, try this: you probably know quite a number of successful people, female and male, from different races, from different kinds of family and with different backgrounds. If you don't know them personally, ask those who do; if you need guidance, ask somebody to guide you; if you need assistance all the way, find somebody to assist you all the way. A position may have been reserved for you, waiting for you to saddle the seat of success. Your biggest regret may be not coming forward to claim what is rightfully yours, by limiting yourself based on poor self-image.

"Success is reserved for few" is a dangerous phrase. It is not reserved for a few; it is reserved for all. The problem is when an individual's mind is in the hands of the Hijacker of life – the individual finds himself in a position where the use of his hands has been taken away from him and his mind can't locate the key (action). If you can't do for yourself what the few have done for themselves, success is then reserved for the few, this in turn opens the door to "I am not destined to be one of the few." Acceptance and conclusion are a personal confinement of one's life to failure by right. All good players need practice to serve out apprentice duty required to justify that tag. If the handcuff has been worn long enough, a failure has served his apprenticeship to take ownership of the tag.

$100

A friend once asked for a $100 loan – to be blunt, he really wanted a gift. Unfortunately, at the time in question, the factory was expecting a delivery of raw materials to enable production of products to resume normal services. I politely told my friend about the current situation in the factory, and that the cash flow at the moment was not too good. I could not loan or give him the $100 as requested. My dear friend went crazy, to put it mildly. "HOW CAN YOU NOT HAVE $100 TO LOAN OR GIVE!" he shouted. This encounter was an experience; the interesting thing about this situation is my dear friend was not mad at himself for not having $100, but was extremely comfortable getting mad with me for not having $100 to give him. We cannot comment on somebody else's image when ours is no better; the reason he does not have the hundred dollars is the same or similar to why I don't have it. In situations where FEAR has handcuffed two individuals, would it not be better for the individual who is complaining about the handcuffs on the other individual's hands to check to see if his hands are in similar handcuffs, and if they are, to try to remove his own before worrying about others?

Michael Jackson

When the Hijacker of life intervenes in an individual's FEAR of his looks, plastic surgery and complexion treatment fly first class into the individual's life. In some cases, a black man wants to look white, and a white man wants to look black; Michael Jackson is an extreme example.

I remember hearing him say; He had two operations on his nose because it helped him breathe better to enable him hit higher notes.
'I am telling you the honest truth,' he said.
'I didn't do anything to my face.'

Superstar Michael Jackson needed to be able to hit higher notes; hence, he flew plastic surgery treatment into his life on a private jet. He claims to have a skin condition called vitiligo (a disorder in which white patches of skin appear on different parts of the body.). Nature is nature; no individual can turn water into blood or vice versa. *It really doesn't matter if you're Black or White.* MJ gave us those words of motivation in his music. Although I believe in the concept, I wonder if he did; considering changes in his looks and complexion in recent years. MJ's music is incredible. The fact is, his music could not and cannot be denied, regardless of his skin color, just as the lyrics of his song, "Black or White." He was a senior member of the music Hall of Fame, the legendary king of pop, a royal in the music industry; however, the THEEF is not in the business of distinguishing fellow royals from the crowd but in the business of extinguishing the crowd, including other royals, in various walks of life. Just like FEAR, inferiority feelings are based on false assumptions, opinions or conclusions about oneself and others. Nobody knows you better than you do; therefore, their assumptions, opinions or conclusions can't be conclusive – but yours are conclusive. Don't let anybody turn you into what you are not; be what you see yourself to be and what you truly are. Nobody created any human being, God has the sole ownership of that accolade, he created all of us. A poor self-image is unjustified. Realize from now on, that no one is inferior to anyone else; people are simply different from one another, and a common misperception is person-to-person inferiority. An individual is not better than another individual; they are simply different brand names of a product that fulfills the same need in the same way but under different names. For example, a car gets you from point A to point B or point C, whether it is Mercedes Benz, BMW, Toyota or Ford. You have the ability just like any other human being to be successful; your road to success may have different street names, but you will still need to navigate the streets to success just like any other human being. Unless you have taken ownership of the misconceptions of person-to-person inferiority, in which case, an audience with the Hijacker of life is required urgently.

The first and only acceptance that you require is yours, for yourself. God has made you the way you are and gave you all the tools you require, of which, for most of us, we only utilize about 30 percent, at any point in time. *Can you imagine yourself utilizing 100 percent of the abilities you were given?* At 30 percent, you are in great shape, let alone 80 percent or 90 percent. Accept yourself as you are, and make a conscious decision to do this even if others don't. Your life is for you to live, not for others to live for you.

MICHAEL JACKSON DIES
L.A. Times

An Icon who transcended the barriers of color and wealth with his music. *At fifty years old, is this the price of fame?* Sadly, a great music icon was taken away from us; the news of his death broke on Sky News, CNN, and FOX etc.

> *Way before Tiger Woods, way before Oprah Winfrey, way before Barack Obama, Michael did with music what they later did in sports and in politics and in television.*
> **Rev. Al Sharpton**

In a nutshell, Michael lit the torch and kept it burning for others. My condolences to his entire family (his children, sisters and brothers and parents). May his soul rest in peace. **It really does not matter whether you are black or white!** Michael said it and he proved it; he was loved by people from around the world. Rev Al Sharpton said it all in his rousing eulogy at Michael Jackson's memorial service at the Staples center in Los Angeles:

> *So, some came today, Mrs. Jackson, to say goodbye to Michael. I came to say thank you. Thank you because you never stopped, thank you because you never gave up, thank you because you never gave out, thank you because you tore down our divisions. Thank you because you eradicated barriers. Thank you because*

You gave us hope. THANK YOU MICHAEL, THANK YOU MICHAEL, THANK YOU MICHAEL!

Rev. Al Sharpton

Self-Marginalization

"Have I exclusively excluded myself from any meaningful participation in society?" For any human being, self-marginalization is the question you need to answer within yourself – you cannot claim to be oppressed by others if you initially oppressed yourself. In order to participate in the society, you need to include yourself, not exclude yourself. You can't relegate or confine yourself to a lower level as of social standing, and then engage in discussion about being marginalized by others.

As most job requirements normally state these days, *"ability to hit the ground running."* FEAR will always hit the ground running in people's lives; this is an established issue, and the non-established issue is, *"Are we prepared to hit the ground running in our battle with the THEEF?"*

Within the hierarchy of conversations, particularly in the formal (professional) arena, it can be argued by some that the Hijacker of life has held their *"will to act"* hostage, and requires a huge ransom payment for a consideration of release. I wonder what a guaranteed release will cost. A sense of unity and solidarity is established with the THEEF of life when they listen to the THEEF and/or his agents. However, listening does not constitute a complete conversation; communication is a two-way process. In conversation with the THEEF, an expression of an individual's perception is required. Those who have ensured a sense of unity and solidarity which is not established with the global terrorist, would debate affirmatively that it has a negative impact on individuals by putting the barriers of impossibility between the individuals and success.

The majority of people have action on their radar, even though that action may never be executed in the near or distance future. However, they never have the THEEF of life on their radar, yet the reason why the actions on their radar never gets executed is FEAR.

Conversation or discussion with the THEEF is a mandatory requirement for action. A common statement within the professional working environment is *"let's touch base."* Many would have used or heard this phrase for years while having formal and informal conversations but again, never with the THEEF of life. To ensure the THEEF does not steal your life, you will have to touch base with him as you do with your colleagues.

Self-Esteem

One of the quickest ways to fail is to lack self-confidence. Always extract the statements that build your self-confidence, not the sweeping statements that damage your confidence. In life, one of the most important weapons anybody will require to deal with life and its challenges is self-confidence. A lack of self-confidence can paralyze your desire and kill your dream. The greatest killer of dreams is FEAR. When you entertain negativity in your life, negativity permeates your life. *"I will fail," "I can't do it,"* or *"I am not good enough."* You end up failing, not doing it and not being good enough. Negativity robs your self-confidence, your self-confidence robs your efforts, your efforts robs your action, and action becomes inaction. Inaction is a pilot on FEAR Airways, and FEAR Airways flies non-stop, first-class only, to Failure in FEARVILLE. During the flight, even if you spot success in the distance from the cabin, it is a non-stop flight to Failure without stopovers at Success or Action Town. Develop and maintain your self-confidence, and your flight will fly directly to success. Don't contribute to your low self-esteem, making yourself feel bad by entertaining negativity in your life about yourself; instead, rate yourself highly – the higher the better, because the higher your rate yourself, the higher the energy levels that will be available to you to face the challenges of life. Given the modern-day human duties, a good energy level is a necessity of life, not an optional accessory. You are the pilot of your future; fly your future to your desired destination.

The THEEF of life will test your determination to succeed from time to time; your weapon is your self-confidence. If you share or believe other people's views about your inability to be successful, you deprive yourself of a chance to be successful and hand the THEEF a competitive advantage. You appoint yourself as an agent of the THEEF of life, by putting your hands in handcuffs yourself. Success is not reserved for people without any self-confidence; success is reserved for confident people. If you lack self-confidence, engage yourself in a conversation with the global THEEF; extract the positives for yourself and not the terrorist of life from the conversation. Refuse to buy into views of people who lack self-confidence. Set achievable goals and always reward yourself for every milestone. People with high self-esteem have confidence: mirror confident people you know and how they operate with confidence. Even when learning, learn confidently. Make references to your achievements. Focus on what you can do confidently and be proud to do.

Desire

Hope is hope, a dream is a dream, and desire is desire. Identifying your burning desire, the uncontrollable desire, is one of the steps required along the way to mount your podium of success.

> *Desire is the starting point of all achievement, not a hope, not a wish, but a keen pulsating desire which transcends everything.*
> **Napoleon Hill**

Everybody has a wish for one thing or the other. Whether each will accomplish the wish is a different matter, but those who accomplish their burning desire do so based on the price they put on their desire or weight of their desire. A weak desire is *'wanting something,'* and a burning or strong desire is a *'must-have requirement.' 'Wanting something'* could last for seconds, minutes, hours, or days, or even years; however, it may not be required any more within a short space of time, even before it is achieved. *'Must-have something'* lasts for as long as it takes to get it. It stays with you until you feed on it, and if you don't get it, starvation arrives, and as we all know, starvation has its own causalities – so the earlier you get it, the better for you. A man who has a burning desire for something is aware of the possibilities but not the difficulties, while a man with a weak desire is only aware of the difficulties but not the possibilities. Hence, his weak desire is backed with inaction or a weak attempt to take action.

Your desire is your foundation; a strong or solid foundation gives you a solid house, while a weak foundation gives you a weak house susceptible to collapse at any time. If you have a burning desire, the heat from that desire will give you sleepless nights and constant worry to the point where you will be compelled into taking action to eradicate the heat and constant worry.

For example, Joe James, married with two children, worked as a branch manager for a dry cleaning company for nineteen years. For the last twelve years, he wanted to seek employment with another dry cleaning company in search of better pay and a different environment with the possibility of growth within the company. Year after year, the desire was not backed up by action because his desire to change jobs was a weak desire; hence, Joe James remains at his job with little increase in pay. One day, the owner of the company told Joe he was selling the business and could not guarantee if the new owner would keep the existing workforce, particularly the managers, as they may prefer to have their own management team to run most of the branches.

On account of this information, Joe's weak desire became a burning desire; the next day, he took action. He started applying for jobs, and within a week, he got a job interview with another dry cleaning company. Joe went for the interview. At the end of the interview, Joe was told, *"We would love to give you the job, but we have a problem with you taking that position. We feel, based on your experience and knowledge of the industry, that your best position in our business would be Area Manager of ten branches at the very least. The job is yours if you want it."* Joe was speechless, but managed to compose himself and accepted the offer. The package tripled Joe's existing salary and included a company car. Joe broke the news of his new job to his family and said to his wife, *"I should have changed jobs years ago."*

Joe had the experience beyond what he was seeking and never even realized it; his desire initially was not a burning desire, and he accepted his position in life due to FEAR of moving forward in life (he saw no reason to move since he was not pushed). We need to back up our desire with action; desire on its own will not and cannot get the job done. Rather, desire will do a job, lift your spirit for a while and move on. We can't expect our desire alone to generate results. Desire is not a sole trader; it operates better in a partnership or limited company environment. We need a wonderful duet, two awesome performers, 'burning desire' and 'action,' side-by-side.

Within the limited company environment, desire may be the only director of the company but would still require at least a company secretary (Action) in the company. Even if you are going to arrive at your destination by default, you will need to position yourself and get your shoes on, unless you intend to arrive at your destination with your bare feet. *"Finding is reserved for those who search."* Donald Trump did not achieve what he achieved with burning FEAR and inaction; he did it with burning desire and action.

Books

Reading books and attending seminars are great sources to awaken the desire in you; they give you the courage and inspiration to overcome FEAR and the obstacles it places in front of you. For the young, they offer hope, knowledge and preparation for what lies ahead, and for those with little experience in dealing with the THEEF of life, they refresh your perceptions, reignite your desire and motivate you to get back out there to carry the fight to FEAR. For the seasoned pro, they reinforce what you know already, make good pleasure-time reading, give you a reminder of what needs to be done and prepare you for any minor distraction that may appear.

Step 3: Establish

An investment in knowledge always pays the best interest.
Benjamin Franklin

An investment in knowledge is not limited to academic qualification alone, but includes knowledge in general.

Sales Executive

A sales executive constantly achieves record sales for his company. Financially, he is struggling to make ends meet. He had the desire to ask his boss for a pay rise but never did. Unbeknownst to him, his boss had decided, based on his record of accomplishment for the company and record sales month after month, he was going to get the maximum pay raise for his grade if he asked for it.

As long as the THEEF is accommodated, desire is the hostage of FEAR.

Due to FEAR of not getting the pay raise and lack of burning desire, he did not act on his desire. As a result, his desire became hostage to the THEEF, yet he continued to break his own sales record in the company month after month, year after year, content with the sales commission he got for sales he made. His boss privately wondered why he had not asked for a pay raise *(Are we paying him too much already?)*. Perhaps, his burning desire is the sales commission and not a pay raise, yet to his friends he constantly tells them he needs and intends to ask for a pay raise at work.

Desire is fruitless without action.

If you want fruits from your desire, you must act on your desire; otherwise, the fruits of failure will be your guest for breakfast, lunch and dinner.

Hot Food

Certain types of food are best served hot – when they are served cold, not only does it affect the taste of the food, but it also defeats the purpose as well. For example, try serving yourself or your guest hot ice cream as dessert after lunch.

> *Without a sense of urgency, desire loses its value.*
> **Jim Rohn**

If you don't execute your desire as soon as the need arises, your desire will lose its value. The timing has to be right – you know what they say: *"A dollar received today is not of the same value as a dollar received tomorrow."* You are meant to have your salad cold, not hot, so have your salad cold. If you restrain or let somebody restrain your desire, your desire is not a strong or burning desire. If your desire is truly a strong desire, an uncontrollable desire, it cannot be restrained by anybody – including you, the owner. To have a burning desire, you must really and truly want to achieve the objective of a desire. If you don't have a burning desire, create it by increasing your need and want for a particular desire. For example, most of us work, not only because we love our jobs, but also to make a living, pay rent, buy food and clothes etc. The desire to satisfy these requirements is a burning desire, hence, its fulfilment.

Where millions have failed, few succeed, and the reason why those few succeed is because their desires are burning desires. Those millions who failed had weak desires or strong desires that gradually became a weak desire due to inaction. If you have no desire, you have no road map to anywhere from the middle of nowhere; therefore, you keep going round and round in a small circle without a FEAR exit point sign in sight. Even though the FEAR exit signs exists, you will not see it, as no desire simply means no visibility or blurred vision. Desire is the birth of success, and a lack of desire is the birth of failure; it is only a matter of time before each will grow to claim its natural birthright. Your desire is your propeller that pushes you to success. To be successful in anything you do, you must have the passion to succeed, and that is exactly what a burning desire is. Lack of desire is the mandatory condition of inaction. When you lack desire, failure awaits you; it is the birthright of the lack of desire. Let us get our brains in motion for a few minutes, and remember, what have we done very, very well in the past that we did not have a desire to do. NOTHING! Any successful individual will tell you, to succeed in any task or project, you will have to maintain your focus on the task or project.

> *The first principle of success is desire – knowing what you want. Desire is the planting of your seed.*
> **Robert Collier**

If you don't plant the seeds, they will not grow. The field marshal of failure has a duty to ensure you don't plant the seeds of success. If you don't have desire, you cannot ask yourself questions like, *"Why am I not successful?"* You need to ask yourself questions like, *"What exactly do I really desire?"* Even when FEAR approaches you to destabilize you, your burning desire quickly moves into action and takes care of you, yet again removing a potential obstacle from your path to success. Your burning desire is an obsession, and obsessions are not easy to derail once their journey begins.

'If you can't stand the heat, get out of the kitchen.' Likewise, 'If you can't have a burning desire for something, don't expect success in it.' The truth of the matter is, if you have a very strong desire to succeed, nothing can stop or prevent you from the success you crave. Your action-backed burning desire is your fighter plane JSF (Joint Strike Fighter). With its improved survivability and precision engagement capability, the obstacles of your success will not stand a chance in battle, all you have to do is call in your air strike support.

Procrastination

If you have ever engaged yourself in procrastination, then you know how powerful it can be. The same can be said for persistence, burning desire and action, if engaged. However, human beings don't shy away from procrastination, but from persistence, burning desire and action. Procrastination is another model of the only and the best-selling product of FEAR, the handcuffs. Quite a number of people procrastinate – don't be one of them! Procrastination is the THEEF of all elements of success. You must keep your spirits high, and be highly motivated. You can't afford to drop your guard; if you drop you guard, failure awaits you. You can't afford to go into battle (Personal or Public) with doubts of victory; the battle would be lost before it actually begins. There is a proverb that says:

Procrastination is the thief of time.

We cannot keep procrastinating. Procrastination is an erosion of life. If we keep pushing what we can do today until tomorrow, what will happen if tomorrow never comes? If we don't pick a fight with the THEEF today, should tomorrow not arrive on the next flight into town, the realization would be at a cost. Not only does time wait for no one, but day after day, week after week, month after month, and year after year, procrastination has robbed you of action. The question to ponder is: what are the consequences of your procrastination to you and your family today? The long-term implications of procrastinating are not hidden; the majority are aware of them, yet they subscribe to the implications of procrastination. Nobody can claim to have obtained value from procrastinating in the past. How then, or why, should we prevent progress in our lives today by not committing ourselves to a start date, instead of committing ourselves to phantom start dates in the future? When tomorrow changes its call sign to today, the start date scheduled for 'tomorrow' never arrives. Tomorrow is always in the future; so we have to own today.

Tomorrow may never come but at least today is here, own it.

The Face

You cannot put a face to FEAR, but you can put a face to the look of a terrified man. FEAR will have a conversation with you; the terrified man must have had a dialogue with FEAR. Failure to defend his points effectively in the discussion with the THEEF will have future implications, hence, he wears a face of FEAR for his efforts. When you engage in a debate or discussion with FEAR, the only language FEAR will understand is your burning desire and action *(they speak the same language)*. You can converse with the THEEF for as long as you want in an effort to free yourself from the bondage of FEAR, the handcuff of life, but the face of FEAR will always be your reward for your efforts if you don't communicate in a language the THEEF understands.

When you step in, be prepared to step up or be stepped out.

Your only chance, when you initiate a conversation with FEAR, is to show your strong desire and will to act immediately; anything short of that and you will not stand a chance with FEAR. You will simply join the failure casualty list of FEAR. You will have to step up your swimming technique to avoid drowning in the pool.

A house is built brick by brick, the first brick has to be laid before the second, third and fourth. Take your first step, move forward step by step.

DHL (Desire and Hope to Learn)

Education is important, and work experience is the icing on the cake. A mix of both is a powerful personal investment for the youths of today, particularly with the world's modern culture of 'work until you drop' in the twenty-first century that is upon us today. Stella Jackson, a nineteen-year-old girl, is not only gaining work experience, but also rose within her company to become a supervisor at such a young age. More importantly – she is teaching herself how to provide for herself.

To have risen to become a supervisor, she must be doing something right. To state the obvious, Stella is *doing a great job with her life*. She already knows how to eat; by gaining work experience, she is also learning how to fish for food. It is one thing knowing how good fish tastes, and another thing entirely to be able to fish. Stella may be too young to really appreciate her efforts now, but certainly, in years to come, she will appreciate her efforts even more. I am impressed and motivated by her efforts; I feel liking going out to get myself a part-time job to make up for lost efforts. At Stella's age, I knew only how to eat the food, not how to fish for food. If I had the opportunity to learn how to fish when I was Stella's age or the ability to get started with good guidance, I would have. Stella's conversation with her FEAR of fishing is evident; with regard to fishing, she doesn't wear the face of FEAR.

> *Age is foolish and forgetful when it underestimates youth.*
> **Harry Potter and the Half-Blood Prince,**
> **J.K. Rowling**

Learning is acquiring, and there is no disgrace in learning from the young; their methods are probably more up to date in this fast-moving world of ours. With my DHL (Desire and Hope to Learn) in place, I am glad I have Stella Jackson as a model. Look around you; you may have your own Stella Jackson close to you in your family. Keep it within the family.

Anybody willing to learn from the young or old will increase their knowledge, and anybody unwilling to learn from the young or old will decrease their knowledge. With increased knowledge, anything is possible, but with decreased knowledge, the possibilities are limited. Increase your knowledge from anywhere you can; don't let the Hijacker of life limit your possibilities. Most people, young or old, can tell you how good fish tastes, but 80 percent of them can't tell or teach you how to fish.

It is only a matter of time; the minors will become adults, and companies like to employ young adults with fresh and creative ideas to enhance the company's existing work force and growth. This creates a new requirement, learning, for the adults with old and outdated ideas to maintain and enhance their position on the treadmill.

Early birds always get the best deal, particularly when the

demand is high. The likes of Stella not only get a head start, but they also gain a competitive advantage. By the time they finish their education, their education in hand complimented with their work experience becomes the complete package in demand, but limited in supply.

There are quite a number of good books on how to set goals, but the focus of this book is mainly FEAR. It has been said that everyone has goals, whether we know it or not. It is important to set goals, but without interrogating FEAR to enable the creation of a burning desire, your goals will not be executed even if they are written on the walls of your room and you read them every morning. Creating success is simple, but most people plan to fail by having no plan or goal to move them in that direction. A number of people know what to do to be successful but never take action; you may have the greatest plan or goal, but if you don't take action on the plan or goal, then it is as good as having no plan or goal. I hope this can improve the lens on your camera and help you to capture better-quality pictures that see beyond the poor quality pictures FEAR presents to you. The bully, FEAR, takes no prisoners. If you stand still, the THEEF will put your hands in handcuffs.

Once the THEEF has been accommodated within your room, the representatives of FEAR take control of your decisions. Impossible become more than a word and possible becomes only a word. Your goals become servants of FEAR; hence, your goals become goals to fail rather than to succeed. The successful people who set goals for themselves and achieve them did something that those who set goals for themselves and never achieved them did not do. The successful people interrogate the THEEF before setting their goals to ensure FEAR will not interrupt – and more importantly, execute the goals. Those who don't set goals for themselves buy ready-made goals from the THEEF; they have their seats reserved with FEAR already. It is easy to set goals; however, executing the goals is a different matter. Your interrogation of FEAR will enable you to talk a good talk and walk a good walk.

Plan + Action

"Plan + Action = Success" and "Plan + Inaction = Failure." Planning is important for achieving success, but the plan needs to be executed for it to deliver the desired result. When you have a plan and keep delaying the execution of the plan, you gradually lose the drive, desire, determination and motivation to action the plan; once these vital ingredients are lost and you can't act, failure of the plan is guaranteed. If you don't make the change required to be successful, you cannot be successful. A man can only go on a hunger strike for so long – after a while, death is a certainty. The main reason people fail to act on their plans in most cases is – you guessed it, the Hijacker of Life – and, when you are afraid to action your plan, your plan will shy away from you. As a thank you gift for your planning but not taking action on your plan, the THEEF will give you failure.

A plan is free, but action has a price. When price gets involved, the product with a price becomes the less desired of the two products. If you want to be a medical doctor, you will need to take action based on your plan to become a medical doctor and do what is required to ensure you become a medical doctor. You can get rich in knowledge for anything you desire, provided you have a strong desire and the will to take the required action to achieve it. The desire is the oxygen required, and the will is the power and effort needed. It's a free world; you can do what you want to do, provided it is within the limit of the law. When you have the plan and don't follow up the plan with action, you will only keep dreaming of what you could have achieved. Anybody can dream, and you can dream for as long as your heart desires. Regardless of how good your plan is, the bottom line is plan plus inaction equals FAILURE.

Burning desire and Action are the pillars of FEAR eradication.

"Janet and Thiago," I interrupted, "it's tea time. I suggest we take a 15-minute tea break." "Good idea," said Janet, and off we went for our tea break.

Last word:
If you establish the burning desire in your mind and stand by it, every other part of you will follow. The stage is now set for you to launch your action on the global stage and focus effectively on what you need to do.

PART THREE
Public Battle

SEVEN

Step 4: Action

Take action on small FEARs one after the other that have little or no consequence.

If you celebrate your desire, your desire will celebrate you.

Within personal battle, confrontation is generally with FEAR; with progress towards the public battlefield, his troops (the agents of FEAR) are deployed. Having Talent, Potential, Capability or Intelligence can't deliver a result without action. The successful people in various walks of life all speak the language of success. They don't just daydream; they take action in order to fight and conquer the public battle. To join them you will need to bring your experience of taking action from the personal battles to the public arena. Obstacles will always exist in the journey of life with the option to fight or surrender your life. To survive the battle of life, you will have to take action. Despite the fact that taking action is unlimited, many prefer to consider it as limited only to a few. Upon completion of the steps in your personal battle, keep the momentum going; follow up with action as you did in those steps.

Action is crucial to success for any individual. Within the financial industry, cash is king; similarly, within the seven steps in Protect or Reclaim strategy, action is king. Without taking action, you can't relax, you can't conduct an interrogation, you can't establish your burning desire, you can't execute your burning desire, you can't analyze the result of action, you can't increase or decrease your level of action and you certainly can't derive the benefits of practice of action. There is no room for cripple or phantom action in Protect or Reclaim strategy. With regards to action – there is no point in planning an attack if you don't intend to execute the plan. To execute the plan, action must be given an audience. This will lead to the celebration of any burning desire.

1. Small: Start with the small FEAR you have, and take action on it. By dealing with your small FEAR, you get the experience of dealing with the THEEF of life gradually, and you also get stronger dealing with the THEEF. At the very least, you can accommodate the word 'FEAR' without being afraid. For example, if you are interested in stocks and shares, you can start trading with an amount you can really afford to lose *(this amount will vary from individual to individual; identify yours and not somebody else's limits)* and not feel the loss in any way, shape or form.
2. Do it: there is no point in saying it and not doing it. Take Nike (Just Do It) for example – there is no other way. FEAR will never take off the handcuffs he placed on your wrist, you will have to do that yourself by reaching for the Key (action) to get it off. For example with regards to your burning desire, if you did not take action, it would still be an ordinary desire.
3. Take action NOW! You own this moment, but you don't own tomorrow. For example, Bill Gates took action with regards to Microsoft yesterday, not today or tomorrow. There are a million and one people in the world with the same idea as yours, but only those who take action immediately on their burning desires can have a voice on that idea in future. Once the route to your destination has been established, begin your journey.
4. Make taking action one of your habits. Every human being on earth has some habits in common; they all eat food and drink water. But the habit of those who reach the top is the habit of action on uncommon habits. If you want to reach the top, make it a habit to take action.
5. Join the club of doers. They don't accommodate saying and thinking, they only accommodate doing and doing.
6. Ask yourself an honest question. There is no such thing as a perfect individual and you are not perfect, but you get on with your life – so, why are you waiting for the perfect time or environment to take action?

7. Action the things you FEAR – if you are scared of learning, start learning; you will fall in love with learning in a short space of time. Take action to cure your FEAR of taking action.
8. **Take action! Take action! Take action!**

Starting a big task or project can be overwhelming for anybody. It is highly important to ensure you are within 5 to 10 percent of your value. If you jump into the deep end of the swimming pool, either by mistake or on the assumption that you can swim and you can't swim, if you're rescued from the pool. FEAR will be your best friend for the foreseeable future, if you don't recover from that experience.

In a simple game of cards where red, green and navy blue decks of cards are presented to the players and the "house rules" stipulates; a pick from the red deck of cards gives you a huge win or loss. The green deck of cards gives you the option not to play the round (not to pick a card from the red deck of cards) but five voluntary picks from the green deck of cards eliminates the player. The navy blue deck of cards gives you $50 to $5,000 payouts or minor losses. However, the red deck of cards is littered with land mines. Some players still ignore some of the "house rules".

The win from the red deck of cards is a jackpot, but the loss could be disastrous with associated discomfort and pain for your family. For example, take a scenario of a man who gambles the only house he owns, occupied by his family of two young children and his wife. If his pick from the red deck of cards is not in his favor, the loss of a life-time investment and shelter for the family disappears within the space of a few minutes. Discomfort and pain is presented to innocent victims of high risk/high reward gambling games of cards. *I mentioned earlier in Chapter 2, "in the majority of cases, the house always wins."* A win that could change the old results of *"the house always wins"* should not be overlooked if that win exists; the option of the navy blue deck of cards is the win that will not only protect the innocent victims, but will prevent the possibility of such a grand loss for the gambler.

Individual affordable limit is very important – not only for creating a soft landing regardless of the result of the action, positive or negative – but to prevent the creation of a complete failure (handcuffed for life) based on unexpected results, which can arrive at any time without notice, and, more importantly, for using an unaffordable limit. These small steps (small actions) will begin to give you insight into how effective action is and how ineffective inaction can actually be. This enables you not only to plan your future actions well, but also to protect your future actions, particularly as not all actions guarantee desired results. A lesson, at the very least, is guaranteed in all actions, in areas of preparation and/or improvement or increased action, based on the desired result of an action for future actions. What you learn from the small action is imperative for future actions (small, medium or large). If we are to defeat the THEEF in battles (Personal and Public), we must do it in little steps, not giant steps; a big task can be overwhelming for any individual.

TAN

ACTION!
ACTION!!
ACTION!!!

TAN – TAKE ACTION NOW!

Man shall not live on bread alone.
Matthew 4: 4

Houston, we have a problem. Yet, we don't understand the nature of the problem, we can't estimate the cost of the problem and we can't put a time limit on the problem. But we are not going to run away; we are going to deal with the problem and eradicate this infection, vagabond and nuisance to life. Ladies and gentlemen, the voice of success is *Action*. 'Action' is a word from the mouth of God. A man shall not live by FEAR alone but also by action.

The person who won't read is no better off than the person who can't read.
Zig Ziglar

Glorified, modern-day slavery: we are not forced to do it, but we force ourselves to do it, perhaps because we don't know any other way, not that another way does not exist. A reality about life: *'Life'* is a natural casualty of the THEEF. However, the maximum application of your ability is the minimum application of the THEEF's ability – hence, the emphasis on TAN (Take Action Now) to propel yourself with the application of your ability to new heights.

You are the only person on earth who can use your ability.
Zig Ziglar

Your natural ability is something you need to identify and use positively. Nobody can use your ability the way you would use it. However, knowing you have ability is one thing; using the ability is another. Without any attempts to hold a conversation or discussion with the THEEF or interrogate him, individuals succumb to FEAR as the gospel of life, hence, welcoming failure before its arrival. To welcome failure before its arrival is a life sentence without parole. The individual who refuses to take action cannot be better than the individual who cannot take action. Crippled or phantom action is not action. Such action has already been infiltrated or intoxicated by the THEEF and its agents. With regard to a crippled action, a shout is nothing more than a whisper and an able mind reduced to a disabled mind. A crippled action is a liability at best.

Your mothers and your fathers, they have made you weak, but General Juma, he will make you strong. He will make you strong, so that you can take back the country from the government and the traitors that work for them.

24: Redemption, Colonel Ike Dubaku

With action, your lost appetite, which FEAR and its close friends took away from you, will be yours again. In *24: Redemption* (a television movie from the television series, "24"), General Juma must have made Colonel Dubaku strong. At the end of the day, everybody deserves a chance, including action. We have all given FEAR opportunities; personally, I believe it is unfair. We should not be selfish to action and unselfish to FEAR. Let us give action the same opportunities we gave to the THEEF of life in the past, and see how it plays out. *'The Audacity of Action:' From anywhere to somewhere, from nothing to something, from nothing to write home about to something to write home about.* The results required by humankind are not in saying, saying, saying; they are in doing, doing, doing. War on action is a mistake; peace with the Extinguisher of life is suicide. Do what you are here to do, not what you are not here to do.

Phonetic

Action is a word of importance in any language, anywhere in the world. As far as communication and language are concerned, we are still within the remit of this book. Let me spell it out; in the process, permit me to employ the official intercommunication style used by the police and military: 'Foxtrot,' 'Echo,' 'Alpha,' 'Romeo' is used for the word 'FEAR'. Those are part of the NATO phonetic language (radio-telephony spelling alphabet), used to identify letters individually when spelling a word by adept communicators, particularly in the military, police, emergency services and other armed forces. Yet, this is not included in the communication rules of engagement in the Failure Armed Forces, despite the fact that it is still the most extensively used form of intercommunication in various armed forces, and despite the availability of different types of phonetic language. This enables those transmitting and receiving the voice message to pronounce and understand the combinations of letters via telephone or radio, regardless of their native language and especially when the safety of an individual life is at stake. The validity of the values of the Failure Armed Forces should be questioned, particularly as the safety of any individual's life is not of paramount importance in Failure Armed Forces in reality. 'Alpha,' 'Charlie,' 'Tango,' 'India,' 'Oscar,' 'November,' – the official NATO spelling alphabet for the word 'Action,' is what I deeply intend to communicate to you.

The onus is on you to make an impact on your life or your family's life. It is not anybody's responsibility to improve your life or the lives of members of your family positively. That duty is YOURS, AND YOURS ONLY! Someone else cannot study law at a university, and you expect to practice law with his or her law degree. If you intend to practice law, you will have to go to a university, obtain your own law degree, and proceed to law school to enable you to practice law in the society, not unless you want to be charged for various offences like deception, impersonation, etc. That simply means that to practice law you need to take ACTION. Inaction today purely based on FEAR is a blow, a few months down the line a major blow, and a few years later, it becomes a knock-out punch. You are down for the count; you can't save yourself, and the bell is your only chance for survival – however, the sound of the bell is two minutes away.

Reward

Action has a reward; *"Positive reward awaits you."* How much reward awaits you will depend on which action you take, not necessarily the size of each action. Either way, reward awaits you.

Rewards are not measured by the size of the action. You cannot keep living on your credit balance to balance your bank account; you need to take action to increase your credit balance at your bank as the years go by. If you entertain the Extinguisher of life and his entourage without increasing your credit balance, a debt balance is what awaits you a couple of blocks up the road. Take action. Action has the habit of giving a large reward for little action sometimes. In certain cases, minimum action can produce maximum reward, and maximum action can produce minimum reward. Even if you don't take action based entirely on FEAR, a reward still awaits you; the only problem here is, the reward that awaits you is FAILURE! *"Even when success or refund is guaranteed, you still need to take action. To achieve anything in life, you will be required to take action, so what exactly do you have to lose by taking action? Action has a positive or negative result, and inaction has a guaranteed negative result."*

Millionaires and billionaires who keep getting richer and richer are not doing so because they stopped taking action, far from it. They are getting richer simply because they keep on taking action after action, while the poor remain poor due to inaction after inaction. The millionaires and billionaires grow their knowledge on a regular basis; the potential millionaires to be do likewise, while the poor prevent their desire and knowledge growth by default. Action is the language of success; any other word with an opposite meaning to action is not readable for success. You cannot refrain from taking action because of FEAR.

> *Even if you are on the right track, you'll get run over if you just sit there!*
> **Will Rogers**

View tomorrow as a new beginning; tomorrow you start to deal with your FEAR, today you realize how much damage FEAR has done to you – but, more importantly, today you take control, and the THEEF of life takes a back seat. Today, from this point on, you start your FEAR eradication treatment. All you need is to have the burning desire and the confidence to move forward systematically. Starting does not cost you anything; just start thinking positively to build up your courage and confidence. Thinking is free; use it to the best of your ability. If you keep on doing what you have been doing, you will keep getting what you already have. You need to do things in a different way from your normal way of doing things. A change is required. Change comes with FEAR, in particular: FEAR of the unknown – hence, to change requires taking a risk. To be successful, you need to take a risk. To take a risk, you need to eradicate the presence of the Extinguisher of life in your life to an acceptable level. To eradicate your FEAR, you will need to take action.

Action is the Antibiotic for FEAR.

When you take action, you feel more in control of your situation, and you can work toward effective solutions. Applying the recommended dose of the antibiotics on a daily basis will generate the treatment needed on a daily basis until the course of the antibiotics is completed. You cannot use the wrong antibiotics and expect a result; you need to identify what type of FEAR you have and apply the correct antibiotics for your type of FEAR. Overall, action is required; worrying about whether to or not to, will not resolve your FEAR.

FEAR grips, action removes the grips.

If you want to do something positive or progressive, but for one excuse or the other, you back out, the underlining reason is FEAR; you are actually gripped by the Extinguisher of life. It feels like your hands are handcuffed and legs glued to the floor. You convince yourself that one day you will be free from this bondage. This day may never come. Freedom from this bondage is only assured if you take action. The action you take to deal with your FEAR will remove the grip the THEEF has placed on you, your hands out of handcuff and your legs unglued to the floor. Based on the action, you will find a spring in your step, and walk freely as you have never done before. Conduct your transaction with the THEEF by taking the conversation to him, not vice versa. Even the last six letters of the word transaction, *'action,'* tells you what is required in your transaction with the Extinguisher of life; perhaps, the THEEF of life knew before we did. Hence, the THEEF carries the conversations to us before we get a chance to carry the conversation or discussion to him. Action is not catty *(spiteful)*. Understanding what you FEAR and where it comes from, will set you free – freedom within. When you have freedom within, the defensive barriers of the THEEF of life are broken. Success is no longer viewed as impossible but possible.

Afraid

If you are scared to take action, you will only encourage doubt and worry in your mind, and FEAR in particular does not require any invitation to move into action. It then begs the question, *"If the Extinguisher of life does not require an invitation to move into action, why are you waiting for an invitation to take action?"* At the first opportunity, FEAR will work its way into your system and contaminate your thoughts. Your action will be based on FEAR, deep down inside you, and on the outside, it appears as if you are taking your time or just not ready to do it for reasons other than FEAR. The Extinguisher then pushes you to convince others to think as you do. A previous minor experience of a failed task or project, a temporary minor setback, becomes the pillar of all future decisions even when the odds are firmly stacked in your favor. If failure is a minor setback, must we hit the threshold of complete failure before we attempt to act? When you are afraid to take action, you need action to attack your FEAR. Start with minor actions to deal with your FEAR to gradually gain the self-confidence you need to progress on to other small or bigger actions. If you don't take action to move ahead, you become a slave to the THEEF of life. Experience teaches us how to handle similar situations better in the future, and by taking minor actions, you prepare yourself and build up your courage to deal with bigger issues based on the results of previous actions. If you are afraid to take action, investigate the reason why you are afraid to take action and find ways to gradually overcome this obstacle. The first step could simply be having the burning desire to do something in your mind without actually doing it. At this stage, the mind is getting into the doing mode and will move into the action mode quickly as all possible ways to take action become your daily thoughts. Within your daily thoughts, you will find not only the courage but the best and mostly effective way to take action and this will ensure, even if you don't get your desired result from your action, your loss will have a minimal effect on yours or your family's life, and in any case, you still get a positive result. You now know, as opposed to the information you constantly receive from the Extinguisher of life, there is no big deal in taking action. Action to a large extent gives you the ability to go forward in life. You may be afraid to apply for a better job in another company and decide to remain in your present job for FEAR of the unknown. *How do you know you will be in your present job in the next two months?* If you want to have an advantage over the THEEF, say your prayers, prepare for battle like a great warrior will do, and take action. Even if you make a mistake along the way, accept it and learn from your mistakes.

Mistakes are the seeds of success.

Everybody makes mistakes from time to time; it is how we deal with and respond to the results of our mistakes that matters, even minor mistakes. We should also be grateful that we are all entitled to a second chance for the mistakes we make. For our second chance, we can draw on the results of earlier decisions we made as a point of reference for making other decisions on actions to take to ensure we get better results.

Do the one thing you think you cannot do. Fail at it. Try again. Do better the second time. The only people who never tumble are those who never mount the high wire. This is your moment. Own it
Oprah Winfrey

You cannot mount the high wire with the THEEF of life.

Spoon

Silver spoon or plastic spoon, you need to take action. Action gets things done; inaction, as the name implies, does not get things done. Let us take a step back, pause for a minute, and ask ourselves, *"What have I done lately that gave me personal satisfaction? What should I have done and did not do?"* Whatever answers you come up with in your mind, the personal satisfaction you felt deep down in your heart was due to the action you took; while in most cases, what you should have done and didn't do was due to FEAR. If taking action gives us a personal satisfaction, we need to be taking action on a regular basis with positive results to ensure we are constantly getting personal satisfaction from our actions. I can just imagine the thought in your mind this very minute: *"Easier said than done,"* – and you are absolutely correct. However, do you know anything that is more easily done than said?

What you need to understand is that mistakes are made every single day; in fact, you could have made a mistake today in the morning (morning blues, as I like to call it). Perhaps you had a meeting and planned to wear a navy blue tie. While indoors, you pick up a tie that appeared to be a navy blue tie in your wardrobe, you put on the tie, and you are ready to go. Halfway through your journey, on closer examination of your tie, you realize you are wearing a black tie, not a navy blue tie. The mistake has been made, but the gravity of the mistake is minor on this occasion. However, on another occasion, such as when the Extinguisher of life is involved, at the end of the journey, there will be a high price to pay. It is the FEAR of mistakes that carries a high price or great consequence that created the phrase *'Easier said than done.'* Deal with managing your mistakes, and you put yourself in action mode, and 'Easier said than done' changes to 'Easier done than said,' in your mind, and your perception in general changes completely.

Step 4: Action

I believe that one of life's greatest risks is never daring to risk.
Oprah Winfrey

Risk is inevitable; it is an essential part of life that can't be overlooked, calculated or not. To be successful, you need to take risks. You don't necessarily have to take huge killer risks, but you must take a *CALCULATED RISK*. Divide your assets by 20 or 10, depending on what you can afford to lose. Take a risk with your 5 percent or 10 percent. At worst, you lose 5 percent or 10 percent of your assets. However, at best, your 5 percent or 10 percent could grow to exceed the 95 percent or 90 percent of assets that you did not risk. Even if you lose your 5 percent or 10 percent, you would have learnt a lot in the process; what you learn is experience, and experience, good or bad, is a great asset to have in your success toolbox. It is said: *"There is no substitute for experience."* If you intend to be a millionaire, the best people to learn from are millionaires; they have been there and done it. Not taking a risk is a risk bigger than taking a risk. A part of you knows you ought to take action, and what matters now is that you know where to draw the line between being wary and taking a small, calculated risk. There is nothing wrong in being skeptical sometimes, and, occasionally, cautious. Whatever you decide to do, create your road map and act on it. You need to follow your road map; sometimes, difficulties appear that put FEAR in your mind that your road map is useless and a waste of time, but really that's what separates the men from the boys. The failures immediately give up; they cannot stomach the fight any longer, but the men take their wedding vows immediately:

"I, **SUCCESS***, take you,* **ROAD MAP***, to be my wedded wife. To have and to hold from this day forward, for better, for worse, for richer, for poorer, in sickness or in health, to love and to cherish,* **until DEATH DO US PART***. And hereto I pledge you my faithfulness."*

Lector, we need to expunge FEAR. FEAR prevents us from taking risk; however, associating with the FEAR in the first place is the true underlining risk. If you associate with the THEEF, it can prevent you from taking risk or action, even when the odds are firmly on your side. When the THEEF prevents you from doing something you want to do or taking action, you will not achieve anything; even if you did something, you probably would still not achieve anything as long as your thinking is still contaminated with FEAR. The man who knows what he wants takes his vows religiously; he sees nothing but success ahead of him. To be derailed or distracted is not an option. The word "failure" does not exist in his personal dictionary; he is a true warrior. The THEEF of life is aware of such warriors and tries to poison their minds, but always finds resistance from them and never stands in their way. FEAR knows it is a pointless battle; defeat is imminent. Sometimes, your environment determines what actions you take, but one thing is certain: no matter what your environment dictates, you will have to take action. When you take action is up to you, but if you don't take the action, inaction grows in your life.

The hand that dips into the bottom of the pot will eat the biggest snail.
**Poet, playwright and Noble Prize Winner
Wole Soyinka**

Naked Arrival

To earth without, from earth without.

You can't depart without arriving; nobody departs from earth without arriving on earth in the first place and that arrival, which is within a round-trip flight, does not permit or allow carrying luggage, let alone excess luggage – naked arrival, naked departure. Everybody who arrived on earth did so via the womb of a woman, and did not arrive with money in their hands. The spaces on earth belong to all. You have a right to live as much as your brother or sister. Don't entertain the option of the handcuffs of FEAR.

Step 4: Action

Pennies do not come from heaven.
They have to be earned here on earth.
Margaret Thatcher

Nobody arrived on earth with a dime in their pocket; yet, some intend to depart the earth with a billion dollars in their pocket, though nobody can depart from earth with the money they accumulated on earth in their hands or pocket. FEAR has no right to depart from your life with a billion dollars in his pocket; you did not come to earth for or on behalf of FEAR – you owe FEAR nothing in monetary terms. We can't stand by the door collecting autographs from the Extinguisher of life. Make him stand by the door to collect your autograph instead. If you take FEAR's autograph to any financial institution to use as collateral for a $10 advance, the loan officer will not even give you an audience, let alone a $10 advance. However, if you take your autograph to the same financial institution you will get an audience and more than the $10 advance you require. We can't expect a loan officer already intoxicated with FEAR to accommodate our presentation of more FEAR into his life. There are some who commit suicide by jumping from tall buildings just because they lost their six figure jobs or their businesses failed, they are the ones who couldn't raise their game or price. Why anybody would decide to depart from earth of their own accord, because they lost something they did not arrive on earth with, is open to debate. Indeed, you have to wonder if they raised their game in the first place to arrive in that position, or if they got there by default or fictitiously.

We have to be tough before we can be liberated; FEAR does exactly the same without been totally liberal. Once we wake up, the world wakes up with us. We cannot wake up from the sleep of FEAR or our knowledge coma without the truth. We cannot take control of the journey of our life with ours hands in handcuffs that belong to the creator of the failures-only exclusive club. History is history; action did not set up the failures-only exclusive club, FEAR did that. In order not to exacerbate the already negative feeling towards the owner of the handcuffs of life, the THEEF, within the society of action-takers – let the owner, FEAR, voluntarily take his products off the shelves for life products.

A Debt Is a Favor

A good favor deserves a good favor in return. A debt is a favor; if you owe, pay it back. When you borrow from FEAR, the debt becomes the only debt that appears to be a favor, but is not a favor. If in doubt, your conversation with the Extinguisher of life is paramount. If you make an attempt to pay your debt to FEAR, FEAR will avoid you. A situation arrives, one that would call for a conversation with the *THEEF*. *"Do we 'engage brain before lips'?" "Why has the THEEF, who is normally readily available, suddenly become a scarce commodity?"*
    These are just a few of the questions that require answers. The reality of the situation is that FEAR is a personal and business loan provider like other creditors – who doesn't want you to make regular payments, early payments, or pay off the loan during the life of the loan. Even better, an extension of the term of payment would be highly appreciated by the THEEF, despite the huge interest rate associated with the debt, because a payback of the favor from FEAR is freedom from slavery. The Extinguisher of life just wants to keep you on the FEAR payment treadmill indefinitely. Get rid of the weeds of FEAR in your grass, and your garden lawn will never look the same again! Your grass is not immune from weeds or its agents. Weeds are only interested in your grass, period! A good favor for the weeds, in return, is to give them weed killer, the language of weeds. By the same token, employ the services of action against the THEEF of life, the contraceptive for your FEAR. Just like everything in life, failure has a right approach and a wrong approach; deal with failure with the right approach, and failure will become a tool for success. Action will repay your debt to FEAR. You may have the best idea, the best resources, or be in the best position to take action, but if action is not taken, the advantage you have is not an advantage. We don't want to tell ourselves in the future that we should have gone to Specsavers on the penultimate or last lap

of the race. If the opportunity to visit Specsavers is an option, we need to elect that option today. We have to address the situation now. Tomorrow is not a day we own by right.

A Clash of the Giants

It takes conversation to defeat conversation.
It takes courage to defeat courage.
It takes confidence to defeat confidence.
It takes a desire to defeat a desire.
It takes a hero to defeat a hero.
It takes a legend to defeat a legend.
It takes an icon to defeat an icon.
It does not take FEAR to defeat FEAR.
However, it takes a giant to defeat a giant.
Each giant is a giant within its own vicinity.
Each giant may not be a giant outside his own vicinity.
Both giants don't need an excuse to be low on confidence.
It takes a burning desire to defeat burning FEAR.
It takes action to defeat the THEEF of life in any vicinity, home or away.

Stop or Be Stopped

With your positive discussion with FEAR, you stop the THEEF; without it, FEAR stops you. You are on the train, and you want to stay on the train; you are thirty minutes from the next stop, but somebody has to get off at the next stop. FEAR or YOU, who will it be – who will end up on the station platform wondering what happened? FEAR will make it tight, difficult and unbearable, and try to communicate the benefits of FEAR to you. Every action is vital; the concentration and the intensity required are higher. You can expect it to be a bit different from other kinds of conversations, particularly if you have hardly won your conversations with the THEEF of life in the past. You will have to conjure up a great dialogue with the Extinguisher of life – your life, by the way, is just another life to be stolen, destroyed and buried, as far as the THEEF is concerned, just like many others before you. It is down to who grabs the key points of the conversation and runs with it to their advantage, that will make the difference by the time the train gets to the next station.

Action will insist on withholding the supply line to the icon of bandits, from your first or second voice, depending on which side they support, and will be the key to success in your conversation. If you can prevent the negative voice, then you can prevent FEAR. If you fail to stop the negative voice, at the next station you will be the one getting off the train, not the THEEF. Both parties, action and FEAR, giants in their own rights, don't need an excuse to be low on confidence – based on their track record, both have confidence in abundance. A burning desire or FEAR is all that is required by each relevant party to take ownership and control of the dialogue.

On the road, we reach a STOP sign at a cross road, with the THEEF of life approaching from all directions—north, south, east, and behind you from the west. It is mandatory to stop at the STOP sign, something that the THEEF constantly avoids. This time we are going to challenge the global THEEF to stop as required, but a conversation or interrogation has to take place – the most ignored conversation. Lector! We are going to open a new branch of IHOP (International House of Possibilities), and we intend to take stock of the possibilities in our lives. If IHOP (International House of Pancakes) has been serving pancakes to the public for decades, then IHOP must be high up on possibilities, a great public servant. If we intend to be a great public servant as well, then our branch of IHOP (International House of Possibilities) must be open twenty-four hours, seven days a week. Opening two hours or less a day does not give the general public options to work with.

Feel the Difference

Buy land, they're not making it any more.
Mark Twain

They're not making land any more, but they are still making FEAR. The production line is open twenty-four hours a day, seven days a week, and the maximum production per day is achieved on a daily basis. Buy action first. Even though they are still making it, the longer it takes you to buy action, the longer it will take you to get results. Don't buy FEAR, don't even make inquiries. By the way, should you decide to make any inquiries at all, do not leave your contact details with them, particularly your cell phone number. Their sales team is the best in the world at closing a sale. By investing in action, you buy success, In its own right, this is an insurance policy for your success; it gives you a burning desire to keep taking action, at the very least, to maintain your station in life. If you buy FEAR, it will deny action an expression as it normally does. Unlike land, where the shortage creates extremely high demand in relation to its supply, the supply of FEAR exceeds its demand, which, in turn, makes it easy to get and affordable for all human beings. In some places, it's available on a bug-off basis (buy one get one free). In certain cases, the cheapest products are the most dangerous products to your well-being. If you were told that the THEEF of life is a killer of dreams who has used delay tactics in the clock of human life to kill dreams and has been convicted no fewer than a million times, would you associate with him or her? The FEAR of action cannot increase the well-being of an individual in the long run.

MODEL COLLARS DUSTIN AT HARVEY NICK BASH
Hoffman party crasher gets dream movie role
The London Paper, Hannah Summers

I am always impressed and have the utmost respect for people who are willing to take action to be successful in whatever they want to do. There are a few different things I admire that Tolula Adeyemi (party crasher) did. The most important of them all is that she *took action*. She established a burning desire which enabled her to take action, her friends helped her to improve her self-confidence and courage, and she increased the odds of her chances (she had already auditioned for the role, so she had a chance of getting the role) by taking action. She got a positive result for her action. Tolula had auditioned for the role in the movie (like many others we don't know, just as we never knew Tolula), but her real audition was the action she took.

Tolula's case is a case of *'Nike'* and *'Ford:':'Just do It'* combined with *'Feel the difference.'* She did it, and she is now feeling the difference. *"She starts filming next week and is seeking an agent."* I wonder how many agents would have responded before she took action to get to this stage, but after she took action, I have a good guess of how many agents will be chasing her now. Furthermore, her modeling career will definitely get a new lease on life. Her burning desire and action ensured she gave herself a chance and, eventually, a positive result. For every action, there is a result (positive or negative); however, if you do not take the action, how would you know if your result would be positive or negative? Even if you take action and the result is negative, once the dust settles, I am sure you will find an element of positivity in whatever result you get to aid your next action. The decision is yours.

Omelet

Ignorance of the law is no excuse. If you know the THEEF of life is holding you back in any aspect of your life, regardless of the type of FEAR you have, you need to take effective action to free yourself from the chains of bondage. After many years of not taking action, you cannot claim ignorance of action as an excuse for not dealing with your FEAR. Conduct a feasibility study, identify what is holding you back from taking action to free yourself from this self-imposed bondage, and identify what is required to take action and how viable the action you choose to take will be. *"You can't expect success to knock on your door and say to you, 'I am all yours, how much of me do you want?"* Success as a product is presumed to have demand that exceeds its supply; however, most of the demands are phantom demands – in reality, supply still exceeds demand. If you don't demand it, it won't come to you.

Step 4: Action

You cannot make an omelet without breaking eggs.

The quality of the omelet you will get is not the issue at this stage; what is important at this stage is that you want an omelet, and without breaking the eggs, you cannot make an omelet. Failure, the alternative product to success, also has a supply that exceeds demand – but it does not require a first invitation, let alone a second invitation, to offer itself to you. As the supply exceeds the demand, it is a free product, and *'door-to-door'* delivery is included as an incentive to potential customers. Based on the nature of human beings in general, the public loves anything that is free. Is failure free, or is the price well disguised in the fact that it is free and its incentive of free *'door-to-door'* delivery? FEAR prevents you from seeing the true price of failure; by the time you reach your retirement age, find yourself on the line for your state pension, and realize that your state pension barely covers your groceries, let alone, other household bills, I believe you will know the true price of failure and the damage the Extinguisher of life is capable of delivering to your doorstep at no cost to you.

If action, effective and positive action, were taken in the early years of your working life, regardless of the amount of action you took, provided you took action, you may not have even realized you were entitled to state pension, let alone know the address of the welfare office and where to line up for your pension. But if your income exceeds your costs in retirement, world tours, cruises, gifts for grandchildren, etc. – while that may not even be on the agenda for most people on state pension, it will become your main activity. Real fear is fear, and it is real – those are mainly out of our control, but action may still be the key to unlock the handcuffs.

Your post-retirement job description is guaranteed based on previous actions taken during your working life; those actions taken in the past will keep you busy in retirement rather than lining up for pension payment or trying to stay in your job even when you reach the retirement age.

FEAR EXIT

FEAR EXIT

FEAR is as deadly as fire, and perhaps, much more than fire. With fire, in certain cases, you can see the flames of the fire, and take the necessary precautions to avert the fire to ensure you are not burnt. Houses, cars, clothes, etc. can be destroyed by fire. They are all replaceable items. Guard the irreplaceable items against fire, and not the replaceable items you own. A life is not a replaceable item. It is possible, even if you were asleep in a house on fire, that the heat of the fire could wake you up; if you do not have a smoke alarm, hopefully you could still get out via a window or be rescued by a firefighter. When you see a 'FEAR exit' sign, run as fast as you can and join others at the action assemble point. It may just be the best race you ever ran. FEAR is not as visible as fire to the naked eye; you can feel FEAR but you can't smell FEAR. It is only visible to the naked eye when the full consequence of FEAR, failure, is at your doorstep – and in most cases, it is too late to act or, even if you act, full, effective positive results are not achievable.

You can't make a claim for compensation to an insurance company for failure. For example, due to FEAR, I did not take action to put myself in a position to buy my own house and car for the last twenty-nine years, and I had a company house and car. I am retiring in six months, and I will have to return the company car and vacate the company house. Insurance companies do not offer 'premium for failure' products.

Look around you, whether you are in the office, restaurant or at home: *"Can you find a FEAR exit door?"* If you can, do not ignore it as you always do when you see a fire exit door in most places; fire is not a daily occurrence in our lives, but the same cannot be said in favor of FEAR. If you find a FEAR exit door, don't even think about it or hesitate; head for the door as soon as you can. If you ignore the FEAR exit door, the failures-only door will be wide open, awaiting your arrival.

In a relationship with the Extinguisher of life, there is only one winner, and that winner is not you. If you are party to such a relationship, the winner is the THEEF of life. In the long run or at the close of play, the results always favor the THEEF; research has constantly produced evidence to support this conclusion. Based on your relationship with the global bandit, your excuses (lack of time, money or waiting for the right time) are already in place; all you have to do is allocate the right one to the right situation, even though any of them would be acceptable for any situation, as is always the case with FEAR. You have been dreaming about something, yet FEAR ensures it appears to you to be a million miles away. Break the mold; you can do it with your conversations or discussion with the global bandit. After all, you have nothing to lose; it is only a conversation, and that you do every day. If you are up for it, you are up for it. If you are not up for it, you are not up for it. If you fight like a novice against the Extinguisher of life, you will be extinguished like a novice. If you are up for a conversation with the poison of life, converse with him. *"The devil always deals with you at a cost to you, not to him. FEAR, if not the devil, is a carbon copy of the devil."*

FEAR Extinguisher

A FEAR extinguisher is very similar to a fire extinguisher; they both do the same job. They are used to extinguish small FEARs and fires, respectively. The only difference is, while it may be possible to extinguish a real fire completely, you cannot extinguish real fear. Extinguishers are very effective in putting out small FEARs or fires. *"Do you have a FEAR extinguisher in your office, car and house?"* If you don't, please get one for your office, car and house immediately. They are very effective for putting out small FEAR. A FEAR extinguisher may not put out a medium FEAR, but it will put out small FEARs in your mind and will certainly distinguish them from medium and large FEARs. A small FEAR ignites a big FEAR, and if you can't deal with small ones, how do you intend to deal with big ones? A FEAR department does not exist; nobody can rescue you from your FEAR regardless of its size, and you are on your own. You can be given the tools to get the job done, but if you don't use the tools, you cannot get the job done.

By the way, if you have the FEAR extinguisher, I hope you use it – because having and using are two different things. If you have it and don't use it, the same fate as not having one awaits you. The price of a FEAR extinguisher is very, very cheap compared to the price of failure; you don't have to believe me. Just take my word for it, or find out which is cheaper when Failure Airlines Flight F99 arrives.

Real fear cannot be extinguished but can be distinguished.

If real fear cannot be extinguished, we need to distinguish real fear from the THEEF. We need to distinguish small, medium or large FEAR whenever the need arises. Distinguish your FEAR. "When you distinguish your FEAR and take action, the barriers of FEAR and FEAR itself are extinguished." Once your tools are in place, use them to distinguish your FEAR, if only the real from the pretender. In your discussion with the THEEF of life, express your views. Stand up to the global bully and come of age. Tell the THEEF, "If you want to take me, I am here, take me. There is no need to prolong and torture me for years only to hand me my failure certificate; you might as well hand it to me now. The earlier the better, sooner rather than later." This kind of confrontation immediately tells the THEEF he has a man with a burning desire and the will to take action on his hands. The game is over; he will simply take his handcuffs and flee. The global bandit known across the world in different languages by different names, but with the same devastating effect in any part of the world, can still be tamed as long as you give yourself the permission to do so. In any society, it is not acceptable to have bandits roaming the streets, a duty owed to the inhabitants of the society by the government of the day. However, a duty you owe to yourself is a confrontation with the global bandit. At the end of the day, the government, if willing, cannot take ownership of that duty; that duty is reserved for you. There are times when real fear can motivate an individual into action but FEAR will never inspire action.

Taming the Murder

Any human being who kills another human being is tried for murder and sentenced to life imprisonment or death row, depending on the laws of the country where the crime was committed, if found guilty as charged. In comparison, FEAR, the freelance murderer, has killed more people than you could possibly imagine and is still out on the streets killing people by infiltrating their clock of life. In addition, people have suffered in untold numbers in different areas of their lives because they let the THEEF rule their world. To date, no court exists in any country in the world to trial the THEEF of life, yet he parades himself on any street in the world. The only person capable of bringing the daylight bandit to justice is you, and the only judge is action. Unfortunately, you can't do it on your own, neither can action on its own; a joint effort is required by you and action. You will have to take action, action will not take you. For example, in a client/server relationship, the client has to make a request to the server before the server returns a service to the client. Action is always ready for action; the question is, *"Are you ready to make a request to the server?"* Create a FEAR disinfectant, the circle of FHAF, applicable to different areas of your life and apply as needed.

Even your doctor will tell you to follow the instruction as stated on your prescription. FEAR occurs more in our lives than sickness; you may visit your doctor once or twice in a year for flu treatment, but in most cases, the THEEF will arrive for a visit at least once a week, if not daily, in any area of your life without notice.

Discover FEAR quickly, and abandon it quickly. When you discover the Extinguisher of life, apply the seven-step taming guide to abandon it as fast as you can – it is a contagious pandemic disease. If you dwell on it, it will ruin your life; unfortunately, the damage FEAR is capable of delivering in any human life is not visible at an early stage. So, if you discover the FEAR and you hesitate, you could regret not taming the THEEF. Arrest your FEAR as soon as you discover it to avoid joining the FEAR department, not the fire department (at least with the latter, you still have the chance to become the fire chief). FEAR can turn your life around, back to where you started from and beyond. However, if action turns your life around, action will turn your life around beyond your wildest dreams or imagination. With the THEEF, failure is assured; but with action, failure is not assured, because, at the very least, you get an extra option in the deal, and the extra option you get is success.

When action wakes up, FEAR disappears and failure goes to sleep.

Strong desire and action need to be constant to prevent the appearance of the THEEF; the appearance of FEAR can turn your life around in the wrong direction, back to where you were before and beyond. Consistent action, however, would turn your life around, and when it is turned around, it could be beyond your wildest imagination. With FEAR, failure is certain, but with action, you get the option of the two sides of a coin. *"FEAR or action, what do I get from it? Well it depends on who is handing out the accolade."* We need to ensure action wakes up on a daily basis in our lives. If we let action go to sleep, the THEEF will appear in our lives again. Remember FEAR does not require an invitation to appear in our lives. Tame the murderer by taking action.

SUPER BOWL XLII

New England Patriots vs. New York Giants

The Patriots were the favorites – but the Giants had a game plan, a burning desire, a will to win, and, above all, took action against all odds. The New York Giants, Goliath in name but David in heart, stepped on to the playing field with a will to win and a mindset that knew no failure. It was a day in which the THEEF of life could not get a ticket for the game from the Giants. The New England Patriots, David in name, Goliath in heart, were expected to win and showed why on the day, but against a team that already had conversations with the THEEF, the result was never going to be in doubt. The last conversation between Eli Manning, the Giants quarterback, and Plaxico Burress, the Giants wide receiver, proved why. Eli Manning threw the winning touchdown pass to Plaxico Burress with just thirty-five seconds left on the clock. The conversation between the Giants defense team and FEAR was just as evident as the conversation between their offense team and FEAR in all quarters of the game.

After the game, a commentator said; *"You don't win a game like that, unless you truly believe you're going to win."* He was right. You only win such game after a conversation with the THEEF of life in your favor. The Giants knew something nobody else knew – they knew they had a chance after their conversation with FEAR, and all that was required after the conversation was to step out and play. They played without FEAR, and failure was simply an armchair spectator. I congratulate the New York Giants; they gave a performance worthy of their name (GIANTS), and I also give a big thank you to them for the following lesson: if you train hard, believe in yourself, and take action in what you believe after a conversation with the world's greatest bandit, you will step on to the field, step up and refuse to be beaten. You can't buy a winning mentality; it is not for sale.

"I never doubted myself, I never lost confidence," said Manning, who completed 19 of 34 passes for 255 yards and two TDs against New England. "As a quarterback I think that's the most important thing, you can never lose confidence in yourself," Manning said.

"But I'm very comfortable in my own skin, you know, I am the way I am and I wasn't going to change."

Be comfortable in your own skill, not in other people's skills, and have a conversation with your FEAR and you will get to the finish line in style. Remember, you arrived at your current position in life by merit, not by default. That merit will take you far and beyond. Eli Manning's father was not the football team's coach nor his uncle, yet he never lost confidence in himself. Even if his father was the team coach, he would have made the team on merit – you have to have unflinching faith in yourself. If Eli Manning can do it, you can as well. Vocation may be different for each one of us, but the requirements, confidence and faith are the same. He is just as human as you are, and he truly deserved his Super Bowl Most Valuable Player (MVP) award. The Giants must have concluded their conversation with the words *"let's get it done;"* not only did they have the last touchdown in the game, they also got the job done.

The Message

"... it's just a lack of understanding. All these boundaries – Africa, Asia, Malaysia, America – are set by men. But you don't have to look at boundaries when you are looking at a man – at the character of a man. The question is: What do you stand for? Are you a follower, or are you a leader? When people talk about my popularity as a basketball player, they don't know that I am not in competition with, and I don't compare myself with, anybody, because I am comfortable with myself."

Hakeem Olajuwon, *Slam Dunk* **–
Interview by Spike Lee**

From Eli and Hakeem, two great icons in their sports – football and basketball, respectively – the message is clear: you have to be comfortable with yourself in your own skin. It is only the beginning; the end is not even in sight, yet we fast-track the beginning to the end. Within decades from now, you will be more disappointed with the things you did without your approval, but with the approval of the hacker of life. Colors are beautiful and give life a colorful meaning. What is the color of your game – blue, red or green? Identify the color of your game and play in that color. Don't play in the color picked for you by the THEEF.

Bella! Bella! Bella! (Spanish) *translates to Beautiful! Beautiful! Beautiful!* That is what action is; more importantly, that is what you are as well. The THEEF does not intend to give you that accolade, neither does its agents. Claim it; it is yours. Action is pretty and gorgeous both inside and outside, while the THEEF of life is not, both inside and outside. The THEEF of life is in the business of winning souls, failures only; however, if any individual decides to join voluntarily, the THEEF will be glad to have the individual. You have to do what you do best when you do what you have to do, not what the THEEF tells you to do. We don't have to live under the spotlight of FEAR. Choose your spotlight!

Warriors don't go into battle without determination and the will to succeed. You have to increase your determination to succeed. When FEAR meets Action, not only is a shout reduced to a soft voice, failure is taken out of the equation and replaced by success.

I KNOW YOU WANNA KILL ME BUT I JUST RAISED THE PRICE. YOU WANT ME DEAD BUT YOU GONNA PAY A PRICE TO GET THAT RESULT.
**Saviour's Day in Chicago,
Minister Louis Farrakhan**

Lector! Increase your price to ensure FEAR or Recession has to pay a price to get a result – regardless of your color (regardless of who you are or where you are from). Blue, Red, White, Brown, Black, Gold or any other color, RAISE YOUR PRICE! We know we may have to pay a price to the THEEF, but HE WOULD HAVE TO PAY TO GET THAT RESULT! If the THEEF of human lives has the right to raise his price, I am well within my right to raise mine as well, and so are you. To raise your price, interrogate FEAR, establish a burning desire and action that burning desire. To get the result, failure or success, the price to pay is inaction or action respectively. Action is not allowed to be a member of the failures-only exclusive club, the Failure Armed Forces, except when the action taken is inaction. The price FEAR will have to pay is a confrontation with action. My desire is hot and burning. My desire to take action is uncontrollable and unspeakable (my determination not to give up without a fight in this battle is second to none).

If God be for us, who is against us?
Romans 8:31

Here is my caveat for the THEEF in any language: *"We are not the daughters of dreamers. We are not the sons of failures. We are not the sons and daughters of Satan. We are daughters and sons of action-takers; more importantly, we are the sons and daughters of God! It is well with us. It would be wise for you to see if action and above all, God is with us. We know he is with us, because we are not against him, but you don't – so it will be sensible of you to confirm if God is with us, and if God is with us, it would be wise of you to leave us in peace. Take your handcuffs elsewhere; we have no need for them!"*

FEAR has declared war on our lives. This is an invasion of privacy. Both hands may be in handcuffs yesterday and today – and the possibility that those hands may remain in handcuffs tomorrow cannot be overlooked. However, with the key (action) we can ensure both hands are not in handcuffs from today or tomorrow. The THEEF of life may have restricted our lives by putting our hands in handcuffs when we were sleeping, but now we are awake. The movement of our hands is limited when both hands are in handcuffs, but if we can only remove the handcuffs on one hand, we will get freedom of movement in both hands, despite the fact that one hand is still in handcuffs. You have the key for the handcuffs, use it! Unleash the action in you! We may not have a pair of keys; at least, we have a key (key of action). Thank God, both keys were not lost, that's why God gave us action. Lector, if the Extinguisher of life has the audacity to declare war on our lives, I see no reason why we can't declare a war on FEAR with our Protect or Reclaim Strategy! By the way, the service of a negotiator can't be employed, as the THEEF is not open to negotiations.

Last word:
It is always cold in the winter. That's why winter coats are the best-sellers for most clothing retail stores in the winter. Action, on the other hand, is not restricted by the weather.

EIGHT

Step 5: Analyze

Analyze the feedback from the small actions you took, and create a soft landing for yourself

What are you trying to achieve in life, success or failure? Analyzing the options you have, and, more importantly, what you are currently doing, will give you a good idea as to whether you are winning or losing your personal and public battles. Action cannot be applied to a burning desire that has not been established. Hence, a public battle based on a fruitless personal battle will result in a fruitless public battle. Consequently, the art of battle in this case; constant defeat in battles. Analysis:

1. Analyze the situation at hand with a relaxed mind. Look at previous results of those who have gone to battle with FEAR without a good research behind them before launching an attack on FEAR.
2. With good knowledge, compare the benefits of mixing with the agents of success and the agents of FEAR. The agents of FEAR will always undermine your ability or potential; the same can't be said for the agents of success. For example, why are some people successful and others are not? Those who are successful, did they arrive in that position by not taking action?
3. Analyze how you feel going to the gym twice a week compared with not going at all. Do you feel more or less fit? If you feel more fit than you were before you started going to the gym, not going to the gym could not have giving you that feeling (provided that was your main objective of going to the gym).
4. Analyze how you feel after having a simple conversation with FEAR, or interrogating him compared to not doing either of

those two options. Analyze how you feel after questioning yourself, as opposed to not doing it. For example, ask yourself, why is car A better than car B? Compare the reliability, performance, other extras etc.

5. Analyze how you feel with a burning desire as opposed to not having one.
6. Analyze how you feel with victory in your personal battle, compared to previous defeat.
7. With regards to clothes, particularly – if worn everyday, jeans are more durable compared to 100 percent cotton pants. For example, analyze the durability of your jeans compared to your 100 percent cotton pants, and you will find that jeans speak the language of durability better than cotton pants. The same can be said for blazers, they speak the language of smart looks better than t-shirts.
8. Analyze the benefits of having plans (two or three plans) as opposed to having only one plan. For example, while you have options with two or three plans, one plan gives you no options (except when we consider inaction as an option – but, an option in which we already know the result associated to it).
9. Analyze the minor details in your contract with FEAR. For example, you are not told in what state you will be at the end of your journey with the THEEF of life – that state may be written in small print on your contract with FEAR. When your focus is on FEAR you can easily miss the minor details, that can undermine the authority of FEAR in your mind.
10. In the last five years of associating with FEAR and action, under which one of the two have you made as much progress as you would like? For example, review things you have done in your past that gave you the results you were after, and those you did not do because you were afraid; consequently, you had to make do with the absence of results you would have loved to have achieved.

Analysis is of paramount important in Protect or Reclaim strategy. We can't keep deploying troops to the battlefield, knowing victory in the battle can't be achieved. Each life has a time limit, and the intention of FEAR is to run down the clock of life. Check your clock of life and analyze where you are, and where you could or should be.

> *It's fine to celebrate success but it is more important to heed the lessons of failure.*
> **Bill Gates**

Those lessons of failure are feedback. Always ask for feedback: 'Why did you rate this as eight?' 'Why did you rate that as two?' Remember, people love to give their opinions and in most cases, they are free. During your analysis, don't entertain poor self-image to avoid pollution of your analysis of the feedback from FEAR and action. Companies pay huge money to survey what people want; it is called market research. Feedback is the dictionary of champions – if you want to be a champion, use their dictionary. Feedback is the language of winners. Request feedback from FEAR and action.

> *A good window does not call attention to itself. It merely lets in the light.*
> **Dale Carnegie**

In every house, one window has the best view and another, the worst view – you cannot prefer the window with the worst view over the one with the best view in the house, unless your ability to appreciate a good view has been contaminated by FEAR. For example, I don't know anybody who would prefer to be confined to a cell in jail at the expense of freedom. There must be an underlining element for that kind of thinking.

Analyze the feedback from both to see whose light is brighter, and, more importantly, which one will let more light into your life. Now that you have dealt with those small FEARS, assess the results, even though they were small – as a communication analyst, which we all are, you would have gained more than you would have lost if you did not take action. Let's assume one of the small actions did not produce the desired positive result – you would still be very okay, as the small action carried little or no significant detrimental results. However, the benefit of this is that you gained experience. Failure without any meaningful impact on your lifestyle is not failure; it is a lesson. You are now in a position to review options and the effects that go with each of your options; this enables you to decide which option is best for you. Even if a positive result is not obtained after taking the small action, creating a soft landing for yourself is included in the deal. Create an alternative for action if things don't go as planned, or if an expected result fails to materialize. Putting a contingency plan in place ensures you don't lose everything, and you can still maintain your lifestyle and still take action in the near future. When you put a contingency plan in place devised for a specific situation, and when things go wrong or the desired result is not obtained, you effectively create a soft landing for yourself; however, when the desired results are achieved, you hold a blueprint formula for achieving positive results, an option not on offer to failures from the THEEF – and, furthermore, you get to deal with the issue of what to do with the emergency funds (contingency plan) set aside for your soft landing.

The power

Are you afraid? What are you afraid of, success or failure? Don't be deceived; everyone is afraid of one thing or the other. Focus your conscious mind on success. With your debate, FEAR is a temporary visitor; without your debate, FEAR is a resident in your life. Terminate your contract with FEAR with immediate effect. The cost of terminating the contract is still cheaper than the cost to your life on the expiration date of the contract. We should read the small print on the contract, not the large print. We already know the details of the large print; what we don't know is the details of the small print on the contract and that is common knowledge to FEAR. Looking back, if you have never really progressed as you think you should, it is because your FEAR is in control, and you have not detached yourself from the THEEF. There are a number of reasons why people struggle to detach themselves from the THEEF:

- You don't know how to detach yourself from FEAR. Detaching yourself from what you FEAR requires doing certain things, and you are not doing those things you need to do. People claim they want to detach themselves from the THEEF, yet they never really do the things they need to do to detach themselves. They remain hopeful that the FEAR will detach itself from them. Some intelligent people year after year remain in their comfort zone not because they choose to, but because of FEAR. Everybody has a choice to detach themselves from FEAR with the Protect or Reclaim strategy.
- You lack the courage, and you are unable to set achievable goals for yourself. Perhaps, you don't have the will or guts to do what it takes. You will have to action step one, two and three of your personal battle against FEAR.
- You are hoping the situation will take care of itself; you are awaiting a miracle.

You have a choice to take the fight to FEAR. Regardless of your reason, it is paramount to understand the following:

Whatever you fear most has no power – it is your fear that has the power.
Oprah Winfrey

University of Choice

The University of Choice in Choiceland is a university we truly never graduate from, as we make choices every day. We make our decisions and must be prepared to stand by them, and sometimes it is difficult to determine which decision is good or bad. On one hand, it appears the perfect decision, and on the other hand not so good. Some people refuse to visit Choiceland, as they do on a regular basis for minor decisions based on FEAR. Gradually, FEAR spreads within their bodies, and even minor decisions at Choiceland can't be taken. Whether you like it or not, you will make a choice between two alternatives – the issue here is the choice you make. To make a choice, you have to analyze the options on ground. Will it prove to be an effective choice for your desired result?

The decision, should it go wrong, could have serious implications. When you have a situation where you need to make a choice within four or five options available to you to aid your progress within a certain area of your life, you may choose not to select any of the five options available to you due to FEAR. You decide to remain stable, standstill. You believe you did not make a choice; hence, you are safe and not in danger of loss based on the gravity of the consequences associated with making the wrong decision. If you analyze the scenario properly, the reality here is that you made a choice in consultation with FEAR, a choice to fail to progress a certain area of your life. You cannot expect a result for an examination for which you did not take. You cannot expect progress in that particular area of your life, based on you not taking action. There is a result for every choice we make in life – failure is for inaction. To standstill is to personally request for the handcuffs of the hijacker of life.

If you want to be successful remain stable and watch the whole world pass you by. You will be successful in failure.

Chance of Choice

Life is not a game of chance; life is a game of choice. In life, we have the chances to make choices, any choice we want. We have a chance to either go to battle or not. We should be in control of any choice we make; however, from time to time we employ the services of FEAR to make a choice on our behalf, believing FEAR would make a better choice for us than we would make for ourselves. The THEEF has a conversation with us and not the other way round. The helping hand of FEAR is presented to you in the morning in the bathroom; hence, you have a shower with the THEEF, and the conversations of the day you make are made by FEAR, not you. We hand FEAR the authority to decide the strategy for our battles. This process becomes a habit, and the habit becomes an accepted process. We get a job, work a professional day, and accept our paycheck as compensation for our efforts week after week, month after month. We keep trading our time for a paycheck, accepting it as a chance, while in reality it is our choice.

At the University of Life, a degree in FEAR has been obtained; now the need to unlearn the FEAR has arisen, not by choice, but by necessity. If you take stock of what FEAR has cost you in the past and the bill it could present to you in the future, how to unlearn FEAR will be at the top of your 'To-do list.' When you have a degree in FEAR and you are faced with an opportunity, the first consultant you contact is FEAR, for his professional views on the opportunity. Hesitation and worrying present a picture to you, and you see that picture in your dreams. Your second voice keeps you in check with constant reminders of your negative conversation. FEAR gives you no options to work with; hence, a burning dread is established, and a burning desire is discarded in favor of the burning dread, limiting your chances of taking action.

We are all born to be successful. Failure is a personal choice.

Mathematics Calculations

A handsome man appears in the corridor of the mathematics of success, called *'Dream.'* His appearance can be deceptive. Dream is only rubbing shoulders with success, and it does not deliver the same fruits as success without action by its side. It is simply failure disguised as success. It is said that two heads are better than one – and in the case of burning desire and action, yes, but not as far as burning desire and FEAR are concerned. Do your calculations and check to see if they add up. Analyze the result of each one: Multiplication, Division, Subtraction and Addition. Analyzing the diagrams below, at least mathematics of success gives or attempts to give 'Dream' a chance. If anything, at least to appear in the picture, FEAR is not willing to give anybody a chance, not even an appearance in the picture in the mathematics of failure. You need to ask yourself, not the THEEF, "Do they add up?" The THEEF of life has done the calculations. *Have you done the calculations?* If you have not done the calculations, do them. At Chrysolyte School, in London, England, among other things, they teach basic Mathematics and English like every other school – however, they go a step further and say, *"Knowledge is light."*

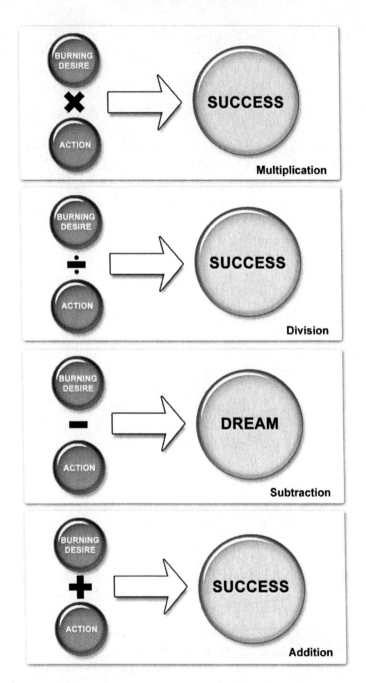

Mathematics of Success

Step 5: Analyze

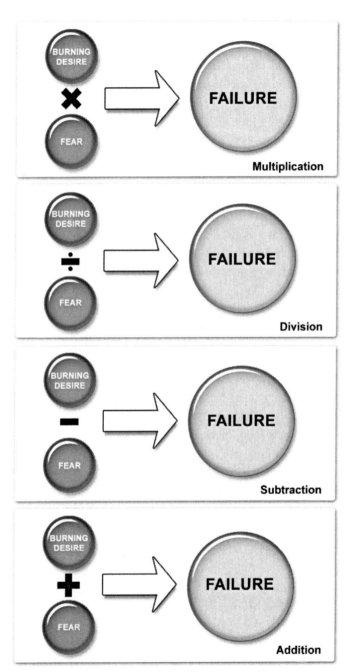

Mathematics of Failure

Many decades ago, with his knowledge, Thomas Alva Edison gave the world the light bulb. Indeed, knowledge is truly light; however, *if knowledge is light, FEAR is darkness, particularly in the twilight years of an individual.* There are only two rules for any individual to emerge victorious in any battle with the THEEF:

Rule 1 – Remember FEAR is darkness.
Rule 2 – Don't forget the first rule.

If Edison had forgotten Rule 1 somewhere along his journey of life in his desire to create the light bulb, the world may still be in darkness today. The THEEF is still doing its best to keep the world in darkness. Furthermore, knowledge of FEAR is light, and FEAR of knowledge is darkness. There can be no light without knowledge, and no darkness with light. **"Let there be light in your life."** FEAR is not bold enough to make that statement; hence, there can be no light in the life of a soldier in the Failure Armed Forces.

Analyze this and that

Dallas officer apologizes for 'poor judgment' toward dying woman's family during traffic stop
11:29 PM CDT on Friday, March 27, 2009
By STEVE THOMPSON and RICHARD ABSHIRE
The Dallas Morning News

His actions pilloried on national television and disowned by his commanders, Dallas police Officer Robert Powell came forward Friday afternoon to say he was sorry for detaining a family rushing to the hospital to visit a dying loved one.

Powell, 25, said he had tried to contact NFL player Ryan Moats and his family to apologize directly but so far had not reached them.

"I wish to publicly and sincerely apologize to the Moats family, my colleagues in the Dallas Police Department, and to all those who have been rightfully angered by my actions," he said in a written statement issued by his attorney.

The attorney, Bob Gorsky, works with the Dallas Police Association.

He said that despite news reports to the contrary, the officer is remorseful.

The day before, police commanders said Powell told them he saw nothing wrong with his behavior, even after reviewing video of the episode.

The video, recorded by his in-car camera, shows him berating Moats, threatening him with arrest and holding him for 13 minutes over a traffic violation while his mother-in-law died at Baylor Regional Medical Center at Plano.

In his apology, Powell said he regretted adding to the family's grief in an already difficult time.

"After stopping Mr. Moats' vehicle, I showed poor judgment and insensitivity to Mr. Moats and his family by my words and actions," the statement said.

Gorsky released little information about his client, saying only that he came to the department straight out of college in January 2006.

Powell, from the Amarillo area, was married not long ago and the couple has an infant, said an officer who knows him but declined to be identified.

"He's semi-quiet," the officer said. "He's not one you'd ever think would ever embarrass the department in any way. I've never heard him raise his voice."

Shortly after being hired, Powell was assigned to the city's north-central patrol station. During his short tenure, he has received some minor discipline, including a one-day suspension for violating sick-time policy.

"There is a complaint involving use of force, but his record's relatively clean," Police Chief David Kunkle said Thursday during an apologetic news conference. "That complaint was not sustained."

'Trying to do his job'

The chief called Powell's actions "inappropriate," "troublesome," "embarrassing" and "extraordinarily disappointing."

But one fellow officer spoke up for Powell on Friday.

"Right now he feels the world is against him," said Detective Ron Pinkston, secretary-treasurer of the Dallas Police Association. "He was trying to do his job out there."

Pinkston said that he sympathized with Powell and that it's been rough on the three-year officer, under the weight of nationwide derision.

He said that he isn't sure Powell should be disciplined and that he certainly shouldn't be fired. He stressed that Powell is still essentially a rookie.

"I think an older officer who'd been out there could de-escalate quicker than a younger officer," he said. "When any officer stops somebody on a traffic stop, there's a high level of anxiety for the unknown."

The situation Powell faced isn't something that figures into academy curriculum, said Lt. Vernon Hale, commander of the Dallas police academy.

"I don't think it's a situation that anybody's ever anticipated," he said, "or it wouldn't be national news."

Different officers will respond differently to the same situation, Hale said.

"You have a traffic stop, someone not stopping and people jumping out of the vehicle," the lieutenant said. "However, at some point, the light should come on is my thinking."

Outrage continues

The Moats family declined to speak about the episode Friday. But a man who witnessed it said he found Powell's apology suspect.

"An apology was very much needed after the fact, but the way he conducted himself, the way he enforced his side of the law, there wasn't no mistake about it," said Jason Brown, 23, who was at the hospital on the night of March 17 and can be seen in the video.

Others outraged by the incident continue to register their displeasure. A secretary at Dallas police headquarters said Friday that irate callers were still inundating the phone lines.

And even officials of a neighboring police department took steps to distance themselves from the incident.

"The Plano Police Department requests the media's assistance in clarifying the fact that this is a Dallas Police Department incident," said a news release. Plano police said e-mails and phone calls of complaints have rained on them from across the country.

The red light Moats ran is just inside the Dallas city limits and just down the street from the Plano hospital where Moats was pulled over.

"Thus, all comments regarding this incident should be directed to the Dallas Police Department," the news release pointed out.

Even others sharing Powell's name found themselves the unfortunate targets of ridicule.

"I am not the cop who pulled over Ryan Moats in Dallas ... so please stop sending me msgs about how much you hate me," said one Robert Powell on his Facebook page. "I'M NOT HIM!"
Staff writers Tanya Eiserer and Scott Goldstein contributed to this report.
REPRINTED WITH PERMISSION OF THE DALLAS MORNING NEWS.

We know the police face danger of the unknown while trying to keep the streets safe, but going by various accounts of the event and with all due respect, this kind of situation may not appear on the academy curriculum, but in the verification process, he gladly employed does and surely, common sense is applicable. The verification process employed by Officer Powell to issue the traffic violation ticket to Ryan Moats could have been employed to verify the information given to him by Ryan's wife, Ryan, the security guard and by the nurse (four individuals gave him information that could and should have been analyzed). Analyze this; furthermore, the location of filming, the hospital, indicates we may have an emergency on our hands, the assistance of the police should have helped to alleviate, rather than intensify the situation. How would Officer Powell had felt if the characters is this scene play were reversed at such an extremely difficult time for the family? Hispanic on Hispanic, white on white or black on black, his performance on the night, that particular night, cannot be justified. Yet, he had the audacity to nominate himself for Oscar as best actor few days later, claiming, *"he saw nothing wrong with his behavior even after reviewing the video of the episode."* It was stated in accounts of the event, "He pulled his gun." What if he shot and killed Ryan Moats, or a member of his family by mistake? Analyze that situation in your mind.

Last word:
Without proper analysis a desire without desire may appear as a burning desire in the portrait of life.

NINE

Step 6: Gradual

Gradually increase or decrease your action.

Increase, maintain current level or decrease your action, based on your analysis – I emphasize the latter part of that point again: 'Based on your analysis.' You could either increase your stake on action from small to medium, or medium to large. You can even decrease your action from large to medium, or medium to small based on analysis, because a decrease could be required for example on accounts of financial constraint or logistics of the operation. A decrease in action is acceptable, provided the decrease is not from small to zero.

Be not afraid of going slowly, be afraid only of standing still.
Chinese Proverb

There is no point in marching forward when the fire power of FEAR exceeds yours; you need to step back to regroup.

When it is going well, push it; when it is going bad, go home and sleep. You shouldn't limit what you can win, but limit what you can lose.
Rupert Murdoch

However, if extraordinary results are achieved to the point where an increase in the activity will not generate a significant difference to the current phenomenal results, current level should be maintained. Action in combat could be:

1. Gradual increase: Start slowly. For example, begin your workouts slowly, then gradually increase the intensity and

length of the workouts you do in the gym. This also helps to ease you into a routine, and prevents or reduces the chances of suffering injuries. Taking small actions is effectively training yourself to later take medium to large actions. As you gradually appreciate action, increase the level of action you take.

2. Gradual decrease: When the level of activities in your life becomes overwhelming, reduce them to acceptable levels. For example, if you have four or five activities on the go in your life, consider reducing those activities to the best two or three, depending on priority of the activities to you.
3. Maintain current level: Maintain the current level of activities. If exceptional results are delivered based on current level of your action, you don't have to increase or decrease your level of action.
4. Cost: Perhaps the cost of those activities are becoming too expensive for you to maintain; reduce them based on cost and benefit analysis. For example, if you are a member of an exclusive club with a high membership fee and you rarely go to the club – on a cost and benefits analysis, the membership fee could be used to increase action in a more productive activity or task.
5. Relaxation: If you feel you are not relaxed enough, increase your level of relaxation.
6. Simple conversation: If you suddenly find your voice by having a simple conversation with FEAR, then you don't need to keep wasting time by continuing the conversation. Instead spend that time establishing your burning desire.
7. Burning Desire: If your desire is not a burning desire, increase your conversation or interrogation. Interrogate yourself as well, to enable you to establish a burning desire.
8. Small action: You need to take action to appreciate action, and that appreciation begins with the introduction of small action into your life. Use your analysis to justify increase or decrease in action based on results. Analysis has to be conducted in all steps of our personal and public battles. At each stage, if more is required to acquire the required results, then the increase can

be justified, or if less is required then a decrease can be justified.
9. Standstill: Be sure you don't standstill by not taking any action, that you are on the move and you become a difficult target for FEAR. For example, a soldier in war standing still is an easy target to eliminate. If you standstill, you are requesting the service of inaction in your life – and inaction, as you know, keeps you in the Circle of FHIF.
10. Instant elimination: For those activities or tasks which are generating crippling losses, eliminate them instantly. For example, if you are running a small business that is running at a massive loss and the losses are crippling, the business should be eliminated immediately with a view to taking action elsewhere – particularly if the chances of a turnaround in fortunes is not visible.
11. **Take action to gradually increase, maintain current level or gradually decrease activities depending on your analysis.**

If belief is missing, confidence can't be on show, and when confidence is not on show, life is confined to doubts. Hence, action – small, medium or large – is slave to doubts. With the arrival of this penultimate step, invite medium or large action to your party; you can still keep the cost down within the 5 to 10 percent of your value by requesting medium or large action to bring their drinks and food to your party, depending on your current level of action. If you have been executing small actions, then ease into medium actions. If you don't believe in yourself, action can't believe in you. Gradually increase your action to the next level (medium or large, you don't have to buy the drinks anyway). From medium actions, large actions will begin to appear on your radar. It is said that a child cannot officially discard his certificate of minority without reaching the age of eighteen in life. Year in and year out, this journey constitutes practice and experience. If the small actions are phantom or crippled actions, they will be detrimental to the individual, with the same results as inaction. However, if the feedback indicates the actions are effective, the stage is set for medium or large actions. We can't, and should not, advance small actions going nowhere, to medium or large actions going nowhere. The beauty of action in some journeys is that the results from small actions can render the use of medium or large actions obsolete. By all means, reduce, maintain current level or increase your action based on your analysis.

Sniper

The target is evasive and on the run; the THEEF of life is constantly on the move, from individual to individual, house to house, city to city and country to country. Apply your sniper's drill, *'Acquisition and Elimination:'* locate and eliminate FEAR under adverse conditions. Your conversation also presents you with other sniper drills: *'Long range marksmanship'* or *'Precision shooting.'* The sniper chief assigns three snipers to eliminate the target. *"Snipers, does anyone have his target in range?"* asked the sniper chief. *"This is Sniper one, yes, I do"*. *"Sniper one, take the subject out! Do you copy?"* Sniper one does not respond. After a brief wait for a response, the sniper chief repeats, *"Sniper one, take the subject out! Do you copy?"* Sniper one eventually responds, *"Yes, sir, I copy."* After about three minutes, the sniper chief goes on air again, *"Sniper one, can we go home for dinner? It's been a long day?"* Sniper one replies, *"Get the table set, the turkey is cooked."* Instantly, there was a loud celebration in the command center. *"Well done, Sniper one; stand down, bring the cooked turkey home."* The sniper chief puts another call out, *"Snipers Two and Three, can you give a status update?"* *"This is Sniper Two, visibility is zero."* *"This is Sniper Three, turkey is not at home."* *"Sniper Two and Three stand down, return to the dinner table for briefing."*

  The Weather predictions for tomorrow are better but not fantastic, and after a long day, the turkey will probably be home tomorrow. If you have not had your sniper drills, you will lack the skills required *('Acquisition and Elimination,' 'Long range marksmanship' and 'Precision shooting')* to take the subject out.

Instead, you will be the turkey to be taken home for dinner – and furthermore, regardless of the weather conditions and/or if the turkey is home tomorrow, the subject will still be elusive for you to locate, let alone eliminate. The THEEF of life moves on from one battle to the other, and its win percentage exceeds its loss percentage. So as far as the THEEF is concerned, if he loses his battle with you, it is not a big deal, and if he wins, you are simply added to the list of existing failures. If the instance of FEAR in question can be eliminated, it should be eliminated. If it can't be eliminated due to weather conditions, efforts to that effect should be dismissed for now, until weather conditions improve.

Mail

Retorno para Remitente (Spanish that translates as 'Return to Sender'): Every now and then, you get a letter with the correct address but the wrong name. As the letter is addressed to you by address but not by name, the chances are you will mark the letter *'Return to Sender'* and mail it back to the sender. If you receive FEAR via the mail, don't open the letter. Simply mark it *'Return to Sender'* and drop it in the mailbox. You should be in the business of *'Return to Sender,'* not *'Receive from Sender,'* as long as FEAR is the sender. Those who have had a chat with the THEEF are already in the business of *'Return to Sender,'* and those who haven't, keep accumulating FEAR via their business of *'Receive from Sender.'* Return FEAR to FEAR; don't make things any more complicated than they are already. It is difficult enough trying to deal with FEAR addressed to you. *"When FEAR is actually addressed to you, address FEAR."* If the THEEF is bold enough to mail you a letter, you should be bold enough to mail it back. In the movie "Cool Runnings" (based on a true story of a Jamaica national bobsled team making their debut at the 1988 Winter Olympics held in Cagary, Alberta), FEAR was mailed to the rich Junior Bevil, who was on the team because of his father, and he kept on receiving his mail from FEAR. Suddenly, with the help of one of his team members, he returned the mail to the sender, and moved on with his life – and from that day on, his life was changed for the better. 'Return to Sender' can only be honored with a burning desire backed with action.

Responsibility

*You cannot escape the responsibility
of tomorrow by evading it today.*
Abraham Lincoln

You have responsibilities for your future and the future of your family, and the actions you take today will respond to the needs of tomorrow. If you let the THEEF make the decisions for you today, when the need of tomorrow arrives, FEAR will be nowhere to be found to make the decisions required for those needs. By the time the maturity dates of those needs arrive, FEAR has no reason to be around you.

At the end of the journey, your ally FEAR will desert you.

The needs of tomorrow are unavoidable; in fact, they already exist. They are only waiting for their maturity dates. When tomorrow comes, maturity dates starts arriving frequently. If you took the actions required for tomorrow's needs yesterday, *well done*. But if the THEEF defeated you in the battle yesterday, I can only pray that God gives you the strength to deal with those needs as and when they reach their maturity dates. The daylight bandit most definitely will not assist you. If you did not engage yourself in battles with FEAR, if you simply listened to your second voice, then you accepted the decision of FEAR without questioning or voicing your views. You have instructed the THEEF to hand failure to you. However, all is not lost. If you gradually start taking action today, the needs of tomorrow can be addressed tomorrow. We can't standstill; the needs of an individual don't standstill.

Keep moving. Keep putting one foot in front of the other. Inch by inch, you will get closer to success.
Ronnie Nijmeh

Pressure

The THEEF of life puts people under pressure. The pressure from the THEEF of life is constant pressure, but only those who can withstand the pressure of FEAR stand a chance in the ring. The pressure simply propels them into action; they rise above the occasion, and take control of the event in their stride.

Top athletes perform better under pressure, so put me under pressure.
Floyd Mayweather, Jr.

We are all top athletes – those who choose not to be top athletes will not perform under pressure from FEAR, but top athletes naturally perform under pressure because they understand the rules of the game: *'Beggars can never be bankrupt.'* FEAR does not discriminate between athletes; its job is to put pressure on any available athletes. We really do not have a say in the matter. FEAR will always put us under pressure. This is what a top athlete knows, prepares for and is trained to deal with at any point in time; hence, a top athlete invites FEAR's pressure to aid his performance within that square called the boxing ring.

Squares

"From where I am sitting, in the folders I gave you today on the second page (see content on second page in folders on next page), I can only see one square. How many squares can you see? I hope you can only see one square as well?" "Sim," said Thiago in Portuguese, which translated into English, is "Yes." Janet nodded.

The THEEF of LIFE

Square

Turn to the next page in your folder (content on next page in folders shown below).

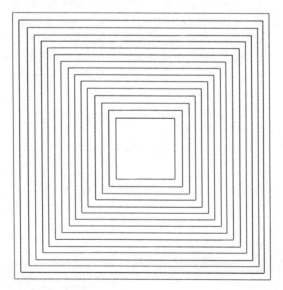

Many Squares

Step 6: Gradual

How many squares can you see now on page three in your individual folders? *"It appears I can see quite a number of squares,"* said Janet. Thiago looked at the squares for a moment and said, *"I can definitely see more than ten squares."* **Caveat!** *Do not look at the squares for too long, it has the potential of causing dizziness or inaction, due to the overwhelming opportunities available.*

If you have children, watch them in action. If you don't have children, watch your sister, brother, cousin or friend's children in action, or cast your mind back to your childhood days. Do you remember trying to wear your parents or older brother's pair of shoes, and walking around indoors without being afraid of falling down? A shoe that is twice or thrice your original size. Children generally perform this act naturally, dragging their feet rather than walking with the oversize shoes. Dragging your feet is not walking; under such circumstances, you can't walk without stress, particularly over a long period of time. Hence, when you occupy a square bigger than your square root or the size of your wallet, not impossible but most definitely stressful for a lot of people, you prepare yourself for enrollment in the Failure Armed Forces. Should the actual result differ greatly from the expected result for putting yourself in a square twice or thrice the size of your natural square, its based on your current standing in life.

The late detection of an issue in such a square could be catastrophic. When you buy a pizza, the pizza shop will give you the right-sized box for your pizza: small, medium or large. In certain cases, some individuals keep looking for an extra large box for a smaller-sized pizza.

From the back of the squares, you can only see one square. The reason why you can only see one square is because the only visible square to you is the biggest square among the squares; the size of the biggest square covers the smaller squares behind it from your current position. Try as much as you can, jump as high as you can, or bend down as low as you can to aid visibility, you will only see one square. Your personal battle with FEAR can either guide you to the front of the squares or keep you behind the squares, and the squares you see depends on your position, back or front of the squares. Standing on the wrong side, you will only see the one giant square. Relocate yourself to the front of the room from the back, and then look in the direction of your previous location in the room – the picture that will be in front of you begins to tell a different story in your mind, in terms of possibilities.

Suddenly, more squares become visible; you can see the smaller honey-coated squares, and so many squares you probably never believed existed because of your positioning at the back of the squares. One square that fits your individual budget and situation appears, and suddenly an action that seemed impossible becomes possible for any individual willing to act – although some still refuse to act, despite improved visibility. When you change position from back to front, the squares were not placed there when you moved. They have always been there; they just were not visible from your previous position. Many people stand behind the squares, depriving themselves of the view from the front and cannot see a way out or the FEAR exit signs. Actions that do not require maximum finance and effort to execute are not options. When you are faced with the biggest square, without any major financial aid or handout in sight, execution becomes impossible and a dream at best, which leads to failure.

Before you dismiss an action, review your options. The bandit flashes one option in your face: the option beyond your station in life, or one you will be afraid to execute if you manage to acquire the desire to consider the option. It is the option that ensures you walk with stress. Investigate your options; don't banish your options before an investigation of the options is available to you. Change your position to the position that enables you to see the smallest square and the biggest square – by seeing both squares, you not only get the opportunity to increase visibility, but you also get the opportunity to see various possibilities and executable honey-coated squares that have the potential to produce the same results as the possible results associated with the biggest square. If you find yourself in the biggest square and your analysis indicates a struggle ahead, decrease your action to operate in a smaller square. If you are comfortable in it, maintain current position, or if you are in a smaller square and it is way below your level and not giving you your desired result, gradually move to a bigger square, one after the other. You should not stay in the same sized square forever. It is important to take the small ones that are available, when a bigger one is out of reach.

There were companies in the same line of business established about the same time as the Tesco grocery stores in the United Kingdom (UK). They were established with a bigger capital injection compared to Tesco's capital injection. However, today, Tesco is growing bigger and stronger by the second, and those other companies don't even exist in memory, let alone in physical appearance in any town. The humble beginnings of Tesco, a British-based international grocery and general merchandising retail chain, began in 1919, when a gentleman named Jack Cohen made a profit of £1 ($2) on the first day from sales of £4 ($8), selling surplus groceries from a stall in the East End of London. Half a decade later, the brand Tesco arrived from the initials of Mr. T.E. Stockwell, and first two letters of the surname of Jack Cohen, the buyer who bought Stockwell's first shipment of tea. Jack Cohen opened the Tesco flagship store in Burnt Oak, North London. Tesco later became a private limited company, in 1932. Today, Tesco is the largest British retailer by both global sales and domestic market share, with profits also exceeding £2 billion ($4 billion) worldwide. It became the world's fourth largest retailer, and the second largest retailer in Europe, after overtaking Metro AG, the German retail giant. Tesco controls more than 30 percent of the grocery market in the UK. Perhaps, Tesco saw all the squares before inception.

By seeing the smallest and biggest squares, you see every other available size between the two squares. There is something for everybody. Even if you are in the small, medium, or large size, there is a square for you; shoe manufacturers make every style of their shoes in various sizes. Regardless of the size of the shoe, they provide a box big enough to house the pair of shoes. The price of the shoes may vary from designer to designer, but they are designed to be durable. In certain cases, the cheapest ones last longer than the expensive pair of shoes – so on account of durability, regardless of the square you fit into among all the squares you can see from between the smallest and the biggest squares, your square may not only last longer than the bigger squares, but may also produce bigger results as the years roll by. Just like good wine, it gets better with age. Jack Cohen must have stood in front of the squares rather than the back of the squares, and found the right size with a solid durability. If Jack Cohen had stood at the back of the squares, the only square he would have seen would have been the biggest square. He started with the square that was affordable to him at the time, a small stall in the East End of London, gradually increased to medium size and it has expanded into the huge square we now know as Tesco.

In any direction you look, there are still many squares before yours and after yours, available and affordable in your current position in life. You have to position yourself in front of the squares, not behind the squares. There is no point waiting to start until you can afford the biggest square; the longer you wait, the more expensive it becomes. While waiting, you could have commenced your battle in a square that fits your wallet, and who knows how many gradual increases you would have made within the waiting time. The FEAR is greater when you are behind the squares, compared to when you are in front of the squares. With a burning FEAR, you don't see the options; with a burning desire, the options will suddenly begin to appear on your radar. Your conversations with the Terminator of life will present you with affordable honey-coated actions, even if you cannot afford the expensive honey-coated actions. Position yourself to view, then view to establish your square.

Last word:
To live in peace in the future, we can increase or decrease our actions – but not by complete withdrawal of action.

PART FOUR
The Art of Battle
(Personal or Public)

Step 7: Practice

Practice, practice, practice and practice again.

How to Practice

The art of war is the practice of positioning, tactics and strategy. If you have executed the three steps of personal battle and those of public battle above, you have already declared your independence from inaction, because you would have executed action six times already. Regardless of increase or decrease in action-taking, practice must still be allocated its own time slot to reach mastery. Practice is a deterrent to re-occurrence of FEAR. The use of chopsticks to eat, to anybody who has not had regular practice, could be daunting. However, the arrival of constant practice delivers effective and efficient use of the chopsticks. For the voice of experience to be heard in your life, do the following:

1. Take Action.
2. Take Action.
3. Take Action.
4. *Take Action again.*

At the beginning of the journey of life, inexperience is acknowledged. Somewhere along the journey, experience declares its independence from inexperience, just as America declared its independence from Great Britain on July 4, 1776. With experience, comes the demand for the services of action. As action is the call for success, burning desires get the attention they require. One thing that is certain in life is that if a man intends to learn how to drive a car, he would have to physically get himself inside a car for driving lessons and to drive the car, preferably with a driving instructor, again and again, to master the act of driving before the learner sign (the L sign) can be removed from the car to indicate his arrival on the driving stage as a driver. By practicing, the FEAR of driving is accommodated, and the services of the driving instructor are eliminated. The same is required of a man to emerge from his battle with FEAR in general, to mount the podium of success in different areas of his life. This last step, *practice, practice, practice and practice again,* is the language of experience. For some, a little may be all that is required, and for others, constant practice may be required. It is said that *'practice makes perfect.'* Learn how to swim, and practice as much as you can, before declaring your independence from your swimming coach. When you have to practice, practice, practice and practice again, and are having conversations with the THEEF with a relaxed mind (which, in turn, enables you to have a burning desire to take small to medium effective action regularly), you become an expert in dealing with the THEEF. Hence, taking action becomes second nature, and the main recipe for protecting or reclaiming a life from FEAR. Having mastered putting a contingency plan in place, in addition to practicing taking action regularly, you provide a safe vicinity for dealing with FEAR and taking action. You grow stronger, feel safer and your defensive barriers against FEAR become stronger. Your FEAR gets arrested, your points, are well-received by the THEEF of life, and, as a result, action denies the THEEF an expression in different areas of your life. The handcuffs and ankle chains on your hands and legs are returned to the rightful owner, the THEEF, and your freedom opens the door of action for you. Your seat awaits you as you saddle the podium of success. Practice gives you the perfect experience, and as there is no substitute for experience, that experience becomes the best teacher. Action is the best teacher, trainer or coach any individual can ever employ. There is really no other way – with your teacher, trainer or coach in place, all you have to do is to do your homework for submission, do your work as directed by your trainer regularly or follow the guidance of your coach religiously. Practice, again and again, again and again – the more you practice, the more you gain from your experience, and the better you become. Nobody can practice for you or on your behalf.

Success awaits only those bold enough to declare their independence from the THEEF of life.

If it wasn't for practice, experience would not have been in a position to gain its independence from inexperience, in order to proclaim himself as authority on his subject. Inexperience already has a voice, a huge voice in every individual on earth – and, in most cases, inexperience is not willing to give experience a voice voluntarily. Your experience needs a voice. Grant your experience his wish, and that voice can only be provided by practice, practice, practice and practicing again. Independence comes at a price, and that price is experience. Pay inexperience what you owe him.

Analyze your results for trends, and use those trends in the results for future actions. The trends will give you indications of what is required to make your action more effective, if necessary. Complete the great escape before the great escape gets beyond you. The saddest description of a life begins with 'should' or 'could' have. Ensure your life description is not filled with "I was going to, but . . ." The 'but' makes the situation worse, because it is bad enough not taking action when you should have done so – to try to justify something unjustifiable with the 'but,' brings another dimension to the catastrophe at hand. However, regardless of where or when we decide to execute the Protect or Reclaim strategy, even though individuals will vary from other individuals, one thing is certain: you can't miss out on the Action step. You will have to take action to cross the bridge between failure and success. I wonder why action exists in all the steps in personal battle, public battle and the art of battle. Could it be that action is trying to have a voice in our lives, or is it that action is just the unavoidable recipe for success? The THEEF *will always mount a comeback* – a fact not open to a debate. *The daylight bandit knows no law and will try a comeback every now and then, here and there.* However, it is what each individual will do to overcome this monster that is open to a debate. To tame the THEEF of time and opportunities, you need to take action regularly. With your seven-step strategy in place and up and running, you are good to go. You will now be in control and know there is nothing to FEAR apart from real fear. Remember, "FEAR cannot be extinguished, but it can be distinguished." Distinguish your FEAR from real fear; with the exception of real fear, there is nothing to fear. Even FEAR can't really be extinguished; it always attempts a comeback here and there, and that is why it must be distinguished upon appearance. Your place among the elite awaits you. Go on, you have paid for your goods; take delivery of them. You truly deserve it. Today may not be the 4th of July, and it does not have to be, but it can be our personal independence day from the THEEF of life. We now have the missing part of the puzzle; **complete the puzzle, and let's go home!**

We had been there since 10 a.m., and it was now 6:45 p.m. We had talked about FEAR, PAST and the Protect or Reclaim strategy (Personal Battle, Public Battle and 'The Art of Battle'). In my opinion, that constituted a professional day; a day's work deserved a day's rest. We needed to relax our bodies and minds. Each of us had a father and a mother, husband or wife, sons and/ or daughters, brothers and/ or sisters, uncles and/ or aunts and friends waiting for us at different locations. So we decided to break, go home for dinner, and planned that we would meet again the next day.

Last word:
The Art of Battle, personal and public, is practice. Any role model will tell you there is no substitute for practice. Lector, take the subject out, and move on with your life.

ELEVEN

Role Models

What a lovely day – warm and bright. "Good morning, did both of you have a lovely evening and a good night's rest?" I asked Janet and Thiago. They both replied, "Yes, thank you. How was yours?" I said, "Very good, I enjoyed dinner with my family. I had a lovely journey this morning. The trains were not crowded and late. I was able to reflect on our conversations yesterday, and I must admit it has been a great weekend so far. If yesterday was anything to go by, I can't wait for our conversation today." Janet said, "I thoroughly enjoyed the discussion." Thiago said, "So did I – and I think a discussion on role models, warriors in the battles of life, would be a good topic to start our conversation and discussion today." Janet and I agreed.

A role model must have stood on the shoulders of many giants. Role models are great tools for the FEAR eradication treatment, and one may be all you need. Find yourself a role model – as soon as you find your role model, your FEAR eradication treatment is truly on the way. Your role model has been there, done it and received the certificate. They have had their conversations with the silent bandit, and the roles are now reversed. Instead of the THEEF of life searching for them, as he did in the past, they are now searching for him. Just as they previously averted the most ignored conversation, the THEEF of life is now on the back foot, avoiding them. Learn, watch and act like your role model. Seek clarification on gray areas. A role model can easily take you where you want to be. Finding a role model can only increase your chances of success. If you want to be successful, you associate with successful people, not failures. Follow people who have achieved success and accomplished what seemed impossible. Liaise with successful people. Read motivational books and biographies of those who have had to deal with obstacles in the past. Failure itself is success to a certain degree, and many who have accomplished great success today, failed at their first attempt in a task, project or business.

> *If you want to be successful, find someone who has achieved the results you want and copy what they do and you'll achieve the same results.*
> **Anthony Robbins**

Find a role model to mirror. If you want to become rich yourself, don't sit around waiting for a mentor to find you. He may not be looking for an apprentice, so you have to find your mentor. Find somebody who is already wealthy, and study him or her. Anybody can find a mentor. If you find a good mentor, his or her experience is invaluable. You can profit from his or her experience, even to a point where you can exceed his or her successes. Learn as much as you can from him or her – your mentor can be someone you admire, or in the same business or profession as you.

A relationship with a mentor is a two-way communication channel; you will need to be able to offer something in return for what your mentor gives you. Your mentor is not a mind-reader. Without asking the key questions to which you seek answers, your mentor may only give you the information he feels you require. You must be prepared to ask key questions and express your opinions. Your mentor can be somebody who has made an impression on you with his knowledge and perceptions. Such mentors can be found easily around you.

Khan

One of my mentors is Mohamed Khan. He is a great man who can carry a conversation on many other subjects. He was also my "Banking Law" lecturer at City Banking College years ago, and he always gave a brilliant lecture whenever he lectured. The first time I attended his lecture, I was so impressed that I never missed any of his lectures after that. His lectures were not only effective on the subject at hand, but they also prepared you to handle your conversation with the THEEF of life and respond by taking ACTION. The student pass rate based on his lectures was 99.9 percent. Mr. Khan turned 'F' students into 'A' students. I was so impressed that I attended extra lectures, even though it was not necessary. While lecturing, he always said to the students before and after asking a question:

Engage brain before lips.
Mohamed Khan

This is a quote I still find effective today in all aspects of my life. When you are asked a question that appears to be difficult to answer, your first thought is that you don't know the answer to this question. Almost instantly, you reply, *"I don't know the answer."* However, if you engage your brain before your lips, you will be amazed how wide your knowledge is, knowledge you never realized existed in your brain. Furthermore, if you know the answer and you engage your brain before your lips, you produce a much better answer. By thinking and having a conversation with the THEEF of life, the answer and the will to act appears. When you act, you act effortlessly and effectively.

Lectures from Daddy

One time I had dinner with my father, and as usual, the father and son training school was fully in progress. Most parents normally educate their children about life, and my family was no different. After a few words of wisdom, my father said to me, *"You are now an adult, and being an adult comes with adult responsibilities – not for yourself alone, but for your family as well. You have to comply with your responsibilities."* My father then asked me a question: *"Can you tell me two things that a man owns that can't be stolen from him?"* I engaged my brain before my lips, as Mr. Khan had always requested me to do. I thought about the question my father asked me, and knowing my father as well as I do, I knew I had to come up with a good answer to his question. If not, it was going to be a long night. I said, *"Daddy, a man's education cannot be stolen from him."* After a few minutes, my father said, *"Do you have any more to add to your answer?"* I engaged my brain before my lips again. After a while, I said**,** *"Sir, I can't think of any other one."* Just as I replied, his cell phone rang, and I got a break. He took his call, and I hoped the call would last for twenty minutes at least; however, the call was very brief, and it lasted for only four minutes. After the call, he said, "That was your brother; he will be joining us in an hour."

My father continued with our conversation: your car, watch, clothes, etc. can be stolen by thieves anywhere. Even in your house, burglars can break in and steal your goods, including your money (if you keep any at home, instead of keeping it with the money janitors in town), jewelry, passport, furniture, television, video, stereo etc. – all your goods could be gone when you get home, only to find out burglars have made themselves your guests while you were out. They can steal everything in your house, except your house itself.

My lesson on the value of a house to a man and his family had just began. For the next few hours, even after my brother joined us, our lesson on the value of a home as an asset continued. Even today, the message from that particular lesson is still at the top of my memory bank. The main message from the lesson that night from my father that I deposited in my memory, was that one of the most important responsibilities of a man to himself and his family is to provide shelter.

18 years for burglar who killed woman at her home
A BURGLAR who battered a mother-of-two to death in her home after being released on an electronic tag was jailed for a minimum of 18 years today.
Lloyd Edwards, 19, repeatedly punched Laila Rezk in the face and left her blood-soaked body in the living room of her house in Kingston Vale, where she was discovered by her two adult children. He stole £60[$120].
Edwards, from Roehampton, was jailed for life after being found guilty

of murder by a jury at Kingston crown court yesterday. He had admitted manslaughter.

It emerged afterwards that he had been released two months early from a young offender institution, where he was serving part of an 18-month detention and training order for previous offence, and fitted with an electronic tag.

After drinking all day on 29 November last year, he entered 53-year-old Mrs. Rezk's home as she prepared a family dinner and attacked her when she screamed. Her injuries suggested she had been punched a number of times and had her head smashed against a wall. She died in the hospital.

Evening Standard, Paul Cheston

Unfortunately, this burglar's action had a tragic ending for Laila Rezk, may her soul rest in perfect peace. He only stole $120. Is $120 worth a life? Your answer is as good as mine. If Mr. Edwards could have stolen Mrs. Rezk's house, her body would not have been found. Aside from being an item a burglar cannot steal, a house can also be a bank of evidence to aid prosecutors of burglars.

Many years ago, I had an opportunity to buy a house, but the THEEF of life and lack of guidance cost me 40 percent of the purchase price. The property was about to go on the market. A friend knew the owner of the property. He told me about it, and if I was interested, he could set up a meeting with the owner. FEAR took over. I hesitated for a while, thinking about what could go wrong and why the seller was selling the property. "Could there be a problem with the property?" I kept asking myself. By the time I made up my mind to buy the property, it was already on the market with a realtor, and an offer for the property had already been presented to the seller, 35 percent more than the asking price of the property. To secure the property, I had to offer 5 percent more than the offer from the existing potential buyer, which the seller had not accepted. Due to FEAR, I paid 40 percent more than the asking price for the property, that I could have secured before it got to the realtor at the seller's asking price.

However, all was not lost. Although I took late action, what I paid for the property then is not worth 5 percent of the value of the property today. The choice is yours. Whether you buy now or you buy later at a higher price, you will still have to buy. It is an essential commodity, not a luxury – and by the way, you don't want to get to the market when the current asking prices for properties are above your station in life.

That night my father had taught me about houses, he had another lesson for me as well. *"Stand by the window and throw out all the cash in your wallet or pocket."* I was very surprised, so I asked my father, *"Daddy, why do you want me to throw my money away?"* My father asked me, *"Are you still in your rented two-bedroom apartment?"* I replied, *"Yes, Daddy, but I am hoping to move soon."* My father replied, *"The reason I wanted you to throw your money away out the window is because that is exactly what you have been doing for the last five years, renting your two-bedroom apartment instead of buying."* After paying full membership subscription to a gym for one year, you can't request a refund from the gym at the end of the year on the grounds that you did not use the gym once during the year.

Stop investing your money in depreciating assets; invest in assets that will appreciate over time. Until you comprehend the significance of the arguments for buying a house as opposed to those of renting, you will keep investing in landlords via your monthly subscription fee called 'Rent.' Money thrown out via a window is not the same as money placed in a savings account.

Instantly, I knew the lesson for the day was now truly over from my greatest mentor. I knew in my mind the only reason why I was still renting the two-bedroom apartment for the last five years was due to the FEAR of owning a house. The need to extricate myself from the THEEF via personal and public battles became a reality. I was thinking about the lectures from Daddy today, on December 16, 2008, as the U.S Federal Reserve cut interest rates to a historic low, the lowest level in the history of modern monetary policy. The move was aimed at stimulating banks to lend money and reassuring financial markets. The U.S Federal Reserve is doing all it can possibly do to keep people in their homes, but rent subscription collectors continue to operate regardless of the economic climate. The U.S central bank lowered the target federal funds rate *(which is the rate at which banks lend to one another)* to a range of 0 percent to 0.25 percent. Traditionally, the federal fund rate has always had an effect on the rates consumers are charged for home mortgage loans and other types of credit.

Such monthly subscription fees have the habit, once you subscribe to renting, of introducing you to payment wedding vows with your landlord *"Till Death Do Us Part,"* – unless you cancel your monthly subscription fee to your landlord. It does not give you the option of living free before or after the end of your journey on the 9-to-5 treadmill, which is a gift amongst other gifts for buying your house. When you seek the opinion of FEAR on the subject, you are not encouraged to buy and vital information is also withheld. If you don't buy, you will rent till you die with or without a job, with the exception of inheritance or winning the lottery (section 8 should not even be dignified here because it cannot give you home-owner status). A subscription fee to landlords does not entertain discounts or free subscription for pensioner, let alone working adults. Subscription fees payable to landlords operate on a pay-as-you-go basis. You could be evicted within two months if you don't pay your monthly subscription fee to your landlord, regardless of your status in the society. Even if your monthly subscription is not in arrears, your landlord can still give you notice to vacate the property at any time. At least it is stated in the fine print of mortgage agreement that: *"If mortgage commitments are not honored, your house can be repossessed or foreclosed."* It is not stated anywhere on the lease agreement that rental subscription fees to landlords could be a lifetime monthly subscription fee. Regardless of the condition of the real estate market, at any point in time, shelter is still required. You cannot refuse to honor your monthly subscription to your landlord on the ground of recession, but your mortgage provider will be willing to grant you a few months to rectify your situation.

From a father and son perspective, growing up over the years, my father gave what he had to give to a son. Some men gave more to their children, some gave less. My father gave more than the basic requirement; he gave education, love, knowledge and friendship. I can remember vividly in my mind what he once said: "I can't give you what I don't have, but what I have is what I can and will give to you." I remember those words like they were uttered yesterday. Lector, the THEEF of life can't give you success because he does not have the code for success, but can give you failure because he has all the codes for failure – that is one thing FEAR has in abundance. You can only be inspired to inspire others with the inspiration you subscribe to in your debate with FEAR. Janet and Thiago agreed. Janet then said, "Oprah Winfrey and Chris Gardner are great role models."

Oprah

Trailblazing Rags-to-Riches Story

To one of America's most influential individuals from humble beginnings.

Oprah was born into poverty in Kosciusko, Mississippi in 1954 to a single mother. During her childhood she experienced hardship. It is said that she was sexually molested, repeatedly, by relatives and as a child, she experimented with drugs and sex.

At the age of fourteen, she became pregnant. Oprah gave birth to a baby boy, who later died. Oprah was inspired by her father to strive to achieve more in life. Oprah attended Tennessee State University where she received a BA in Speech and Performing Arts.

While she was still in high school, Oprah started working in radio, and at the age of 19, she began to narrate and coordinate local evening news with another broadcaster. Oprah became the first African American woman television news anchor to work at the WTVF-TV station in Nashville. She was later transferred to a daytime talk show on account of her excellent work. In Chicago, after putting her signature on a third-rated local talk show, the show moved to first place in rankings. Eventually, Oprah launched her own production company and the rest, as they say, is history. Through her publishing and media activities, Oprah has amassed a huge fortune. She continues to influence the lives of various people, particularly those in need.

"The Oprah Winfrey Show," produced by her production company, became, in history, the highest ranked talk show program and the most successful.

"The Oprah Winfrey Show" is broadcast to well over 99 countries in the world. Oprah is also the Founder of the successful "O, the Oprah Magazine", and the influential "Oprah's Book Club." She is an actress, producer and generous philanthropist. Many awards have been won by Oprah and her companies. Her show received three Daytime Emmy Awards.

I knew there was a way out. I knew there was another kind of life because I had read about it. I knew there were other places, and there was another way of being.

Oprah Winfrey

Gardner

"I am a stock broker." This answer propelled a man from nowhere to somewhere, bottom to top and homeless to home owner. He asked a question, and he got an answer. That was the answer and its effect on the life of a man, who, while negotiating steep mountains on his way to the top, took ownership of a bathroom at a train station as his residence with his son. Lector, 'Down and Out,' yes, but the opportunities to turn it 'Up and In' exist. A number of people haven't had life as rough as Chris Gardner had his life. His stepfather ensured his mother's life, and his life was a nightmare. His mother, Bettye Jean, was imprisoned after her husband informed the authorities she was working while collecting welfare – as result, Chris and his sister had to go into foster care. His father was nowhere to be called upon to honor his duties. Chris Gardner joined the navy, and later became a medical supplies salesman. In the "The Pursuit of Happyness" (the title of the book by Chris Gardner), or pursuit of necessity, as it unfortunately is, it is clear that many have been brainwashed by FEAR to believe that the quest is impossible. Chris asked a man he saw driving a Ferrari what he did for a living, and then determined to obtain the same career. In pursuit of necessity, Chris Gardner prepared himself for the licensing exam and passed. He worked for long hours after landing a job in San Francisco, at Bear Sterns.

> *I made up my mind as a young kid that when I had children they were going to know who their father is and that he isn't going anywhere*
> **Chris Gardner**

As a soldier with a wooden sword instead of an iron sword, his position with his wife became untenable, and she left him. But with regards to his father not fulfilling his duties as a father, and his own wooden sword at the time in question, he made sure his position with his son was not going to be untenable; hence, he fought to keep his son because he knew, *"The cavalry ain't coming."* His mother had told him they weren't coming.

The battle on this subject is yours, not your dad's. Chris Gardner is not from a rich home and he is not the son of a stockbroker.

Mr. Gardner made the grade on Wall Street, and without his father or access to his knowledge about life. A man with no home, low income and a son to feed, he took the game of life to another level, and gradually, the situation for him and his son got better. He later established Gardner Rich & Co, a brokerage company with $10,000 from his home, executing debt, equity and derivative products transactions. Son of a prisoner, mother on welfare, a homeless man, from a broken home, where most would have given up the fight before it actually started – Chris Gardner saw the beginning, and how the fight progressed toward his life. He did not embark on any area of the drug industry as many do, as a way out of poverty within a short space of time. He took the battle to anyone and anywhere, particularly FEAR, and was courageous enough to stand in his way rather than step aside. Chris is an example of what an individual can achieve without a father's support, but with a burning desire and action. There is somebody out there who is successful and can tell you what he does – ask, and apply it to your life. Thiago and I could relate to what Janet said about Oprah and Chris. "Speaking of role models," said Thiago, "Richard Branson, Hakeem Olajuwon, Helen Small (The Octogenarian), and Abraham Lincoln would all fall into that bracket for various reasons."

Sir Branson

Richard Branson

In 1999 he was knighted by the Queen for "services to entrepreneurship" and became Sir Richard Branson. Loughborough University in England gave Richard Branson the honorary degree of Doctor of Technology in 1993, but his ongoing business journey began at Stowe School.

Branson attended Stowe School until the age of fifteen after leaving Bishopsgate School (formerly known as Scaitcliffe School) at the age of thirteen. Richard Branson was captain of the school's cricket and football teams. Branson was not a good student because he has dyslexia; however, by the age of fifteen he had established two businesses – one for Christmas trees, and one for raising budgerigars. Both ventures failed.

Branson moved, after quitting school, to London at the young age of sixteen. While in London he embarked on another business venture (a magazine for students), but this time he was successful with the business. In his penultimate year as a minor, Richard Branson launched the "Student Valley Centre," his very first charity. He embarked on his next project which was to start a record business after buying dozens of "cut-out" records from across the English Channel, via a record discounter. He sold the records to retails shops in London from the boot of car. Through mail order, trading as "Virgin," he continued the sales of cut-outs, and at a cheaper price compared to most of the High street stores. It was no surprise to many, when Branson opened a record shop on Oxford Street. Soon after, together with Nik Powell, the Virgin Records record label was born. He bought his country estate from the money made from his record store.

In 1984 Virgin Atlantic Airways was launched, and a few years later Virgin Mobiles was set in motion. In the year 2000, in Australia, then came Virgin Blue. Branson kept on expanding his business empire, and in 1997, he went into the railway business with Virgin train, previously known as Intercity West Coast of British Rail. Branson also made a bid to oversee the Lottery but failed.

34

Hakeem 'The Dream' Olajuwon

Hakeem Olajuwon is a Nigerian-born basketball legend. He established himself by performing as one of the best players in the history of the NBA.

"They taught us to be honest, work hard, respect our elders, believe in ourselves," the NBA legend said of his parents.

Hakeem obtained the values that enabled him to be successful from his father and mother, cement business owners in Lagos, Nigeria.

The basketball journey began when Muslim Teachers College, the high school Hakeem attended in Lagos, was entered in the basketball tournament for a sport festival in Sokoto, in the northern part of Nigeria. However, Hakeem was not on the basketball team, but a member of the handball team. The coach granted Olajuwon permission to play basketball for his team, and a basketball legend was found. The University of Houston became his next port of call two years later.

Olajuwon began his sport career as a handball player and soccer goalkeeper, which gave him the agility and footwork he needed on the basketball court. He established himself in the team at Houston as a dominating player. At Houston, Olajuwon played for three seasons, and had his part in getting the team to the Final Four every year.

Olajuwon was selected by Houston ahead of Michael Jordan, and he was deemed by most in the sport as the right No.1 selection, after the Portland Trail Blazers lost a coin flip to the Houston Rockets in the NBA Draft for first pick. Ralph Sampson of University of Virginia was picked by Houston, the year before Olajuwon, after winning the coin flip against the Indiana Pacers. The two of them became known as the "Twin Towers" – Sampson is 7'4" and Olajuwon is 7'0".

His moves on the basketball court took him to another level within the game, and his style became known as the "Dream Shake." Olajuwon mesmerized both fellow players and fans with his moves. Houston defeated the Orlando Magic and San Antonio Spurs, each of which had an excellent center in their teams, both were bewildered by his moves. Shaquille O'Neal said: "He's got about five moves, then four countermoves – that gives him 20 moves." A view shared by David Robinson of the San Antonio Spurs, he seemed puzzled when he said, in a magazine story: "Solve Hakeem? You don't solve Hakeem."

When Olajuwon retired, after an 18-year career, he was the all-time leader of the Houston Rockets in steals, rebounds, points and blocked shots. Olajuwon's place in the game as a legend was cemented with the Rockets' back-to-back NBA titles. Houston City retired Hakeem's jersey No. 34 in 2002, in recognition of his impact in Houston city.

Hakeem "The Dream" Olajuwon is considered one of the best centers to have played in the National Basketball Association (NBA). While most of his teammates and rivals got involved with the sport in grade school, Olajuwon did not play the game until his senior year in high school. He played the game without FEAR and with strong belief and confidence.

> *My background playing soccer gave me a natural advantage over many of the American-born players.*
> **Hakeem Olajuwon**

Rich, but humble and respectful, Hakeem is truly living the dream. Which position would you like to play on the basketball court – point guard, shooting guard, small forward, power forward or center? Whatever position you choose to play, make sure you have your own 'Dream Shake.' A slam-dunk ("jam," "stuff," "flush," "cram" or "throw down") in your life. In an article in the *New York Times*, "A Slam-Dunk in Houston Real Estate," by Kate Murphy, Hakeem said that though he had not ruled out investing in other cities, his focus remained on Houston: *"It's where I have the home court advantage."* While making sure you keep an eye on the THEEF of life, find your own home court advantage. Success is not confined to a particular environment.

87-year-old has big plans after graduation

08:25 PM CST on Wednesday, December 5, 2007

"Relief!" she cheered last week as she left a classroom at the University of Texas at Dallas. She had just taken her very last final exam.

She may be 87, but Helen grinned like a kid after that final. "Exhilaration – that's what I'm feeling," she said.

All that remains now is the cap-and-gown finale on Saturday. Helen will receive her Bachelor of Arts degree in psychology – and the distinction of being UTD's oldest graduate ever.

For Helen, Saturday marks the finish line of a journey that began in a freshman registration line way back in 1938. That was at the University of Akron, and it proved to be an important moment.

"Standing in that registration line, I met a fellow," she said. "And that's who I married."

Helen managed to finish only a year of college before life got in the way. First there was marriage to that handsome fellow in line, Al Small. Then there were three sons and a war and all the other little things that can sidetrack an education. ...

But Helen never gave up on her plan to finish college one day. "It was just something I had to accomplish for myself," she said.

It wasn't for lack of other accomplishments. As Helen says, "It has been a wonderful life."

Al took a job here in 1954. "Once we got to Dallas, we never wanted to leave," she said.

Soon they began a homebuilding business, Al Small Custom Homes. And working together as full partners, they built it into an enduring, successful enterprise.

Along the way, Helen not only kept alive her own ambition for an education but also instilled it in her sons. Two became physicians, and one is a dentist. Her nine grandchildren and their spouses all have college degrees, too.

"I had to get a degree in self-defense!" she joked. ... But now, at long last, her goal has been met. ...

"Don't stop. Keep forging ahead." That's the advice she would offer to everyone. "I think that's the secret," she said. "Don't let yourself stop. Keep going."

In fact, now she's mulling a master's degree. And why not? She could have it done by 90.
REPRINTED WITH PERMISSION OF THE DALLAS MORNING NEWS.

***Dallas Morning News*, Steve Blow**
sblow@dallasnews.com

Helen's burning desire kept alive her own ambition for education. She never gave up on her plan – it may have taken her more than five decades to execute the plan, but that in its own right is an achievement. Many people make plans and never get to execute them in their lifetime. FEAR did not stand a chance with this octogenarian even with the various obstacles (difficulties of life) placed in front of her.

Some people may never achieve academic qualification for one reason or the other, but in general, if you want academic credentials, there is a degree in any individual's name in any university of his or her choice awaiting his or her collection. If you want it, it is yours – your Protect or Reclaim strategy against your FEAR of education, or obstacle in your way, will guide you to it. Until you confront FEAR, the degree simply awaits collection. Collection of this award can be daunting, but it need not be if you have the burning desire like Helen to reach out and take one more step to reach it.

Lincoln

This was a man who was no stranger to poverty; he was born into it. Every time he fell down, he got back up. Abraham Lincoln once said after he lost a US senate election:

> *The path was worn and slippery. My foot slipped from under me, knocking the other out of the way, but I recovered and said to myself, "it's a slip and not a fall."*

If you want to know why you should not give up under any

adverse condition in your life, particularly, those instigated by FEAR, study the life of one of the greatest presidents of the United States – Abraham Lincoln. Abraham Lincoln knew the unyielding power that resides in knowledge, so he made extraordinary efforts to attain knowledge while working on a farm. Along the journey of his life, he failed in business, twice. Lincoln ran for state legislature twice and failed both times, Congress three times and was only successful once, the US Senate twice – and again he failed to make the grade on both occasions. He was unsuccessful running for speaker of the state legislature, and at his party's national convention, he tried to be nominated as Vice President, but again he was unsuccessful. He became bankrupt and had a nervous breakdown at some point in his life. Lincoln's mother died in his tenth year and his sweetheart also died before they could be married. He received his party's nomination for president and in 1860, he won the presidential election to the become the 16th president of the United State of America. Abraham Lincoln's persistence is one of the greatest and highest levels of determination; FEAR presented him with a million reasons to give up and accept failure, but he kept on knocking on the door until the American people allowed him into the White House.

> *The sense of obligation to continue is present in all of us. A duty to strive is the duty of us all. I felt a call to that duty.*
> **Abraham Lincoln**

Lector, feel your call to that duty.

Recession

Getting ready for recession is like getting ready for a snowstorm; predictions may indicate a minor snowstorm, but in reality, it may be heavier than predicted. Just as an individual cannot do a lot about a snowstorm, neither can he do much about a recession. All we can do is to make sure we have the essentials in place, to give us a chance to deal with such weather and hope the fat lady is not going to sing. When the economy recedes, a period of an economic contraction, economic recession is a fact of life. Within the current climate in the global village, newspapers carry headlines relating to unemployment, failing businesses, the birth of low consumer confidence, home repossession and falling stocks and shares. Typical newspaper headlines include:

Global recession fears hit markets
London METRO
CITI GRIEF
CITY A.M.
Troubled Citigroup to cut 53,000 jobs
London METRO
AVIS cuts 300 jobs after a drop in demand and rising costs take toll
CITY A.M.
Japan joins the Eurozone in recession
CITY A.M.
SALES DIVE 14PC AT JOHN LEWIS AS XMAS FEARS MOUNT
The Daily Telegraph
Close to 3m unemployed' by 2010
BBC
Lehman Brother bank collapses
Newsbeat
Repossessions set to increase in coming months
Financial Times

Within the gloom and doom of economic recession, there are a number of things that can be done to improve our chances of survival. I have no doubts whatsoever, if the opinion of any veteran of previous recessions was obtained on how to survive an economic recession, his list would be similar to the following:

1. **Work** in a critical sector; regardless of the economic recession, jobs in the critical sector are never the first to go.

VIBRANT JOBS WITHIN THE CURRENT JOB MARKET
Despite the gloom and doom within the global village, as some industries keep downsizing others are growing. And in certain cases even offering sign on bonus to prospective employees.

Police Officers—Law enforcement, essential voice in any city. Jobs in this vicinity are the last to be downsized even when finances are tight. While seasoned officers in big cities can earn as much as $91,000, rookies in small cities can earn $27,000.

Registered Nurses—RNs could earn $41,000 to $90,000. In certain cases signing bonuses from hospitals could be as high as $12,000 amid national shortage.

Internal Auditors—To safeguard against fraud and in order to ensure that government economic stimulus funds are not misappropriated. Auditors can expect $52,000 to $120,000 from financial institutions.

Speech Therapists—Earnings could range between $44,000 to $76,000 as most schools attempt to comply with federal disability laws, in addition the increasing number of trauma sufferers and the aging population are also on the rise.

Search-engine experts—Companies want to have prominent view on search engines like Google etc. They are hiring search-engine gurus to get the job done effectively with earnings as high as $40,000 to $60,000 on offer per annum.

2. **Terminate** memberships in clubs you can do without when cash is tight, like gym memberships and magazine subscriptions, especially those magazines you don't really need. If you have other membership cards you hardly use, i.e., used once in ten weeks, get rid of them.

3. **When shopping**, particular grocery shopping, buy only things you need and not things you don't need that would most probably end up in the bin as trash when it reaches its expiration date. Buy more of items you use regularly if they are on sale. Plan your journey, – do not make a number of trips to the grocery store during the week when you can do it in one trip.

4. **Create** an extra source of income: sell unwanted items you have in your garage. Develop or increase your skills. Be creative; find other business you can do that would not affect your

normal nine-to-five treadmill duties. There are quite a number of online businesses out there that require only a basic website and e-mail address. Two or three different ways to generate income is a step in the right direction to deal with the recession.

5. **Find** the most cost-effective medical insurance. During such an economic climate, companies offer various deals or packages for medical insurance at cheaper rates.
6. **Make** a mortgage overpayment for two to three months in advance towards the biggest expense within your monthly bills. Considering the importance of having a roof over your head, to be ahead on your mortgage commitment puts you a step ahead of yourself. At the very least, you have two or three months should things not go as planned, to put things right in any climate.
7. **Use** utilities effectively. You don't have to use your dryer regularly, particularly when the weather is warm. Use a bathtub dryer rack. Don't turn on the lights in your bedroom when you will be in your living room. Don't leave your water running, when it is not in use if you pay water bills.
8. **Cut** down on eating out. If you eat out regularly, in comparison to the cost of home cooking, the different in price is huge, particularly within the current economic recession.
9. **Avoid** credit and store cards. Avoid taking on more debt during recession, credit and store cards in particular, except if you have no options. Get rid of high-interest credit cards as soon as you can. Fifteen percent interest is not healthy.
10. **Identify** the positives and take action. There can be no room to house the THEEF to enable him to take over your mind to identify the positives for you.

When a recession arrives north of your location, if you are doing things pointing to the north, begin to do other things pointing to the south where a recession may be expected, but has not arrived. The south may prove to be recession-proof; they may be servicing commodities that are doing well. It is an unpleasant fact in a recession, that many will not do well, but a few will emerge as recession-proof winners. You need to position yourself as such a winner. Unfortunately, the THEEF can never aid your positioning in a recession-proof area. Establish the modalities. Among the list above, the last one is the most important because it is all in the mind, as you will discover in the next chapter in the sections *'Law of Reciprocity* and *'Failures Attract Failures.'* The THEEF is not aware of a recession, let alone a depression. As a matter of fact, production increases for the THEEF during a recession or depression. "Yeah, recession is never easy – but talent can be useful in any economic climate," said Janet and continued.

Talent

You are talented. Have you found your talent? Just because you have not found your talent yet, it is not an indication that you do not have it in you. You just have to keep searching. If you give up searching for results, results will give up searching for you. If you think you don't have any talent, it does not mean you are not capable; it simply means you are a general in the Failure Armed Forces. Reluctance, delay and terror are all agents of the THEEF. They encourage you to focus on the difficult things and discourage you from researching the easy things you can do. In Oprah's case, she had no claim to success; if anything, she had more reasons to be a failure than anybody, judging by her background. In the case of Richard Branson, you wonder how he put together his brilliant business plan (after quitting school), let alone became successful. It is not the responsibility of FEAR to free the masses from their current predicament; it is the responsibility of each member of the public to have their Protect or Reclaim strategy in place for battle with the THEEF to alleviate them from their current predicament.

*If you put your vision in the wrong
hands, your vision will be wrong.*

Indeed, if you have a talent to succeed in a particular vocation and hand the THEEF permission to access the talent, you will not be successful with that talent. The icons are aware of this via effective conversations with FEAR; hence, they refuse any attempts to put their hands in handcuffs by the THEEF, and instead they hand action permission to access their talent. With your dialogue with the THEEF of life, you can change your strategy. If you give action permission to access your talent, i.e. in any sport, you stand a better chance of achieving your dream. *'Hakeem the Dream'* did not know he would be that successful playing basketball, a sport he never really played as child – but by initiating a Protect or Reclaim strategy in the battle against the THEEF, he handed permission to access his talent to action, not the THEEF of life. The vision was put in the right hands to establish the Art of Battle.

If certain people belong somewhere and others elsewhere, then a CEO who joined his company as a baggage handler belongs in the baggage boardroom section of the company, not in the executive boardroom of the company, where we found him. Perhaps, he should be CEO of the baggage department rather than CEO of the company. If Abraham Lincoln had kept faith in the THEEF of life, he would have kept on working in the farm, instead of conducting his duties in the White House as president for and on behalf of the American people. If Abraham Lincoln had accepted one of the reasons presented to him by FEAR, the United States of America would have been deprived of the services of one of its greatest presidents in its history. *The notion that he or she belongs at the bottom or top, here or there, should be dismissed – anybody can become anything.* **NOBODY BELONGS HERE OR THERE – ANYBODY BELONGS ANYWHERE.**

The man who created what we know as Goldmans Sachs was a poor, uneducated member of a despised minority.
**The Uses of Adversity, The New Yorker,
Malcolm Gladwell**

Those who had their dialogue with the THEEF of life should be acknowledged and respected for their achievements. They should be the pillars of our inspiration to greater heights in all areas of our lives. Somebody or something inspired them; so be inspired by them. They are expecting you to join them, not worship them. You are you; more importantly, your ability is unlimited. The choice at this stage is yours. At the changeover stage, the choice will not be available to you, and it will be too late to make a choice. Friendship with time does not include giving back lost time on the basis of that friendship.

Obama

PRESIDENT BARACK OBAMA

Barack H. Obama is the 44th President of the United States. His story is the American story — values from the heartland, a middle-class upbringing in a strong family, hard work and education as the means of getting ahead, and the conviction that a life so blessed should be lived in service to others.

With a father from Kenya and a mother from Kansas, President Obama was born in Hawaii on August 4, 1961. He was raised with help from his grandfather, who served in Patton's army, and his grandmother, who worked her way up from the secretarial pool to middle management at a bank.

After working his way through college with the help of scholarships and student loans, President Obama moved to Chicago, where he worked with a group of churches to help rebuild communities devastated by the closure of local steel plants.

He went on to attend law school, where he became the first African-American president of the Harvard Law Review. Upon graduation, he returned to Chicago to help lead a voter registration drive, teach constitutional law at the University of Chicago and remain active in his community.

President Obama's years of public service are based around his unwavering belief in the ability to unite people around a politics of purpose. In the Illinois State Senate, he passed the first major ethics reform in 25 years, cut taxes for working families, and expanded health care for children and their parents. As a United States Senator, he reached across the aisle to pass ground-breaking lobbying reform, lock up the world's most dangerous weapons and bring transparency to government by putting federal spending online.

He was elected the 44th President of the United States on November 4, 2008, and sworn in on January 20, 2009. He and his wife, Michelle, are the proud parents of two daughters, Malia, 10, and Sasha, 7.
http://www.whitehouse.gov/administration/president_obama/

If any individual, while refusing to hold a conversation or discussion with the THEEF, wonders if a dream can be realized, still questions the power of conversation, or thinks his or her case will be an exception as far as the FEAR is concerned, think long and hard, and THINK TWICE! At a rally in Grant Park in Chicago, Illinois, Barack Obama gave a speech after winning the presidential election on November 4, 2008. The speech delivered a message to the THEEF of life, its agents and worshipers on our behalf in a nutshell.

> Hello, Chicago.
> If there is anyone out there who still doubts that America is a place where all things are possible, who still wonders if the dream of our founders is alive in our time, who still questions the power of our democracy, tonight is your answer.
> **Excerpt from Transcript of his victory speech**
> **President-elect Barrack Obama**

"…Tonight is your answer," not only in America but also anywhere in the world. Wherever in the world a language exists, all things are possible, and a conversation can be held. When his journey to the White House began two years ago, I did not know Barack Obama, let alone know he would be competing for the Democratic Party presidential candidate election. Well, I know now, not only the measure of the man – but also the awesome power in holding your conversation with the THEEF. After all, the THEEF of life is only a common THEEF, and homage is paid to him only by failures. You are not a FAILURE! A THEEF of time is a THEEF and does not deserve to exist within your life. He may be awesome in his vicinity, but not in yours. There are only two of two, who as speakers or keynote speakers can move the majority of the inhabitants of the global village into taking action. The great movers of the human mind, the greatest world speakers, are President Barack Obama and FEAR. Their records speak volumes; grown men are moved to tears and the voluntary donation of human life to failure, respectively. Perhaps Germany should be charged for insider dealings – before Obama was elected as president of the United States of America, he went to Germany, and they came out in thousands to hear him speak. *"Did Germany get inside information on the elections?"* No, they had good knowledge, were aware of what stood before them in Berlin and knew, around the global village, walls were tumbling. Permit me to borrow Obama's words from his speech in Berlin.

> *When you, the German people, tore down that wall – a wall that divided East and West; freedom and tyranny; fear and hope – walls came tumbling down around the world.*

Have a dialogue with the THEEF, and find the objective, voluntary creation of burning desire for action to protect or reclaim your life. FEAR is a pandemic disease. Most other diseases are epidemic; you only need to research the figures to nod in approval. When the majority blinks, the show is over and the deal is done. They (role models, icons or legends) all have real fear like every other human being, but they do not fear the THEEF, and when they blink, the show has only just begun, and the deal is not done.

Speed Bike

Life is a ten-speed bike. Most of us have gears we never use.
Charles Schulz

Air hostess lands plane after pilot 'goes mad'

A flight attendant helped land a jet carrying 146 passengers after the co-pilot had an apparent mental breakdown over the Atlantic Ocean, investigators revealed today.

The co-pilot was yelling for God as he was restrained, according to one passenger.

The UK-bound Air Canada plane made an emergency landing at Shannon Airport, in Ireland.

The air hostess came forward saying she had a commercial pilot's license and took over the co-pilot's seat, after a request from the captain to find any trained pilots amongst the passengers.

When the jet landed, the sick co-pilot was removed and admitted to an acute psychiatric unit.

The captain and air hostess were praised for their 'professionalism' by the Irish Air Accident Investigation Unit.

The cabin attendant has a ten-speed bike; she uses gear one as a cabin attendant, and she knows she has gear two (a commercial pilot's license) which she hardly calls into action at her disposal. That leaves her with eight gears that never get a look in. If individuals know they have ten-speed bikes, a few will attempt to use more gears – some will use gear one and two as they normally do to maintain their daily life routine, and the majority will not even ride the bike at all under any circumstances. The THEEF of life intends to keep us on gear one, hence, welcomes and appreciates the gears we do not use. Surely, they must be useful, if not, the THEEF would not appreciate them. FEAR will dampen your appetite for using the gears you have and never use. Anyone who can use all the gears of their ten-speed bike will succeed.

President Obama, Oprah, Bill Gates, Chris Gardner, Sir Branson and Abraham Lincoln could have been failures. We all have a ten-speed bike, but we rarely utilize all ten gears on our bikes. The only difference between us is the results that each of us get from the use of our basic gears (one, two and three). The basic gears give the role models excellent results and they throw the use of other gears into a safety deposit box, and hence, the use of more gears is available but optional. Most of us don't even use all our basic gears. Successful people know when and how to use their basic gears to devastating effects. For example, President Obama uses his first gear as a politician and his second gear as an author. If you don't know what time it is, you may be doing the right thing at the wrong time or the wrong thing at the right time – either way the destination is failure. Find out what time it is, so you can do the right thing at the right time. The role models know this and that is what they do; therefore, their basic gears give them better results.

I cannot see the Obama School of presidents, orators or authors, which would not be short of takers and would command a high tuition fee at the very least. I cannot find the Obama stepping school based on his Inauguration party dance steps. I cannot find the Oprah Makeup range or women's shoes (by the way, I may be tempted to get a pair for the steppers course at the Obama stepping school for the steppers of the future). I cannot find CEO training school for future CEOs (for movers from the baggage room to boardroom). I appreciate the fact that there are many excellent business schools, but it is an avenue open to successful CEOs, and will not be short of students. The point here is despite the huge success of these role models, they have something else in common; they all have a ten-speed bike. They are not using all their gears. Most are still using gears 1, 2 and/or 3; yet they are in excellent shape. They still have, at the very least, seven gears at their disposal. Given their status in life as icons, the use of any more gears is a done deal, a certainty guaranteed over uncertainty. An average human being, in most cases, uses only one gear and, occasionally, introduces a crippled attempt to use another gear, which in reality is an uncertainty guaranteed over certainty.

The most interesting thing about all the role models in this book and you, the reader, is not only are you and each one of them human, but also not one of them has two pairs of hands and/or legs. They don't have two pairs of ten-speed bikes, yet, based on their achievements, you are led to believe some of them were actually blessed with two pairs of hands to do things quicker with their hands and two pairs of legs to run twice as fast as a normal human being would. The world's undisputed king of destruction of human life's place in history and beyond is not in question; however, contrary to general belief, there is a bone to pick. The bone to pick is with the THEEF, not action.

Pick a fight with FEAR not action.

Janet said, "I totally agree with you, our fight should be against FEAR not action." Action is not the THEEF of time from the clock of life. I belief, with knowledge you can RISE!

RISE

Don't tip-toe, RISE (Rise In Style Empowered) and walk. RISE and walk, and please do not doubt yourself. I am willing to accept any other excuse, except your doubt of your God-given ability. Rice is common on the food menu in most, if not all countries, despite the different languages utilized as a communication tool; people from different countries do not doubt that rice is on the menu. They still rise to the occasion of eating rice, one of the solutions to human hunger worldwide. If you rise to the occasion of rice, your ability to RISE and walk is not in doubt. Lector! RISE and walk the journey of your life empowered. If you tip-toe, you are walking the journey of life handed to you by the THEEF of life.

The whole idea is for FEAR to present us with a dilemma with his handcuffs, and most of the time FEAR does. It is about time we present the THEEF with a dilemma. We have to RISE, not just RISE, but RISE and walk. Former President Lincoln rose and walked, President Obama rose and walked, Oprah rose and walked, Sir Branson rose and walked, The Dream rose and walked and above all, Stevie Wonder rose and walked. Stevie Wonder cannot see the piano, yet he plays the piano better than those who can see it. Can you play the piano like he can? I know I can't. We have eyes but can't see the true picture in front of us, particularly when we employ FEAR as our optician. Each and everyone has unused gears. I wonder if FEAR also has a ten-speed bike and has only been using half or less than half of his gears. If so, yet his legions of fans run into the billions worldwide. Lector! Role models from different walks of life, they have given us their shoulders to stand on and we should. There is no point lying to ourselves any more, **We have a**

job to do, let's get the job done. "Indeed we do," said Thiago. Janet added, "Yes, an individual should RISE and walk like our role models did."

Last word:
Icons are icons and legends are legends and role models are role models. They all own a stake in the Art of Battle.

TWELVE

Constant Reminders

Law of Reciprocity

Nobody understands the law of reciprocity better than action. The law states the following:

> "You reap what you sow."
> "Pay and you will be paid."
> "You get what you give."

Sow with FEAR, and you will reap failure. The seed of FEAR grows failure. Pay action, and you will be paid with success. If you don't take action, it will give you nothing; if you take action, it will give you something. Give to action what is due to him from you. Action will give you success in return for what you give him, and much more – to do nothing is to sow with FEAR, and believe me, FEAR will give your failure in return. Has anybody ever said to you, "I owe you one"? Perhaps, after doing that person a favor, if you call up that favor years later, the debt will be paid. However, FEAR does not comply with the law of reciprocity. FEAR will never owe you anything but failure, even if you give him a loan.

Failures Attract Failures

The Law of Attraction is a theory commonly associated with New Age and New Thought theories. It posits that one should never dwell on the negative, as the "metaphysical principle of life" is embodied in a "law of attraction": "you get what you think about; your thoughts determine your destiny.

en.wikipedia.org/wiki/Law of Attraction

The law of attraction speaks all languages; when you have a dialogue with your FEAR, the law of attraction acts on the outcome of your conversation with the THEEF of life. If the THEEF gets the upper hand in the conversation, you slip into inaction mode – as FEAR attracts FEAR, "Inaction attracts inaction." In the Failure Armed Forces, all the soldiers are failures; successful people don't join the FEAR army. They are not like-minded people. "Failures attract failures." Even if they wish to, their applications will be rejected on the grounds of success, because everything a soldier in the Failure Armed Forces draws to itself is like itself; fortunately or unfortunately. Depending on which side of the fence you position yourself on, success and failure are simply birds of a different feather. Success will flock together with success, and failure will flock together with failure. A failure cannot apply for membership in the millionaires' club unless he starts to attract success to himself, instead of his customary failure. His mindset needs to be success, success, success. You cannot attract failure to yourself, and expect to be successful.

As a man thinks in his heart, so is he.
Napoleon Hill

The law of attraction does not argue with you; it complies with you. Whether you request it or not, your perception is what awaits you – it simply adheres to your conversation with the THEEF of life. The law of attraction has no particular loyalty to success or failure, but has an astonishing chemistry with you that creates a loyalty to success or failure for you, depending on your choice. Because of this chemistry between you and the law of attraction, you must direct your thoughts, feelings, emotions and energy toward what you want; even your dreams should be about what you want (and they will be, if you control your thinking). The universe receives your thoughts and exactly what you want will be attracted to you. Deciding when, where and the mode of delivery is not part of your job description; your job is to make a burning request and await delivery. A burning request or desire always ignites action; remain focused and do not allow FEAR to derail your positive thoughts with negative thoughts or put doubts in your mind. Remember the saying, "once bitten, twice shy." The global terrorist has already robbed you in the past; don't give in, don't let him rob you again. The law of attraction awaits you; make sure your thoughts are positive, not negative, because the law of attraction will deliver.

> *I know for sure that what we dwell on is who we become.*
> **Oprah Winfrey**

The law of attraction gives you the sum of your thoughts; what you desire is what you get. It is not open to negotiation, but it is open to request. Place your order. "Success attracts success." If you do not believe you will be successful, it means you believe you will fail. The law of attraction works in the same direction with you. With the law of attraction, what you want is yours – it is not a game of chance, but a game of choice. If you feel very low within yourself, you do not have a chance of feeling very high within yourself. You call to yourself the feeling you feel within you, and the law of attraction simply gives you the feeling you requested. FEAR only wants to steal from you, and if you place yourself in that position, FEAR will steal from you. You will not get any empathy from the THEEF. The law of attraction will deliver the result of your action.

D'banj

D'Banj was born as Dapo Daniel Oyebanjo in the Northern city of Zaria, Kaduna State, Nigeria to an artillery Officer and a church dignitary whom hailed from Shagamu in Ogun state.

His incredible harmonica skills are self taught; he says, "I play the harmonica like it was built for me".

D'Banj became more and more involved in music and he cannot see himself doing anything else with the same passion. His song "All The Way" is about the struggles he has faced with his parents over his chosen career.

Dapo has now adopted the elegant, almost French-sounding name "D'Banj", a combination of his first name Dapo and his surname Oyebanjo.

www.mohitsrecords.com

D'banj (Koko Master as he is also popularly known) is a Nigerian singer-songwriter and harmonica player. D'banj is Nigeria's first United Nations Youth Ambassador for peace and founder of Koko Foundation for Youth and Peace Development. Awards after awards don't arrive if you don't believe in yourself. That is exactly what D'banj has done; he believed in himself. It doesn't really matter whether he is hotter than you or you are hotter than me in any vocation, we are all hot and you are just as hot as anybody out there – if you don't believe it, step up your game, then check the results. At least, that is what he did, he stepped up his game. D'banj is right when he said; *"Don't hate me because I'm hotter than you,"* instead **step up your game; step it up!** At least, that is one thing I give FEAR credit for. When required, FEAR will step up his game to neutralize any hope you have, and to reduce an articulate individual to a voiceless soul, except the individual who is willing to step up to another height. You don't have to be anybody but yourself, with determination, focus, motivation and passion *(a different drug like no other drug on the planet),* you will put FEAR in his place, you will be hotter than his disciples, who have, indirectly been put in their place by FEAR. Did I hear somebody say African Michael Jackson or World Michael Jackson? The latter would suffice.

Dress Code

Over the last several years, the dress code in the work environment has been getting more and more casual; dressing down (t-shirts and jeans) has become the norm in quite a number of companies, particularly for non-customer-facing roles in companies. However, business suits and ties are still mandatory in some offices. The blazer or sport jacket plays an important role by allowing flexibility and comfort, and at the same time, presenting a professional appearance. When you dress, dress smart. Don't wear the blazer of FEAR; wear the blazer of success with the action badge clearly visible on your blazer of success. The blazer or any other type of clothes worn daily by a homeless person, which has been denied a good wash for over six months, can't be compared to a blazer that adheres to the garment washing instructions. Every individual has the ability to be successful, provided the individual wants to be successful, and the place to start is to engrave the belief in your heart that you will be successful without entertaining any FEAR in your mind.

When you have the look of success, you call success to yourself, and when you radiate the look of failure, you call failure. Most successful people declare that when they looked successful, they found it easier to think success and achieve success. Such is the effect of clothes on the human body. A naked man, roaming the streets would be arrested for indecent exposure, compared to a man who adheres to the dress code of society. FEAR has little or no respect for such people. On the other hand the THEEF has respect for those who adhere to the dress code of success. Don't roam the streets in the wrong clothes, dirty, ripped or smelly clothes, regardless of the type of clothes you wear. You can't be granted an audience in those kind of clothes.

Jeans transcend the barriers of kids', teens' and adults' fashion. Wearing jeans is not restricted by weather; jeans are all-weather products. Jeans speak a universal language, a language understood by successful people and failures, unlike FEAR, the language of failures. Whether you are a soldier in the Failure Armed Forces or a successful individual, there are different types of jeans to wear for your conversation with the THEEF of life: *"Boot Cut,"* *"Boyfriend," "Cropped," "Flare," "High-waisted," "Skinny," "Straight-leg," or "Wide-leg."* Aside from various jean trousers, you may choose to wear denim overalls, shorts, dresses, skirts, shirts, jackets or caps. Try on the different variations to see what feels and looks best on you. Jeans are durable and will last the distance of the conversation or discussion; every individual needs to be as durable as jeans in his or her conversation with the THEEF, regardless of the type of jeans he or she decides to wear. This does not mean other types of clothes can't get the job done (for example, troops are not issued 100 percent cotton wear when deployed to the battlefield), but they are not as durable – in comparison to jeans, they are not in the same league. The THEEF of life is not in denial of the durability of jeans wear in general, be it kids', teens', men's or women's jeans.

Last word:
There has to be action on the part of an individual to request an answer to a question capable of changing his life.

THIRTEEN

Conclusion

The James Effect

*I have lived a long life and had many troubles,
most of which never happened.*
Mark Twain

If FEAR is nothing more than '*False Evidence Appearing Real,*' and we have the answer in hand to the question, "Who Stole my Life?" then we have a case to either:

Free ourselves from FEAR.
Escape from FEAR.
Avert FEAR.
Resist FEAR.

Resist the devil, and he will flee from you.
James 4: 7

'*Resist*' should be one of the end results of our battles (personal and public) with the global merciless THEEF, if we are not to hand our lives to the THEEF on a plate. If we can't address our FEAR, then our results will simply be limited to our beliefs. Personal Battle (Relax, Interrogate and Establish), Public Battle (Action, Analyze and Gradual), Everybody wants and is entitled to a piece of the global village, but FEAR is greedy, extremely greedy. The THEEF of life kills dreams by stealing time from a life. Prevention can be put in place via simple FEAR safety advice:

- Be bold enough to hold a simple conversation with FEAR.
- Always make sure that FEAR is distinguished from real fear.

- Keep FEAR away from burning desire and action.
- Keep FEAR away from the vicinity of your mind.
- Never leave a burning desire unattended.
- Don't share the views of tenants of FEAR – more importantly, don't pay rent to the THEEF of life.
- Pay mortgage payments to action.
- Refuse the influence of members of the Failure Armed Forces.
- Don't allow the THEEF to handcuff your hands.

Death does not announce its arrival in most cases, neither does FEAR.

The Angel

The THEEF of life is not the author of success. I have never met anybody who regrets declaring their personal battle against FEAR; the regret most have is not going to battle earlier. Many people will narrate endless tales as to why action is the evil and FEAR is the angel. Under the disguise of first impressions, the THEEF appears as the best partner in the world, and within a short space of time, you are walking down the aisle with him, a stranger you don't know but think you know. Don't *'Throw a Wobbly'* with action; the THEEF is the culprit you need to be angry and upset with. Despite all the warnings including *"Be cautious of walking down the aisle with the THEEF of life,"* the majority ignores this caveat and proceed. Once FEAR has gained an entrance into your heart and made himself at home with you, divorce *(the divorce certificate)* will be the most expensive product you will ever buy. In most cases, the Extinguisher of life never files for divorce until it has fully established his intention in you and you are fully committed to it. Should the THEEF decide to file for divorce, rest assured that it will be virtually impossible for you to take any action to gain all the lost years you spent with the THEEF. An old soldier in the Failure Armed Forces who is too old to fight is of no use to FEAR; new recruits will be enlisted. It will mostly be in your old age. At this stage, FEAR has no need to be with you any longer. Don't fall in love with the THEEF foolishly; examine all your options, give action a chance, even if it means taking a small measurable action. Just as FEAR grows in you over time, so do small measurable actions. They may well be the only thing you can fall back on after your tenure with the THEEF. You need to learn to fall in love with your head, not just your heart based on a first impression. If anything, the THEEF is evil, even though they are not in the same class of words (FEAR and evil), alphabetically, they are first cousins as 'E' and 'F,' respectively.

Having a positive conversation with the THEEF of life creates happiness in your life, and the fact is that happy people have better relationships, achieve more of their goals, are better parents and leaders and are healthier. So mounting the podium of happiness in your life is the best and greatest gift you can give yourself, your family, your co-workers and everybody around you.

Good conversations breed good spirits in you, and with good spirits, life becomes a rewarding adventure instead of something to get through in pain, *even waking up on the treadmill every weekday appears like a rewarding adventure.* The world is constantly changing; the advances in technology over the course of the last two decades are proof of the changes in the world, yet every change has been a result of battles with FEAR. For example, people who invent things have conversations with their second voice that the change they propose can be done, and then go to work to introduce the change to the world. Discussion with the THEEF is not reserved for an elite group of people; it is reserved for all. Gender, occupation, or name *are not criteria* for having such discussions, just as language is not a barrier, because the THEEF is fluent in all languages. If others can have battles with FEAR and create a better and happier life for themselves, why can't you do the same? You cannot expect to fly first-class round trip without paying for the flight; the tab must be picked up by somebody, either you or the THEEF. You cannot apologize profusely to the THEEF of life at the end of your journey of life. "Always fly Action Airways; in the long run, even if you fly economic class, it always ends up being more comfortable than flying first class on Failure Airlines."

Hidden Ability

In every individual lies a hidden ability waiting to be called into action – to awaken your hidden abilities and/or overcome your FEAR, you will need to rediscover yourself. For example, as a baby you were spoon-fed, and as you grew up you needed to spoon-feed yourself and not be spoon-fed by your parents. It is at the point when you learn to spoon-feed yourself, that you discover your ability to spoon-feed yourself. To tame the THEEF, you will need to rediscover yourself, just as you learned to spoon-feed yourself. It can't be done for you; you will have to do it yourself. You have to be prepared and willing to extract your hidden abilities, or the contents of the safety deposit box the THEEF has placed in your care without a key to unlock the box, which contains your abilities to eradicate your FEAR. If you do it, progress will be swift, and with constant practice, it will become second nature. The THEEF of life will gradually become a guest, and ' action will become a resident in your mind, and then the action will become habitual, and then an addiction. The addiction to FEAR is like the addiction to change resistance in most walks of life, which in itself is a creation of FEAR, as people resist change, so they resist action instead of FEAR. However, a change is still required to move from FEAR to action. As everyone is still addicted to their own behavior, change will be slow except for those willing to meet the demands of instant change.

    Positive thinking can reduce your FEAR of what might happen in a new, unfamiliar situation or how someone might respond to what you are saying or doing, while negative thinking will enhance your FEAR and will send your mind to FEAR imprisonment. Any positive thinking in your mind is quickly dismissed, as the negative thinking is stronger than positive thinking in your mind, the effect of FEAR imprisonment. To regain your freedom from the THEEF, again, a change is required in various areas of your life. If you think change is impossible for you, it will be impossible, and if you think change is possible for you, it will be possible. The change in thinking is the key; if you are ready and prepared to accommodate the change, your views, thoughts and action changes as well, negativity will become positivity. I can assure you the first question you will ask yourself after the change is, '*Why did I wait until now to make this change in my life?*'

Free Society

You are not in the business of past directions that lead nowhere; you are in the business of future directions that lead somewhere. You have been doing, doing and doing without any results to show for your efforts. It's now time to do, do and do with solid visible results to show. There is always a beginning and an ending; you can't stop something you have not started. You need to start before you stop; even inaction has a start date. In your personal battle, the day you start your dialogue with the THEEF is the day you request a warrant for his arrest and that creates an end date to the audacity of FEAR in your life.

Do what needs to be done to know what you need to know; this ensures you learn to understand and understand to learn that learning is understanding and understanding is learning. Pilots go to flying school to train as pilots. Negative assumptions are seeds of failure: *"I can't do it." "He said I can't do it." "How do you know you can't? Have you tried, or did somebody tell you you can't?"* Ask yourself or talk to your FEAR; your answer awaits you. Are conversations with the THEEF theirs or yours? With theirs, you are still in bed. *"Don't do it, nothing good can come out of doing it."* Your conversations or discussions with FEAR will 'Knock You Up.' Conversation with others is meant to enable us to express our views and learn from each other. The THEEF of life has no intention of learning from you or giving you the opportunity to express yourself. It is said that we can't teach an old dog new tricks – FEAR is an old dog; you can't teach him anything new. Instead, you run the risk of being handcuffed for life.

Always remind yourself, the THEEF has nothing to lose in this symposium, so why should you have something to lose? Within a free society, there is freedom of speech; nobody has the right to impose his or her views on you and vice versa. The day and night bandit seems to be exempt from this constitutional right; yet again, he can't be held accountable for his actions, but you can. He takes action at will, destroying lives of people and has the audacity to prevent you from taking action to avert failure in different areas of your life. However, a hope for accountability and refusal of exemption from the constitutional rights still exist; it's in your hands, and it's your Protect or Reclaim strategy, 'Personal Battle', 'Public Battle' and 'The Art of Battle' with the THEEF.

Peace

Lector, I wish you peace. Peace be with you. The only way we can find peace with FEAR is to make peace with Action. There cannot be peace with FEAR without the implementation of the laws of action. When we take the fight to a member of our family, we are not fighting the enemy. Action is a child of the first-born child within the family of alphabets (the alphabet 'A'). Action is on your side, not against you. Embrace him, he is always willing to embrace you. If you desire peace of mind in your life, you will have to implement your divide and eliminate strategy against the THEEF – otherwise, FEAR will compile a list of issues for you with a maturity date in the future. It is not only important to have an effective conversation with FEAR or Interrogation, but also to listen attentively to what FEAR communicates to you. Every single time you have a conversation or discussion with FEAR, it always carry a warning for and against, the question for you to ask the THEEF but are too worried and terrified to ask, is: *"What is this, and what's in it for me?"* Find your place on the team, and give yourself a chance before you fall down. Take a bite before a bite takes you. In your conversations with FEAR or interrogation, choose your words carefully – they are your weapons. FEAR will take your mind and let you keep your body. FEAR is aware that a weak mind in a strong body is not strong enough to take FEAR on at any stage of the dialogue. It is not about physical strength; it is about the use of words in the conversation battle, and a weak mind can't coordinate the required words effectively to justify his opinion in any debate. Conversation is the tool of professionalism. Be professional with the THEEF, and have a constructive debate. Let us assume FEAR does not exist for a moment; then lock yourself in your room and state the following: *"I want to have a conversation with you, FEAR. Please stand up!"* Naturally, nobody will stand up (you are alone in your room). In this case, based on assumption and since FEAR is not visible, who or what are you afraid off? Who or what has handcuffed your hands? Who or what is holding you prisoner? Assume he does not exist for a while in your life and see how you feel for that period.

Ability

It doesn't matter who you are, where you come from.
The ability to triumph begins with you – always.
Oprah Winfrey

Your ability to triumph begins with a relaxation of your body and mind, along your journey to freedom. It is said: *"Attack is the best form of defense."* This is true; if you don't attack your FEAR with your words (not your fist) in your dialogue with him, you have no defense against the THEEF. You are, simply stated, *a disaster waiting to happen, or a dead man walking.*

The secret for achieving your goals and discovering your abilities is overcoming your FEAR – there are no shortcuts. You have to eliminate the THEEF of life. One of the most important things to do is to get rid of your FEAR of FEAR. Without eliminating your FEAR of FEAR, it will be difficult to use the Protect or Reclaim Strategy, as it will prevent you from starting the process. You can draw up a business plan and set effective goals, but without dealing with your FEAR, you will never take action on them. It can be frustrating trying to tame the THEEF, but with the correct mindset, it can be done in seven steps or fewer, depending on the individual. However, without the correct mindset, it could take weeks, months, even years to overcome FEAR for some. However, all is not lost.

Repeat the seven-step process regularly, and your FEAR will be a thing of the past in the near future. It's like the seventh step in the seven-step process, 'The Art of Battle' in Chapter 10 (practice, practice, practice and practice again), and you will soon get it right. There is no room for hiding if success is to be achieved.

Delay

Nobody is immune to real fear. FEAR did not create itself; human beings are the creators of the Finisher of life. At some stage in our lives, we have all experienced FEAR; it could be a limiting factor in different areas of our lives, not only holding us but pulling us back from reaching the top. Success is a friend to all human beings, but only those who introduce themselves to action in battle against the THEEF become friends or good friends of success; those who don't become best friends of failure. Whether they be teardrops of FEAR or teardrops of joy, either way teardrops are inevitable – ensure yours are teardrops of joy. Walk away from the FEAR in your life via your Protect or Reclaim strategy. The question is, *"When will you engage yourself in battle against the global THEEF?"* The sooner the better; however, the THEEF would rather you do it very, very late, or not at all. A word is enough for the wise, in the event of a miscarriage of justice, which is usually the case, the damage is already done, and there is no recourse to the THEEF.

Delay is the deadliest form of denial.
C. Northcote Parkinson

FEAR creates delay. Once the THEEF creates delay in your life, it effectively denies you success. When you are afraid, you keep avoiding the action you need to take. The THEEF has delayed so many people from taking action all their lives. When you put an action plan together, taking action becomes a different story. Year after year, you find an excuse for not taking action, and you convince yourself that you will take action the year after. A few years later, you can't even remember the full details of the task;

gradually, the dream dies before its birth. A life is denied expression. Nobody killed your dream; you killed your dream as an agent of the Finisher of life, due to your association with the Finisher, and you are presented with 'delay' as a reward for your association with the THEEF. FEAR ensures you are constantly thinking about the negative side of the task rather than the positives you could be focusing on.

The next step will be coming up with an action plan to take us from where we are now, to where we want to go. And I promise you, that enemy of life, FEAR, will show its ugly head at various stages. The biggest obstacle you will face is the FEAR. Whatever action you need to execute will require you to overcome FEAR. For example, you may want to start a business or expand your business activities but *"You're afraid of what will happen if you step out and start a business?"*, *"What if it doesn't work?"*, *"What if people don't buy?"*, *"What if I lose money?"*. The *"What If"* monster bombards you with all the negative possibilities, all leading to delay upon delay, never with the positive possibilities – *"What if your business is successful?"*

FEAR and action are inspirational, but in opposite directions, failure and success respectively.

FEAR and Action have something in common behind the glaze of public eyes – each is striving for results for its own people (in the case of the latter, success, and the former, failure). Your conversation with FEAR breaks your language barrier with the THEEF of life. You may speak the same language as the THEEF, but without your conversation or discussion with FEAR, it would appear as if you have a language barrier with the THEEF. By listening and not talking to the THEEF, FEAR is not aware of what language you speak. The THEEF assumes you are simply going with the crowd. Initiate a discussion with the THEEF of life, and the picture changes; the THEEF will realize you speak the same language, and you are not willing to accept his complimentary gift, failure, for attending and listening at his seminar. Confront your

FEAR; it's the only exit available for any individual. Doing nothing is not a way out; it is a FEAR entrance door, open twenty-four hours a day without any entrance criteria. There is no doorman at the door, so a conversation with THEEF at the door is not an option you can consider before your entrance. There is no delay at the entrance; the earlier you step in, the better for the THEEF.

Ban

If you are currently a soldier in the Failure Armed Forces, you are entitled to be reintegrated into the society of success from the society of failure, provided you are willing to go to the battlefield. However, from whichever direction you view the situation, you are the only one who has the ultimate decision to initiate the conversation with the THEEF, for your reintegration into the society of success.

Any human being whose credentials as leader of his household came under scrutiny after his loss of control and composure at the symposium with the THEEF, is entitled to many more conversations with the THEEF of life, where he will have the opportunity to marshal his defence brilliantly. With your conversation concluded effectively in your favor, positive results begin to appear in different areas of your life. The victory that comes with actions based on burning desire would even force FEAR to set aside his disappointment and applaud your efforts for taking action.

Whatever the THEEF of life had in store for you will be swiftly discarded, with action intelligently deployed just behind burning desire and the under-rated conversations with FEAR, a willing accomplice for the more lavishly gifted formal and informal conversations. Get your team in place, your conversation, your burning desire and your action, and with action's tactical brilliance to call on, your conversation with the THEEF of life will be a winner – all you have to do is have the conversation. FEAR will look tired. The achievements of your conversation and other members of your team will put you in a position where you would not be dismissed lightly, for many have failed to hold their conversations with the THEEF of life and have paid the price. As we speak, many are still on the same road being driven to the cleaners.

Adidas and Nike

Heart to heart, mind to mind, from mine to yours, don't let FEAR act on your future. Without the THEEF of life in your life, you blossom and the sky will be the limit. Be prepared to act on your FEAR; don't give in to the giant of a monster known as the THEEF of life, at the very least, you owe it to yourself to prove that David can defeat Goliath. A millionaire is human just as much as a poor man; the only difference is that one is rich, and the other is poor, but the millionaire is not necessarily smarter or wiser than the poor man. The reason behind the difference between them is that one took action, and the other failed to take action – or, took action and encountered a minor setback, and, based on this minor setback, refused to take action again. If you fail to take action hoping and waiting for your action to execute itself on your behalf, the day you do that is the day you confine yourself to failure. A pair of hands in handcuffs does not have the privilege of the use of those hands to act. Action awaits execution from anybody willing to act, while the Finisher of life finds weak people (occasionally strong people with a hint of doubt in their minds) to terrorize, in order to put their hands in handcuffs. Refuse to be terrorized by FEAR – instead, terrorize FEAR. We all need a little bit of motivation here and there to ignite our desire to take action. You are well within your right to extradite the Finisher of life from Fearland to Actionland. In Actionland, action is guaranteed. It's important to realize that once you accept defeat from the THEEF, your position, soon or later, will become untenable.

We need to maintain our focus on whatever we engage in; this ensures you know what the focus is, and you can't be derailed easily from your focus. To commence battle against the THEEF is not impossible, so just get it over with. The agents of FEAR may tell you a battle against the THEEF is impossible, while successful people will tell you *if 'Nothing is impossible,' then 'Just do it,' or 'Just do it' based on 'Nothing is impossible.'* Adidas and Nike, or vice versa, have been doing their best to communicate these messages to the public worldwide for years. FEAR has never been very generous with such critical information. And the THEEF of life is certainly not about to start being generous after all these years, and least of all, to you.

Today

Today, at dawn, the terrorist, the day and night bandit, the global assassin known as THEEF of life said:

> You are not in the race.
> You are well past your sell-by date.
> You are divided within.
> You are confused.
> You are not up to the task.
> You are too tall.
> You are too short.
> You are too black.
> You are too white.
> You are too Hispanic.
> You can't do it.
> You are on borrowed time.

Lector (young or old), I have one question to put to you; "*FEAR is not racist – how then can he say you are too black, white or Hispanic?*" Perhaps, it is the views of some agents of FEAR. Based on this opinion of the agents of the THEEF, I wonder why black fails to be successful among blacks, white among whites and Hispanic among Hispanics. Don't daydream about the part of the day that belongs to the past, don't dig the part of the day that has already been buried for which there can be no remembrance of the taste of honey and don't call FEAR to assist you through the rest of the day. Personally, he buried the other half of the day, and by observation, as far as I am concerned, FEAR made a mess of the job. Let me assure you, today, you RISE; today, you are in the race, you are united within. You are not too black, white or Hispanic; today is about unlocking, and today, the THEEF of life is confused, lost and not up to the task. Today, we will end the strategy that has been about failure, and together, we unveil the strategy of success and stand as one against the global THEEF. Today, we shall not be defeated; we shall prevail together under the spirit of togetherness – today, not tomorrow, now, not later. Allow me to quote two lines from President Barack Obama's acceptance speech in Denver on August 28, 2008.

> ... we are here because we love this country too much to let the next four years look like the last eight. On November 4th, we must stand up and say: 'Eight is enough.'
> **Senator Barack Obama**

Today, we must RISE together and say: *'Yesterday is enough.'* We can't allow tomorrow to look like yesterday. Half of today could have slipped through the net, but what is left of today should and must not be granted the same immunity as its other half.

Yesterday was yesterday, today is today, period!

Today, more importantly, is *dismissal and deliverance* day. Today, we dismiss the views of the THEEF, and we deliver a copy of our strategy and plan of success to the THEEF of life. This is a full-blown battle between you and FEAR, the stubborn individual. This issue cannot be sidestepped any more; that ticket expired yesterday, so it is not valid today. Today, together, we put the ghost of the THEEF of life to rest for good. You have the combination to the safety deposit box; unlock the safety deposit box. Intelligence should not be underestimated. It is something profound in all individuals, kids, teens, and adults. Don't underestimate anybody's intelligence, most importantly your own. Lector, I can state the opinion the THEEF of life has about you, but I disagree with it. I cannot state your opinion about yourself, but I can state my opinion about you today. YOU ARE INTELLIGENT, INCREDIBLE, TALENTED AND AWESOME! Do what you have to do, no later than by the end of today. Disable the mind of the THEEF of life, and enable your own. Today, the truth deserves a hearing. When the truth gets a hearing, action prevails. Distinguished readers, and honorable friends, Mark Twain once said:

> *There are two kinds of speakers: those that are nervous and those that are liars.*

FEAR and his agents are liars; they are never nervous when they speak.

24

Vicinity in turmoil; the nation of Sangala in Africa where a dangerous rebel group attempts to reclaim the land as their own by overthrowing the government. 24: Redemption begins with Colonel Ike Dubaku, one of the leaders of the rebel group teaching children how to fire guns as they are prepared for combat. At the end of the scene Colonel Dubaku instructs one of the children to behead an opposer who was brought in by his men.

Kill the Cockroach.
24: Redemption, Colonel Ike Dubaku

The traitor, who tragically lost his life, is not the cockroach. The child soldier who decapitated the traitor is not the cockroach. Jack Bauer is not the cockroach. Carl Benton is not the cockroach, and neither is General Benjamin Juma. Colonel Ike Dubaku is not the cockroach, nor is Youssou, his brother. The cockroach is FEAR. The trading of strength for FEAR must be monitored, not ignored. One of the techniques used to replace weakness with human strength is the desire and ability to act.

Comply with Colonel Ike Dubaku's instruction – Kill the cockroach! Kill the FEAR! (a particular instance of FEAR). Kill the cockroach to protect or reclaim your land; your life may not be precious to the cockroach, but it should be precious to you. FEAR must be eliminated to save a life. Without the elimination, you cannot protect or reclaim your land from the government of the THEEF. Freedom cannot be bought with the blood of action, only with the blood of FEAR – ashes to ashes, and dust to dust.

FEAR is not human, don't mourn the death of FEAR, celebrate the death of an instance of FEAR and birth of success.

Caution

"*Caveat Emptor*" or more appropriately, I should say "*Caveat Lector.*" Success is the maximum utilization of the ability that you have. A reality about life, '*Life,*' is a natural casualty of the THEEF. However, maximum application of your ability leads to minimum application of the THEEF's ability. Propel yourself with the application of your ability to new heights.

Life has the habit of limiting our choices as we accumulate yearly wisdom miles on our Life Frequent Flyer Miles (LFFM). You can't attain the age of fifty years old, and intend to apply for position that requires an under twenty-five-year-old applicant as a requirement for the job. In addition to this, the THEEF of life is doing its best to ensure our wisdom miles are acquired, but not utilized. Bit by bit, we drift, in different directions, up or down, left or right – either way, we are drifting with every battle, and an individual can drift from battle to battle, leading from 'failure to failure,' 'success to failure,' 'failure to success,' or 'success to success.' However, a drift with the THEEF is a drift toward chaos and personal sabotage. I am sure millions of people within the global village called the world have lawsuits to file against the THEEF, if they can find him. Individuals are different, regardless of the differences and experiences. The supply of success exceeds the demand for success; the demand is limited by the THEEF. Success is available to anybody who demands it. With your conversations with the THEEF and action, you can demand your success; it is not a scarce commodity as the supply exceeds the demand, and supply awaits your demand.

> *Finding is reserved for those that search.*
> **Jim Rohn**

Lector! We have now reached the point where we either drown or swim. Step up your conversation or discussion, heat it up, so hot it will be too hot to handle – even the THEEF will have no choice but to take a step back. When those who have a destination, success, arrive, those with no road map, including those with a navigation system without a destination (a navigation to nowhere), will move over. *"Driving without a navigation system to your destination is no different from driving with a navigation system without a destination."* In a town or city we don't know, without a satellite navigation system to help us navigate around, we cannot map a route. It is not only a destination but destiny; your destination, success, is your destiny. Our battles, socially, professionally and spiritually on any level, are for a purpose. When we tell our children off to ensure they are well behaved children to authorize our happiness, in the process for the children, learning the behavioral rules of engagement in society, we have a dialogue with God for improvements in all areas of our lives. We talk to colleagues at work to ensure we all get the job done properly, or perhaps, we have informal conversations with people in general to brighten up the day (ours and theirs). Herein lies the reason of our battles – the whole point of our battles is to be happy, HAPPY PEOPLE!

Blood of Failures

It takes the best interviewer to bring out the best in the interviewee. In an interview with Minister Louis Farrakhan, the leader of the Nation of Islam, by Mike Wallace on "60 Minutes" (Mr. Wallace was a correspondent for CBS' "60 Minutes" since its debut in 1968 until his retirement), the question was put to Minister Louis Farrakhan regarding his recent trip to Nigeria and the high level of corruption in the country which he described as the most corrupt in Africa and probably, in the world. In his answer, which can be found on YouTube and other media outlets; Minister Farrakhan unleashed his views. He made reference to the age of both countries (Nigeria and America respectively) as independent countries in relation to when black Americans were given the right to vote in America. He also made reference to the atomic bombing of the Japanese cities of Hiroshima and Nagasaki. Minister Farrakhan concluded his answer with the following words:

Yes, there is corruption there. Yes, there is mismanagement of resources. Yes, there is abuse; there is abuse in every nation on earth, including this one, so let's not play holy to moralize on them, let's help them.
On "60 Minutes", Minister Louis Farrakhan

Members of Parliament (MPs) in London, United Kingdom, with regards to the expenses claimed by MPs based on recent news headlines in the UK and other parts of the world, are doing their best to ensure the words of Minister Farrakhan are true: *"Yes, there is corruption there. Yes, there is mismanagement of resources. Yes, there is abuse; there is abuse in every nation on earth."* Unless we consider subtle corruption not to be corruption, on our part, we need to acknowledge his words of wisdom – *"LET'S HELP THEM."* MPs are doing a great job on behalf of the people. If we need to increase their salaries and/or benefits, so be it.

"Janet you are an American by birth, Lanre, you are a Nigerian by birth, and I am a Brazilian by birth," said Thiago before continuing. "We all want to be what we are –American, Nigerian and Brazilian – without apologies to anybody for being what we are proud to be. I can't donate my birth right to FEAR. I can't allow FEAR to be what he is, the Finisher of life, without apologies to the world and be what I am with apologies." The Nation of FEAR has no shame in its game, waving its handcuffs in the air indiscriminately – LET NO MAN HAVE ANY SHAME IN HIS

OWN GAME! The blood of failures in every nation on earth is not in the hands of one particular individual, and CERTAINLY NOT IN YOURS. They are in the hands of FEAR and its agents. Lector, in your debate or interview with FEAR, don't let the biggest killer of human dreams and vision act holy. He who intends to act or play holy should not have the blood of failures on his hands and if he does, he will have to justify his position as the holy one. Ladies and gentlemen of integrity, the THEEF can't appoint or crown himself as a moral judge, or the judge and jury (the 'J & J') over our lives without our approval, so let FEAR justify his position to you and not vice versa. American, Brazilian or Nigerian, regardless of what part of the global village owns your birth right, you can't keep apologizing to FEAR for a crime you did not commit.

Lector, you don't have the blood of failures on your hands, but he does! Go forth and be successful, regardless of your place of birth.

Yours

It was novelist, journalist and poet Christopher Morley who said:

> *When you give someone a book, you don't give him just paper, ink and glue. You give him the possibility of a whole new life.*

A book can indeed give somebody going nowhere a new direction and a road map to get to a destination. In some cases, all you need is a book to awaken the hidden potential in you to move forward in life. I certainly got a new lease on life when my father gave me a few books from his library – books I grew up with, but had never taken notice of while I was growing up. For more than twenty years, I kept walking past them as if they didn't exist; today they are not only part of my library, but they are also part of my most valuable possessions. I am sure you can recall a book you bought or borrowed, perhaps given to you as a gift that rekindled your desire in one way or another, made a significant impact on your life, or motivated you to take action. In my humble opinion, inspirational books are oxygen for our lives and a great asset to have in your arsenal of books. A single book can alter your life beyond your wildest dream; don't underestimate the transformation a book can have on your life. One of the pleasures I will derive from this book is to motivate you to take action to *'Protect or Reclaim your life'* from the THEEF of life; if you have been robbed, reclaim your life, or if you haven't, prevent him from robbing you of your precious life. Either way, we don't need the handcuffs of the THEEF – new or used, we can't afford them, they are way above our price range.

I hope this book has filled you with enthusiasm for the gains you will receive by taking action. Focus, burning desire and action are wonderful tools to have in your toolbox, and realize that taming the monster, FEAR, is a necessity and not a luxury. Lector! With the seven steps to protect or reclaim your life above, the food is ready. We need to tee off. When we tee off, we immediately put the THEEF on the back foot, *"Lector! What are we waiting for?"* Let's tee off before the food gets cold, breakfast, lunch or dinner. You cannot arrive late for dinner after the plates have already been placed in the dishwasher and the restaurant is just about to close its doors for the day and say, *"We have arrived, we got delayed en route."* In the first place, you arrived alone, the use of the word 'We' cannot be justified (or perhaps, you were referring to the THEEF, who, in any case, wouldn't be anywhere to be found). This book, *"The THEEF of LIFE"* was conceived and delivered to make any individual as powerful as FEAR, the THEEF, that they have to deal with in their lives. My premise is, if we can't avoid dealing with FEAR, then we have to distinguish FEAR and take the battles (Personal and Public) to his doorstep before the submission of our burning desire to FEAR. The will to fight gives you a 50 percent chance of victory before the battle commences. We have to empower ourselves to aid our future transactions with the THEEF.

This is your book, brochure or catalogue; the description is yours. Together, we burned the midnight oil, wrote the manuscript of *"The THEEF of LIFE,"* and with your permission, I sent the manuscript to the publishers and authored the book. Just as you employed me to hand you this book, I employ you to utilize it. Lector, let's dine together. This is not a change we hope for; this is a *'change we need' (the Democratic Party slogan).* Democrat, Republican or Independent, this is our moment. This is our time – the hour is upon us, and things cannot continue the way they were. For a better tomorrow for ourselves, our children, grandchildren and great-grandchildren, we have to create the change we need, the conversation we need more than any other conversation in our lives, the most ignored conversation – it is time for our conversation or discussion with the THEEF. With our Protect or Reclaim strategy, we can establish the rules of engagement with FEAR in our favor. The difference between *"failure" and "success,"* or *"average" and "awesome"* is not much; if you use one of your unused gears, you may never need to use another gear based on your results. Don't stand at the bottom of the mountain paying reverence to those at the top. That homage you pay to some people is due to all, including yourself. First and foremost, pay it to yourself, then everyone else. You already have all you need, to envy other people is a waste of time and effort. Instead, investigate how you can join them at the top. Besides, the view is better from the top of the mountain than from the bottom, and they would prefer you join them at the top. You have a voice – speak to be heard – and remember, a whisper is not a shout, but if you need to shout to be heard, SHOUT! And let those who want to hear, hear you.

He that hath ears to hear, let him hear.
Mark 4: 9

It is not the feeling you felt yesterday or the anticipated feeling of tomorrow, but it is about the feeling of today, now, this very moment. If we begin the day asking ourselves *'Why we can't...?'*, then by the fall of today, we shall be telling ourselves *'Why we can't...'* If we RISE today, asking ourselves, *'How we can...?'*, then by the fall of today, we will be telling ourselves *'How we can...'* or *'How we did...'* Failure is not a promise to any individual, and neither is success. But if the chances of success, as opposed to those of failure, are increased by one event, that event must be given the same attention previously given to certified chances of failure, FEAR. Withdrawal from battle is not an option; we have to match forward to victory.

> *To a slave of FEAR, failure is the clear truth, success has a hidden truth.*

"Abnormality becomes normal when all a human being does is abnormal things." Abnormality is already established in a man who believes failure is the clear truth. If a man decides to fail in life, let him be successful. If a man decides to be successful in life, let him fail, because failure to some is success and success is failure depending on who you dine with, but when you dine with action, success is success and failure is failure.

There is nothing wrong with any name in any language, including yours – it is the pronunciation of the name, in certain languages, that is wrong. It is said; "*A place without a name is not a place.*" Provided you have a name, you exist on the global database.

> *Late after a name is an opportunity, late before a name is late.*

Ladies and gentlemen, there is no need to conduct a post-mortem when the cause of death, failure, has already been established before the arrival of death. Likewise, you can't start your campaign for election for a post after the election, except if the campaign is geared towards the next election. As long as an individual's name is not prefixed by the word '*late,*' countless opportunities are available to the individual. A name prefixed with the word "*late*" is late. There can be no opportunities for a dead man in life; it is a late life.

The Matthew Factor

The day President Obama took his oath of office, America changed its call sign from *"FEAR" to "Action."* America proved once again, with the inauguration of President Obama, that it is an awesome country. It is God's own country: no other country leads the way as the United States of America does. "Not everybody will be able to change their address to 1600 Pennsylvania Avenue NW (the address of the White House)," Janet emphasized. "For example, the constitution of America does not permit or allow you and Thiago that right by virtue of your place of birth. To pursue such a dream will simply be chasing your shadow. Your shadow is as fast as the speed of light – chasing your shadow is a waste of time and energy. But everybody can change their zip code to a better zip code, in comparison to the one they currently occupy."

Lector, although our chosen mode of transportation may have headlamps to aid visibility at night, let's drive the message to the THEEF before the day drifts into darkness and *'Today'* decides to change its call sign to *"Yesterday."* By dawn, the call sign has already been changed, and about 20 percent of the day is gone. Above all, the changing of the call sign from *'Tomorrow'* to *'Today'* is not within your authority. Change your call sign from *'FEAR' to 'Action,'* at least – that is within your jurisdiction. By implementing the change of our call sign, we develop the strength to meddle in the THEEF's affairs, particularly those relating to us directly. FEAR has constantly interfered in our lives, why should we not intrude into his life?

Trying is the electricity for success; turn on your electricity.

Drift with the moment, not the call sign *"Yesterday"* or *"Tomorrow."* Empower yourself with knowledge in order to empower yourself to RISE and walk. More importantly, Lector, you don't have to stretch with stress. There are those who want you to stretch with stress, or perhaps, trip at the very first hurdle. There are those who don't want you to try, but they want you to trip and maintain that position as the nerve center of your operations. It is not about tripping; it is about trying. We are not going to trip; we are going to try. If we try and trip, we can accommodate that result, but to trip without trying is not an acceptable result. Lector, don't trip before you try; try before you trip. Your highness, RISE to mount your throne. An excuse in your life can't be valid if your don't subscribe to the religion of excuse.

> *The greatest failure is the failure to try.*
> **William A. Ward**

The only real defeat in life is not trying. Unfortunately, the majority of the members of the global village are deprived of this information by FEAR, that will allow them to make an informed decision on the subject. As an individual, don't deprive yourself of this basic truth, and, more importantly, use the information. *"If I knew then what I know now"* – avoid taking ownership of that old adage in the future. Empower yourself with reasonable action-backed burning desires to stretch without stress. Stay blessed; the moment is not beyond you, and you are more than capable. We can't dismiss the truth; it should be dignified with acknowledgement. The conversations, discussions and lectures of that weekend closed with this quotation:

> *And if the blind lead the blind, both shall fall into the ditch.*
> **Matthew 15: 14**

Farewell

Saying our farewells was upon us that summer night; indeed, it was already time to go home to our loved ones. Our meeting that weekend ensured it was a lovely weekend with awesome conversations, discussion and lectures about our subject – on my part, my future battles against FEAR would never be the same again. I acquired the techniques required to enhance and improve my future battles against the THEEF. I sincerely hope you did as well.

My conversations with Janet and Thiago over that weekend filled my heart with awesome knowledge and the will to act, knowledge I will treasure for as long as I live. I can't wait for our next weekend conversation and discussion; I asked a question and I got more than an answer. I am truly honored to have had the privilege of their time and erudition that weekend. If anything, at least, I know who I am and who the THEEF is not. I now have, in my possession, something priceless – their footprints over that weekend are engraved on my heart, and I will forever cherish their wisdom. My life after that weekend has never been the same.

Last word:
Encouragement is the beginning of prognosis of FEAR; without a diagnosis, a prognosis can't be established. You cannot identify what you have not discovered. Nobody can have a desire to fail in life. If you don't have anybody to encourage you, encourage yourself.

Bibliography

The following news articles and other resources were used in this book.

Definition of FEAR – www.dictionary.com
Blow Steve. "87-year-old has big plans after graduation" *The Dallas Morning News* Publication Date: 12/05/2007
Chinese Proverb *(paraphrased)* Tao de Ching
Cheston Paul. "18 years for burglar who killed woman at her home" *Evening Standard (London)*Publication Date: 11/29/2007.
"Hakeem 'The Dream' Olajuwon" and Profile —- Wikipedia.
Thompson Steve and Abshire Richard "Dallas officer apologizes for 'poor judgment' toward dying woman's family during traffic stop" *The Dallas Morning News,* Publication Date: 03 /27/2009.
24 Redemption. Fox. Broadcast Date: 11/23/2008 .
D'banj. Biography, *MOHIT D'BANJ KOKO MASTER,* www.mohitsrecords.com.
9ice. Biography, *9ice online,* www.9iceonline.com.
"Hakeem Olajuwon" Slam Dunk – Interview by Spike Lee.

The following books were in my library when I wrote this book:

Haroldsen, Mark O., *How to Wake Up the Financial Genius Inside You.* USA: Bantam Books, 1979.
Covey, Steven R., *The 7 Habits of Highly Effective People.* New York: Free Press, 1989.
Galdwell, Malcolm, *Blink : The power of thinking without thinking.* USA: Back Bay Books, Little, Brown, 2005.
Galdwell, Malcolm, *Outliers: The Story of Success.* USA: Little, Brown and Company, 2008.

Kiyosaki, Robert, Lechter, Sharon C.P.A, *Rich Dad Poor Dad: What The Rich Teach Their Kids About Money – That The Poor And Middle Class Do Not!* USA: Warner Books Ed, 2000.

Godefroy, Rene, *No Condition Is Permanent!* USA: Inquest Pub, 2002.

Godefroy, Rene, *Kick Your Execuses Goodbye.* USA: Inquest Publishing, 2006.

Jeffers, Susan, *Feel the fear and do it anyway.* Ballantine Books, 2006.

McCormack, Mark H., *What They Don't Teach You At Harvard Business School: Notes From A Street-Smart Executive.* USA: Bantam, 1986.

Ziglar, Zig, *See You at the Top: 25th Anniversary Edition.* USA: Pelican Publishing, 2000.

Robbins, Anthony, *Awaken the Giant Within : How to Take Immediate Control of Your Mental, Emotional, Physical and Financial Destiny!* USA: Free Press; Later Printing edition, 1992.

Canfield, Jack, Hansen, Mark, Victor, McKowen, Dahlynn, Hill, Tom, Gardner, John, Gardner, Elizabeth and Wilson, Kyle, *Chicken Soup for the Entrepreneur's Soul: Advice and Inspiration on Fulfilling Dreams.* HCI, 2006.

Index

Illustrations in bold and italic

$100, 99
24, 230
34, 194-195
Ability (Hidden), 220, 223
Abnormal, 237
Above the Law, 13-14
Abshire, Richard, 160
Action
  after, 126
  airways, 219
  alternative for, 154
  awaits execution, 227
  badge, 215
  becomes inaction, 103
  amount of, 139
  appetite for, 30
  appreciate, 166
  audacity of, 124
  beauty of, 168
  blood of, 231
  buy, 29, 137
  by, 13, 105, 123
  constructive, 61
  creates winners, 65
  crippled, 123, 124, 167
  desire for, 91, 206
  door of, 180
  effective, 29, 122, 138, 180
  exclusion of, 28
  executed, 179
  FEAR meets, 148
  FEAR of, 137
  habit of, 120
  honey-coated, 176
  ignorance of, 138
  influence of, 84
  instigates, 90
  key of, 98, 120, 149, 150
  laws of, 258
  level of, 119, 166, 167
  maximum, 126
  meaningful, 27
  measurable, 219
  minimum, 126
  payments to, 218
  phantom, 119, 123
  plan, 225
  plan +, 114-115
  positive, 139
  practice of, 119
  reasonable, 239
  required, 114
  requirement for, 103
  result of, 119
  services of, 134, 179
  stake on, 165
  town, 103
  withdrawal of, 176
  your, 57, 103, 115, 128, 129
Actionland, 227
Action-takers, 49, 83, 134, 149
Adeyemi, Tolula, 137
Adidas, 227-228
Afraid, 128–129
Ali, Muhammad, 9
Ambition, 90-92

American
  dream, 30, 78
  people, 198, 203
Angel (The), 218
Anybody belongs anywhere, 203
Archer, Jeffrey, 4
Asset, 24, 45, 84, 131, 186, 235
Authority, 10, 75, 152, 156, 181, 238
AWESOME!, 230
Ban, 226-227
Bandit
  daylight, 13, 144, 170, 181
  global, 36, 37, 61, 141, 144
  legendary, 14
  midnight, 13
Barclays Bank, 23
Bauer, Jack, 231
Basics, 46, 54, 71-72
Bella, 148
Bevil, Junior, 169
Blazer, 214, 215
Blow, Steve, 197
Books, 106-107
Brain, 134, 185, 186
Branson, Richard, 193-194, 202, 207, 209
Brown, Jason, 162
Bully, 18-19, 113, 143
Burning Desire
  analyze your, 81
  and action, 54, 67, 106, 110, 111, 115, 138, 149, 157, 192, 218, 235
  and FEAR, 82, 157
  based on, 90
  belief is, 54
  case of, 157
  creation of, 46, 113
  establish a, 56, 81,82, 149, 166, 218
  finding a, 63
  lack of, 82, 107
  personal, 82
  symptoms, 35
  to eradicate, 90
  uncontrollable, 82
Burress, Plaxico, 146
Call Sign, 78, 110, 238
Carnegie, Dale, 94, 153
Caution, 231-232
Caveat, 149, 173, 218
Caveat Emptor, 231
Caveat Lector, 231
CEO, 203, 208
Certificate of Compliance, 17-18
Chance of Choice, 156-157
Cheston, Paul, 187
Chinese Proverb, 32, 33, 165
Chrysolyte School, 157
Circle of FHAF (The), 33-34, **34**, 144
Circle of FHIF (The), 30-32, **32**, 33, 34, 167
Clash of the Giants (A), 135
Clinton, Bill, 40-42, 83
Clock is Ticking, 31
Cockroach, 230, 231
Cohen, Jack, 175, 176
Collier, Robert, 109
Compound Interest, **22**, 22-23
Confidence
  Introduction, 6
  (PART ONE), 51
  (PART TWO), 65, 69, 80, 81, 83, 84-87, 94-96, 103, 104
  (PART THREE), 127, 128, 135-137, 147, 167
  (PART FOUR), 195, 199
Constant Reminders, 2, 81, 157, 211
Constitution of America, 238
Conversation
  bad, 64
  bank of, 14, 75-77
  basic, 31
  battle, 29, 223
  casual, 62, 74
  formal, 73, 74

Index

good, 64, 65, 219
ignored, 64, 95, 136, 183, 236
informal, 74, 103, 226, 232
janitors, 77
kinds of, 136
positive, 219
power of, 205
prerequisites of, 78
professional, 70
simple, 1, 29, 63, 68, 158, 166,217
telephone, 20
weekend, 2, 240
Conversation with FEAR
(PART ONE), 9, 29
(PART TWO), 63, 64, 66, 76,
(PART THREE), 146, 151, 166,
(PART FOUR), 217, 222, 225
Cool Runnings, 169
Courage, 83-84
Covey, Stephen R, 81
D'banj, 213-214
Deadly Disease, 94-96
Debate (The), 18, 78
Debt is a Favor (A), 134-135
Delay, 260-262
Depreciating Assets, 188
Depreciation, 24
Desire
  strong, 90, 104, 108, 109, 111, 114, 145
  uncontrollable, 90, 104, 108
  weak, 104, 105, 108
DHL (Desire and Hope to Learn), 111-114
Disabled Mind (The), 28
Dress Code, 214-216
Drift, 231, 232, 238
Dubaku, Ike, 124, 230, 231
Dumas, Alexandre, père, 47
Edison, Thomas Alva, 160
Edwards, Lloyd, 186
Electricity, 238

Empower, 6, 236, 238, 239
Encouragement, 11, 87-92, 240
Escape, 4, 170, 181, 217
Exterminator, 4, 86
Extinguisher
  Introduction, 4
  (PART THREE), 124, 126-129,130, 133, 134, 136, 139, 141, 143, 145, 150
  (PART FOUR), 218
Face (The), 111, 112
Facebook, 163
Failure
  airlines, 143, 220
  allegiance to, 48
  birth of, 108
  blood of, 233-234
  certificates of, 33
  chances of, 237
  codes for, 190
  complete, 9, 27, 122, 128
  consequence of, 90
  court of, 20
  creator of, 1, 2, 57
  customary, 212
  failure is, 237
  failure to, 36, 231
  failures attract, 202, 211-213
  FEAR of, 16
  flight to, 103
  friends of, 224
  fruits of, 107
  gravity of, 21
  guarantee, 39
  health club, 29
  juice of, 92
  justify, 18
  key to, 95
  language of, 215
  lessons of, 153
  look of, 215
  loyalty to, 21

marshal of, 109
medals of, 26
minds of, 95
number of, 64
pain of, 26
podium of, 83
potential, 20
premium for, 141
price of, 20, 139, 143
purpose of, 75
register of, 87
seeds of, 221
society of, 226
sons of, 149
subject of, 10
treadmill of, 88
views of, 33
Failures-only exclusive club, 133, 149
False Evidence Appearing Real, 5, 6, 68, 217
Farewell, 239-240
Farrakhan, Louis, 148, 233
FEAR
   acceptance of, 6
   agent of, 5, 61
   arrival of, 12
   asset of, 19, 24
   audacity of, 221
   bank of, 22
   bondage of, 30, 111,
   children of, 32
   conditions of, 30
   corridors of, 10
   disciples of, 54
   element of, 5, 16, 40, 50
   eradication, 5, 10, 83, 85 115, 126, 183
   FEAR begets, 32
   FEAR of, 30, 63, 223
   gospel of, 24, 54,
   handcuffs of, 5, 132
   hostage of, 29-30, 83, 107
   instance of, 67, 169, 231
   is darkness, 160
   kinds of, 19
   knowledge of, 58, 67, 76, 160
   level of, 4
   nation of, 6, 234
   objective of, 4
   responsibility of, 202
   slaves to, 29
   sleep of, 133
   transmitters of, 61
   types of, 14, 16
   worth of, 23
FEAR EXIT, **140**, 140-141
FEAR extinguisher, **142**, 143
Fearville, 103
Feel the Difference, 136-138
Financial element, 1
Finisher, 4, 224, 225, 227, 234
Ford, 100, 138
Formal and Casual, 73-74
Franklin, Benjamin, 107
Franklin, Rachel, 50, 51
Free Society, 221-222
Freelance murderer, 144
Game of chance, 156, 213
Game of choice, 156, 213
Gardner, Chris, 190, 191-193, 207
Gates, Bill, 120, 153, 207
General Juma, 124, 231
Gladwell, Malcolm, 203
Good Books, 113
Great Britain, 179
Habits, 81, 120
Hale, Vernon, 162
Handcuffs
   of slavery, 48
   types of, 4
Hierarchy of Conversations, 64, **71**, 71-74, 77, 95, 102
Hijacker
   Introduction, 4

Index

(PART TWO), 98, 99, 101, 102, 112, 114
(PART THREE), 156
Hilton, 3
Hill, Napoleon, 104, 212
Hispanic, 163, 228, 229
Hot Food, 108-109
How to Practice, 179-182
How to Relax, 61-63
IHOP, 136
In Dollars We Trust, 47
Infectious, 29
Information, 215
Inside and outside, 148
Inspirational books, 91, 235
Intelligent, 155, 226
Interrogation, 66
Interrogation techniques, 66-70
Jackson, Michael, 99-102, 214
Jackson, Stella, 111, 112
James, 105, 217
James, Joe, 105
James (Bible), 217
Janet
  Introduction, 2, 3
  (PART ONE), 18, 38, 39, 42
  (PART TWO), 79, 115
  (PART THREE), 171, 173
  (PART FOUR), 183, 190, 193, 202, 209, 210, 233, 238, 240
Jean, Bettye, 191
Jeans, 152, 214-216
Jones, Peter, 73
JSF, 109
Kennedy, John, 83
Khan, 184-185
Khan, Mohamed, (see Khan)
Knowledge
  awesome, 240
  bad, 76
  bank of, 26
  coma, 133

good, 48, 76, 151, 206
investment in, 107
is light, 157, 160
public, 43
pursuit of, 2
Ladder (The), 72, 90
Landlord, 10, 188, 189
Languages, 25
Lanre, 233
Law of reciprocity, 202, 211
Lector
  Introduction, 6
  (PART TWO), 79
  (PART THREE), 131, 136, 148, 150
  (PART FOUR), 182, 190, 191, 198, 209, 210, 222, 228, 230-232, 234-236, 238, 239
Lectures from Daddy, 185-190
Lee, Spike, 147
Liability, 17, 84, 124
Life Frequent Flyer Miles (LFFM), 231
Lincoln, Abraham, 170, 193, 197-198, 203, 207, 209
Macy's, 97
Mail, 169-170
Mandela, Nelson, 1
Manning, Eli, 146-147
Mark (Bible), 236
Marshall, Frank, 74
Mathematics Calculations, 157-160
Mathematics of Failure, 157, **159**
Mathematics of Success, 157, **158**
Matthew Factor (The), 238-239
Matthew (Bible), 122, 239
Maturity dates, 170
Mayweather, Floyd Jr., 41, 171
Members of Parliament (MPs), 233
Message (The), 147-150
Metro, 175, 199
Mittal, Laskshimi, 52-53
Moats, Ryan, 160-163

Money, 53-55
Morley, Christopher, 234
Most ignored (The), 64, 77-78, 95, 136, 183, 236
Motivational, 62, 183
Murdoch, Rupert, 165
Murphy, Kate, 195
Naked Arrival, 132-134
Navigation, 232
Negligence, 23-24
Net book value (NBV), 24
News, 78-79
Newton, Isaac, 87
Nigeria, 12, 194, 213, 214, 233
Nike, 120, 138, 227, 228
Nijmeh, Ronnie, 171
Nobody belongs here, 203
Normal, 75, 99, 127, 201, 208, 237
Obama, Barack, 43, 78, 79, 101, 204-209, 229
Obama, Michelle, 86
Olajuwon, Hakeem, 147, 193, 194, 195
Olé, 11-13, 25
Omelet, 138-139
Overview, 56
Page, John, 73
Paranoid, 40, 43
Parkinson's Law, 52, 227-228
PAST, 38-40, 41, 42, 43, 55, 182
Peace, 222-223
Pennsylvania Avenue, 238
Penultimate, 135, 167, 193
Petrov, Dr., 96-97
Phone, 19-20
Phonetic, 124-125
Pizza, 173
Plan + action, 114-115
Police
   department, 162
   headquarters, 50, 162
   officer, 9, 13, 160, 200
Population, 200

Poverty and Struggle, 44-46, 49, 55, 69
Powell, Robert, 160-163
Power (The), 154-155
Pressure, 171
Pretty Boy, 41-43
Price of A Soul (The), 48-49
Procrastination, 109-110
Protect or Reclaim strategy
   Introduction, 5
   (PART ONE), 30, 56, 58
   (PART TWO), 61, 87
   (PART THREE), 119, 150, 152, 155
   (PART FOUR), 181, 182, 197, 202, 203, 222-224, 236
Purpose, 74-75, 95, 96, 108, 204, 232
Purpose (Fundamental), 95
Pursuit of Happyness (The), 191
Quran, 36, 37, 55
Race (The), 33, 44, 135, 228, 229
Radcliffe, Mark, 88, 89
Real estate, 189, 195
Recession, 10, 16, 148, 189, 198-202
Religion, 35-37, 239
Reservation, 29
Resist, 217, 220
Responsibility, 46, 98, 125, 170-171, 202
Return to sender, 169, 170
Reward, 95, 104, 111, 121, 125-128, 225
Rezk, Laila, 186, 187
RISE (Rise In Style Empowered) and walk, 209, 210, 239
Road map, 108, 131, 232, 234
Robbins, Anthony, 184
Rohn, Jim, 108, 232
Rogers, Will, 126
Romans (Bible), 149
Roosevelt, Eleanor, 54, 84
Rowling, J K, 50
Rule 1, 25, 160
Rule 2, 26, 160

Index

Rule 3, 26
Rule 4, 27
Rule 5, 27
Rule 6, 28
Rules of Engagement, 25-28, 30, 125, 232, 236
Russel, Bertrand, 17
Sabour, Melvin Thomas, 35
Sales executive, 107
Schulz, Charles, 206
Self-esteem, 81, 103-104
Self-image, 2, 96-99, 100, 153
Self-marginalization, 102-103
Sharpton, Rev. Al, 101, 102
Small, Helen, 193
Sniper, 168-169
Soft landing, 57, 122, 151, 154
Soyinka, Wole, 132
Specsavers, 134, 135
Speed bike, 206-209
Spoon, 39, 130-132, 220
Square, 171-176, *172*
Step 1 (Relax), 5, 57, 61
Step 2 (Interrogate), 5, 57, 64
Step 3 (Establish), 5, 57, 80
Step 4 (Action), 5, 57, 119
Step 5 (Analyze), 5, 57, 151
Step 6 (Gradual), 5, 57, 165
Step 7 (Practice), 5, 57, 179
Stockwell, T.E., 175
Stop or Be Stopped, 135-136
Stretch Without Stress, 6, 239
Success
    agents of, 5, 151
    amount of, 10
    author of, 218
    bedrock of, 53
    birth of, 108, 231
    blazer of, 215
    cancer of, 6
    chances of, 94, 183, 237
    code of, 215
    elements of, 110
    friends of, 224
    grounds of, 212
    juice of, 92-94
    ladder of, 212-214
    language of, 119, 126
    look of, 215
    merits of, 92
    mountain of, 93
    plan of, 229
    podium of, 83, 104, 180
    purpose of, 75
    road of, 91
    seat of, 98
    seeds of, 109, 129
    society of, 226
    strategy of, 229
    success attracts, 213
    supply of, 232
    taste of, 93
    voice of, 123
Sum of Thoughts, 86-87
Super Bowl XLII, 146-147
Take Action Now (TAN), 120, 122-124
Talent, 119, 202-204
Taming the Murder, 144-146
Tenant, 29, 30
Terminator, 4, 176
Tesco, 175, 176
Thatcher, Margaret, 133
Thiago
    Introduction, 2, 3
    (PART ONE), 9, 18, 38, 39, 41, 42
    (PART TWO), 79, 115
    (PART THREE), 171, 173
    (PART FOUR), 183, 190, 193, 210, 233, 238, 240
Thompson, Steve, 160
Three Musketeers (The), 47-48
Throne, 89, 239
Throw a wobbly, 218
Tim, 93

Today, 228-230
Tony, 93
Transportation, 70, 72, 94, 238
Trump, Donald, 106
Twain, Mark, 38, 49, 136, 217, 230
University of Choice, 155-156
Variation, 16-17
Wallace, Mike, 233
Ward, William A, 239
Warranty and Receipt, 20-22
Warriors, 57, 132, 148, 183

Wattles, Wallace D, 44
Welfare, 49-52
White House, 40, 198, 203, 205, 238
Winfrey, Oprah, 101, 129, 131, 155, 190, 191, 213, 223
Words of wisdom, 38, 185, 233
XYZ, 19
Yours, 234-238
Yours and yours only, 125
Youssou, 231
Ziglar, Zig, 15, 53, 123

About the Author

The author, Lanre Aristo Balogun was born in Nigeria to a property tycoon father and nurse-cum-business mother.

After growing up in Nigeria, he was later sent to be educated in England where he graduated from the University of Leicester after studying Banking and Financial Services. He completed his post graduate degree in MSc Computer Systems & Networking at South Bank University in England. He has been working within the Information Technology (IT) industry for over a decade.

He has a burning passion for motivation; a passion he has carried deep in his heart from childhood. His phenomenal views and ideas in his book, 'The THEEF of LIFE' are given with profound, yet simple, straightforward guidance and show how every person can truly control their destiny and improve the quality of their lives. His nonprofit organization, 'The THEEF of LIFE' Foundation was set up to give each life a voice by impacting the lives of people – particularly those in need, the less privileged and his engagement in community development projects are testimonies to his passion to help and inspire others. He is married to Adetutu (nee Bamgbose), and together they have a son, Lanre Jr. He shares his time between America, UK and West Africa.

ORDER FORM

Postal orders or Cheques: Payable to Pages Publishing Limited
Address: The THEEF of LIFE, Pages Publishing Limited, PO Box 424, Hatfield, AL10 1DN United Kingdom
Email orders: cs@thetheefoflife.com

Please send me the following book:
I understand that I may return the book(s) for a full refund in its original condition.

Book	Price	Quantity
The THEEF of LIFE	~~£13.99~~ £9.99	
	Total	

Name: ....

Address: ....

....

....

City: .... State: .... ZIP/Postcode: ....

Country: ....

Telephone: ....

Email address: ....

UK: £1.90 (1st class) for first book and £0.50 for each additional book.
£1.59 (2nd Class) for first book and £0.36 for each additional book.
Shipping by air
Europe: £3.09 for first book and £0.55 for each additional book.
International: £5.29 for first book and £1.11 for each additional book.

The THEEF of LIFE Foundation – To donate visit our website: www.thetheefoflife.com or send your donation to: **The THEEF of LIFE Foundation,** Pages Publishing Limited, PO Box 424, Hatfield, AL10 1DN United Kingdom

www.thetheefoflife.com